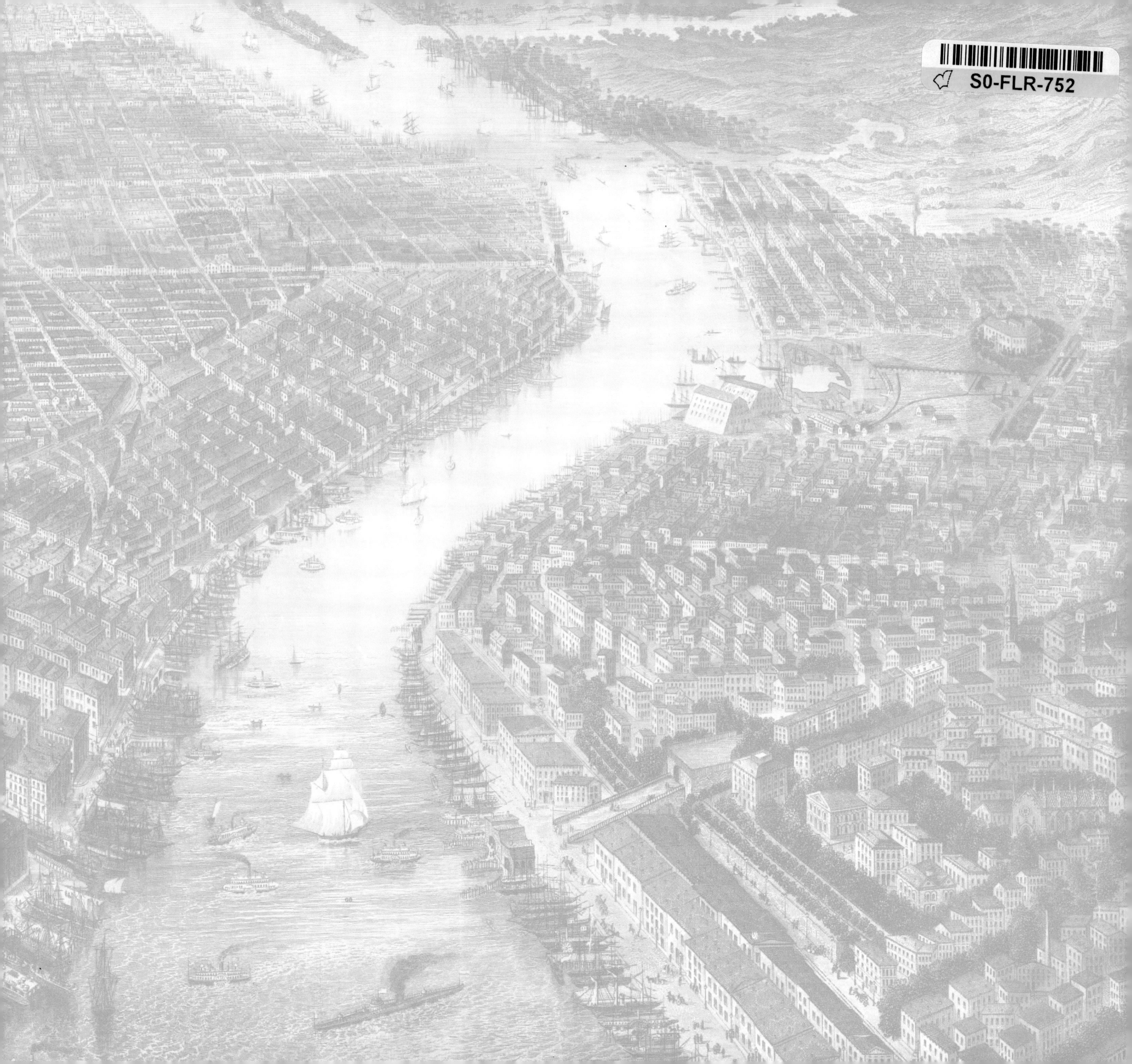

Goldman, Sachs & Co.

ESTABLISHED 1869

Goldman, Sachs & Co., Established 1869

© 2019 Goldman Sachs & Co. LLC.

Published 2019 by Goldman Sachs & Co. LLC.
www.goldmansachs.com

Printed in the United States of America

ISBN 978-0-578-58528-4

All rights reserved. No part of this publication may be reproduced, stored in any information storage or retrieval system, or transmitted in any form or by any means, electronic or mechanical, including photocopying, recording or any other method now known or to be invented, without the prior written permission of Goldman Sachs & Co. LLC, 200 West Street, New York, NY 10282.

Contents

Introduction	2
Beginnings	8
The Music Stops	24
Back from the Brink	34
Transformation	50
Principled Leadership	64
Walls Come Down	84
Turning Point	116
A Global Citizen	134
Evolution	160
The Long View	180
The Partners of Goldman Sachs	204
Image Credits	208
Acknowledgements	211

NOTE TO READERS

This book is a collection of important moments in the history of Goldman Sachs. The images and stories that appear in its early pages authentically depict the firm's past in the context of the world in which it operated at various points in time. Today Goldman Sachs is different in many ways. Just as our business has evolved over the century and a half since our founding, so too has the fabric of our talent. The people of Goldman Sachs now represent 169 nationalities and speak more than 100 languages, reflecting the many countries and communities in which we operate. They bring a diversity of backgrounds, experience and perspectives to the culture that unites us. Respecting our past for what it was and how it helped us get to where we are today, we are heartened to imagine what the story of the next 150 years of Goldman Sachs, shaped by a diverse and inclusive workforce, will look like.

September 2019

Introducing

Goldman, Sachs & Co.

Established 1869

The Firm

The 150-year history of Goldman Sachs is a story of entrepreneurial spirit, innovation, client service and bold thinking. It is a timeline punctuated by extraordinarily strong leaders who have left their mark not only on the firm but on the broader financial marketplace and in the realm of public service. For the past century and a half, it has been — in many respects — a history that parallels the vicissitudes of the coming of age of America and, more broadly, reflects the path to globalization experienced by investors and markets around the world.

Beginning at the dawn of the Second Industrial Revolution, the growth and evolution of Goldman Sachs mirror the events of each succeeding era, with the firm often playing a key role within each chapter. First there was the rapid American expansion West and the incumbent need for steel, railroads and infrastructure — and with it the need for the financial wherewithal and intermediaries to fuel this movement. This was followed by the Allied war effort during World War I, then by the cataclysmic challenges to the financial system wrought by the Great Depression.

The close of World War II launched the economic boom of the 1950s and '60s, as well as the postwar rebuilding efforts that followed. All of this culminated in the increasingly global scope of business and internationally integrated markets at the end of the millennium. Today, in the early stages of the twenty-first century, it has been the challenges and opportunities brought about by the interconnectedness of global markets and the unprecedented pace of technological change that have driven the needs of investors and the strategy of Goldman Sachs — and, more widely, impacted the way the world does business and how people live their lives.

Through it all, the firm has evolved, expanded and played a leading role in providing the advisory services, market making, investment and capital to help promote development and growth essential to all facets of society: corporations, entrepreneurs, individuals, governments, schools, hospitals, nonprofits and small businesses alike.

While the times and challenges the firm has confronted have varied in nature and scope, the core principles of the Goldman Sachs culture have remained largely unchanged. These foundational pillars, formally codified in the firm's 14 Business Principles more than 40 years ago, will continue to form the bedrock of its enduring client focus and success, regardless of what circumstances and events the future brings.

The Beginning

Founded by Marcus Goldman in 1869, the firm opened its doors at 30 Pine Street in the Financial District of New York City. Marcus, a German immigrant, had first settled in Philadelphia but then moved his family to New York, where his enterprise began modestly, serving as a middleman between merchants and commercial banks.

Thirteen years later, he offered a partnership arrangement to his son-in-law Samuel Sachs. Soon after, Marcus's own son Henry joined the firm. When Marcus retired a few years later, Samuel Sachs and Henry Goldman became co-senior partners of the firm that had now become Goldman, Sachs & Co.

Opposite: Page from client services brochure, 1963.

A Partnership Culture

Teamwork has been at the core of what has been, for more than 125 years, a true partnership culture. Partners have not only shared in the successes and losses of the firm, but have collectively helped to debate its future, chart its course and seize upon episodes of opportunity that have presented themselves over the years and decades since its founding. Even in the era that succeeded the firm's initial public offering in 1999, it is this sense of partnership and pursuit of excellence that continue to fuel the firm's focus and the work undertaken every day on behalf of clients.

Integral to the ethos of the partnership has been the expectation to give and to serve; as such, while Goldman Sachs is known for producing statesmen and public leaders at the highest levels, it has perhaps produced an even greater number of committed, lifelong philanthropists. It is unlikely that the modern-day charitable efforts made by Goldman Sachs would have achieved the success and impact that they have without the long-standing philanthropic spirit that lies at the heart of the partnership and the firm.

Time-Honored Leadership

The Goldman Sachs story is populated with a collection of compelling and dynamic leaders: Sidney Weinberg, who steered the firm's survival through the ruins of the Great Depression; Gus Levy, who developed Goldman Sachs' Trading Department and pioneered new industry-wide strategies; John Whitehead and John Weinberg, who jointly presided over exponential growth of the firm as co-senior partners; Robert Rubin and Stephen Friedman, who continued the firm's co-head tradition and guided the firm's expansion into new products and services across banking and securities in the lead-up to globalization; Jon Corzine, the bond trader who helped to establish the Fixed Income, Currencies and Commodities Division as senior partner; Hank Paulson, who oversaw the firm's IPO and entry into consequential new markets, Asia and China in particular; his successor, Lloyd Blankfein, who guided the firm through the global financial crisis and subsequent Great Recession, positioning the firm to capitalize on new strategic opportunities, such as direct consumer lending; and current CEO David Solomon, who has begun his tenure by thinking boldly about the future of Goldman Sachs, what that can be and what the firm can achieve on behalf of its clients.

Opposite: First office at 30 Pine Street, New York City, c. 1900.

PACIFIC.
PACIFIC INS. CO.
NASSAU INS
CALEDONIAN INSURANCE CO.
LOANS

A History of Innovation

Common to all of the firm's leaders has been their collective belief that among the greatest strengths of the firm is its people's ability to think innovatively and creatively — and then execute on behalf of clients. With that in mind, the firm has always considered its culture as one that encourages idea generation at all levels, from the analyst in London to a partner halfway around the world. From the invention of block trading in the 1960s to the creation of Investment Banking Services in the 1970s to the modern-day IPO in the mid-1980s — forever changing the way offerings are conducted industry-wide — and the firm's rapid adoption of technology during the early 1990s, Goldman Sachs has been at the forefront of both developing innovative approaches and putting those ideas to work to better serve the needs of its clients.

The Next 150

As a firm, Goldman Sachs has learned a great deal in the past century and a half, and some of the greatest lessons have arguably been the toughest. Mistakes and missteps are part of any journey, but they become valuable only when they are used to reflect, learn and grow. On one level, Goldman Sachs has changed almost beyond recognition since its beginnings in 1869. What started as a single entrepreneur in a one-room office in Lower Manhattan has evolved into one of the premier financial services firms in the world. But on another level, the spirit of Marcus Goldman very much lives on unabated — a spirit of personal integrity, professional excellence and unwavering commitment to clients. These remain the linchpins of Goldman Sachs' success, and — if past is prologue — will lead the firm purposefully into the next 150 years.

These pages are dedicated to the people who have helped to build the 150-year legacy of Goldman Sachs and to those working today to chart its path forward.

Goldman Sachs 150 YEARS

BEGINNINGS

In 1869, the US Civil War had been over for four years and the nation's transcontinental railroad was completed. As construction on the Brooklyn Bridge in New York City commenced, a German immigrant named Marcus Goldman started a new chapter of his life in a one-room basement office next to a coal chute on Pine Street in Lower Manhattan. The sign on the door read, "M. Goldman, Banker and Broker," although its proprietor could rarely be found there. Instead, he spent most of the day walking the maze of streets in New York's Financial District, buying promissory notes from merchants and manufacturers at a discount and then heading uptown to sell them to bankers for a profit. Guided by an intense entrepreneurial spirit and quickly earning a reputation for reliability and fair dealing, Marcus single-handedly transacted more than $5 million in commercial paper ($95 million in 2019 dollars) during his first year in business.

Marcus started his business at a time when the gold standard was being adopted by several nations of the Atlantic economy and European periphery. Combined with advances in transportation, industrialization and technology, this would pave the way for the first age of financial globalization, between 1880 and 1913. This period also saw a slowly increasing participation by women in the labor force, particularly in manual and manufacturing occupations, but it would be many years until this trend would extend to the field of finance.

In 1882, Marcus invited his son-in-law Samuel Sachs to join his growing enterprise. The addition of Samuel created not just a family business but a partnership that would endure in one form or another for the next century and a half, preserving the innovative spirit of its founder, even as Goldman Sachs grew to become one of the largest financial institutions in the world.

Above: Perspective map of Manhattan, 1867.

Opposite: Portrait of Marcus Goldman, c. 1880.

Entrepreneurialism and grit inspire Marcus Goldman to seek opportunity in a new land

Marcus Goldman was born in Trappstadt, Bavaria in 1821 to a Jewish family led by a peasant cattle drover. He sailed to America as part of a wave of migration resulting from the European Revolutions of 1848 and growing anti-semitism in Germany.

Marcus landed in the United States with his brother Simon and began work as a pushcart peddler in Philadelphia, where he met his future wife, Bertha, and they started a family. In 1869, the Goldmans moved to New York City with their five children.

At that time, Marcus conducted the majority of his business among wholesale jewelers on Maiden Lane in Lower Manhattan and leather merchants and tanners on Beekman Street, reselling their short-term notes to banks and other institutional investors.

Over time, Marcus' reputation for diligence, accuracy and persistence helped grow his business significantly. By 1890, just 11 years after its founding, his company was turning over $30 million in paper annually ($677 million in 2019 dollars).

Marcus served as senior partner of Goldman Sachs until his death in 1904.

Above: City Hall in Trappstadt, Bavaria, the birthplace of Marcus Goldman, c. 1890.

Left: Credit report showing Dun & Company's opinion that M. Goldman & Sachs are "safe brokers," 1882-1884.

Above: Group portrait at golden wedding anniversary of Marcus and Bertha Goldman, taken in Elberon, New Jersey, 1900. Marcus is seated in the middle row, third from right, wearing a hat.

Left: Ship manifest showing the Marcus Goldman family on the Holsatia, traveling from Hamburg, Germany, to New York City, October 19, 1869.

Samuel Sachs joins the family business

When Samuel Sachs accepted his father-in-law's offer to join the business in 1882, Marcus Goldman renamed the firm M. Goldman & Sachs. (The firm would become Goldman, Sachs & Co. in 1888 following the addition of Marcus' son Henry and his son-in-law Ludwig Dreyfuss.)

Born in Baltimore, Maryland in 1851, Samuel Sachs was meticulous, conservative and deeply devoted to further solidifying the company's reputation in the banking community. He believed in growing the business gradually, building upon earlier successes, and remained committed to commercial paper, the firm's most important business, even as the company expanded into self-liquidating transactions, money market activities and arbitrage.

Samuel was instrumental in driving the firm's expansion into foreign markets. In June 1897, he traveled to London to develop relationships with renowned merchant bankers Kleinwort, Sons & Co., laying the groundwork for expanding the business globally. Samuel also built connections in Paris and Berlin, advancing the firm's standing in European markets. He became senior partner after Henry Goldman's retirement in 1917.

Samuel retired from Goldman Sachs in 1929 and died in New York in 1935.

Above: Goldman family tree, c. 1985.

Left: Sachs family tree, c. 1976.

Top: Samuel Sachs, undated.

Bottom: Announcement of Samuel Sachs joining the partnership, 1882.

Above: Henry Goldman, undated.

Right: Announcement of the new name of Goldman, Sachs & Co., 1888.

A second generation of the Goldman family makes its mark on the firm

In 1885, Marcus Goldman invited his youngest son, Henry, to join him and Henry's brother-in-law Samuel Sachs in the family business. Henry was born in Philadelphia, Pennsylvania in 1857, prior to his family relocating to New York. For three decades, Henry's leadership and ingenuity helped transform Goldman Sachs into a leading financial institution. After Marcus Goldman's death in 1904, Henry Goldman and Samuel Sachs became the firm's co-senior partners.

Considered by his colleagues to be an innovative thinker with a measured approach to risk, Henry sought to expand the firm's business activities into new segments. Around the turn of the twentieth century, investment banking and securities dealing were still nascent industries. At the time, most underwritings were executed on behalf of railroads and utilities, and the business was dominated by established players, including the houses of J. P. Morgan & Co., Kuhn, Loeb & Co. and Speyer & Co.

Closed out from the railroads by the entrenched bankers who fiercely guarded their turf, Goldman Sachs instead targeted the growing base of retail companies in need of "industrial financing," providing funding to privately owned businesses, incorporating them and selling their equity to the public. With Henry at the helm, Goldman Sachs led numerous significant offerings for some of the country's largest retailers, profitably expanding into uncharted waters.

Henry Goldman retired from Goldman Sachs in 1917 and died in 1937.

> THE FIRM OF M. GOLDMAN & SACHS HAS THIS day been dissolved by mutual consent.—December 31, 1887.
> MARCUS GOLDMAN,
> SAMUEL SACHS.
> HENRY GOLDMAN.
>
> THE UNDERSIGNED HAVE THIS DAY FORMED A copartnership under the firm name of GOLDMAN, SACHS & CO.—January 3, 1888.
> MARCUS GOLDMAN,
> SAMUEL SACHS.
> HENRY GOLDMAN,
> ja3 1t   LUDWIG DREYFUSS.

25th ANNIVERSARY

1894: Coca-Cola, the International Olympic Committee, and the "Velocipede"

Goldman Sachs turns 25 during the US economic depression of the mid-1890s

In 1894, Coca-Cola was sold in bottles for the first time in Vicksburg, Mississippi. In Paris, the International Olympic Committee was founded at Sorbonne University. Karl Benz's "Velocipede" became the world's first mass-production car, with 1,200 units. Construction was completed on London's Tower Bridge, and Albert Turpain sent and received the first radio signal using Morse code.

At the time of the firm's 25th anniversary, Goldman Sachs' offices were located at 9 Pine Street and 10 Wall Street, mere steps away from the New York Stock Exchange. The firm dealt in commercial paper and government securities. According to Walter Sachs, sales of commercial paper had risen from $31 million in 1890 ($883 million in 2019 dollars) to $67 million in 1894 ($2.02 billion in 2019 dollars).

The United States was in the midst of an economic depression triggered by the Panic of 1893, forcing the US Treasury to issue bonds worth $262.32 million ($8.01 billion in 2019 dollars) between 1894 and 1896 to increase the nation's gold reserves. In November of 1894, Goldman Sachs was one of the bidders in the US Treasury auction for its second $50 million bond issue. When economic recovery eventually arrived in 1897, the firm would leverage the opportunities presented by a growing and rapidly industrializing American economy, expanding into equities trading, foreign exchange and the underwriting of issues of stock and debt for industrial and retail corporations.

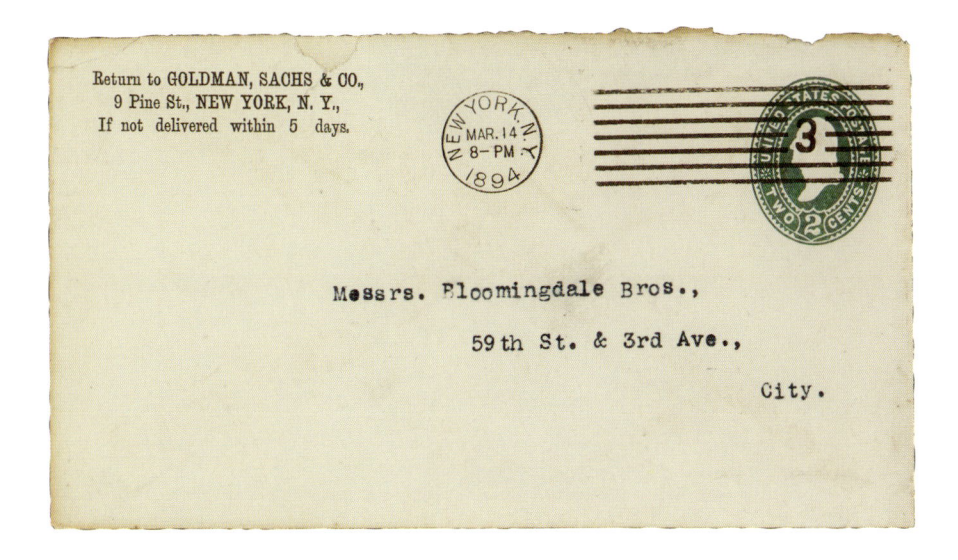

Top: Tower Bridge, London, 1894.

Bottom: Envelope from Goldman, Sachs & Co. to Bloomingdale Brothers, 1894.

Above: Floor of the New York Stock Exchange, c. 1889.

Goldman Sachs joins the New York Stock Exchange

In 1896, Goldman Sachs joined the New York Stock Exchange (NYSE) as a member company, and Harry Sachs (Samuel Sachs' brother, who had joined the firm two years earlier) became the first partner to have a seat on the NYSE. That same year, the Dow Jones Industrial Average (DJIA) was first published in *The Wall Street Journal*.

Goldman Sachs partners with Kleinwort, Sons & Co. of London, expanding into Europe

Near the turn of the twentieth century, as the firm's business continued to grow, Samuel Sachs pursued overseas expansion into Europe. He was enamored of both the continent and its marketing opportunities, traveling there frequently. In 1897, Samuel arrived in London with a letter of introduction to the established merchant bankers Kleinwort, Sons & Co. The Kleinworts and their firm had roots in Havana, but in 1858, Alexander Kleinwort opened a London acceptance house named Drake, Kleinwort & Cohen.

Herman and Alexander Kleinwort knew little of the American firm represented by Samuel Sachs, but based on the endorsement of noted New York financier August Belmont, Jr. (head of the banking firm August Belmont & Co.; sponsor of horse racing and dog breeding; and backer of transportation projects, including the New York City subway and the Cape Cod Canal), the Kleinworts agreed to the joint endeavor. The relationship proved successful from the outset and thrived for decades. Goldman Sachs and Kleinwort worked closely together on joint accounts in London, Paris, Berlin, Amsterdam and Budapest. They focused on foreign exchange and stock arbitrage, both of which were regarded as profitable and growing businesses at the time.

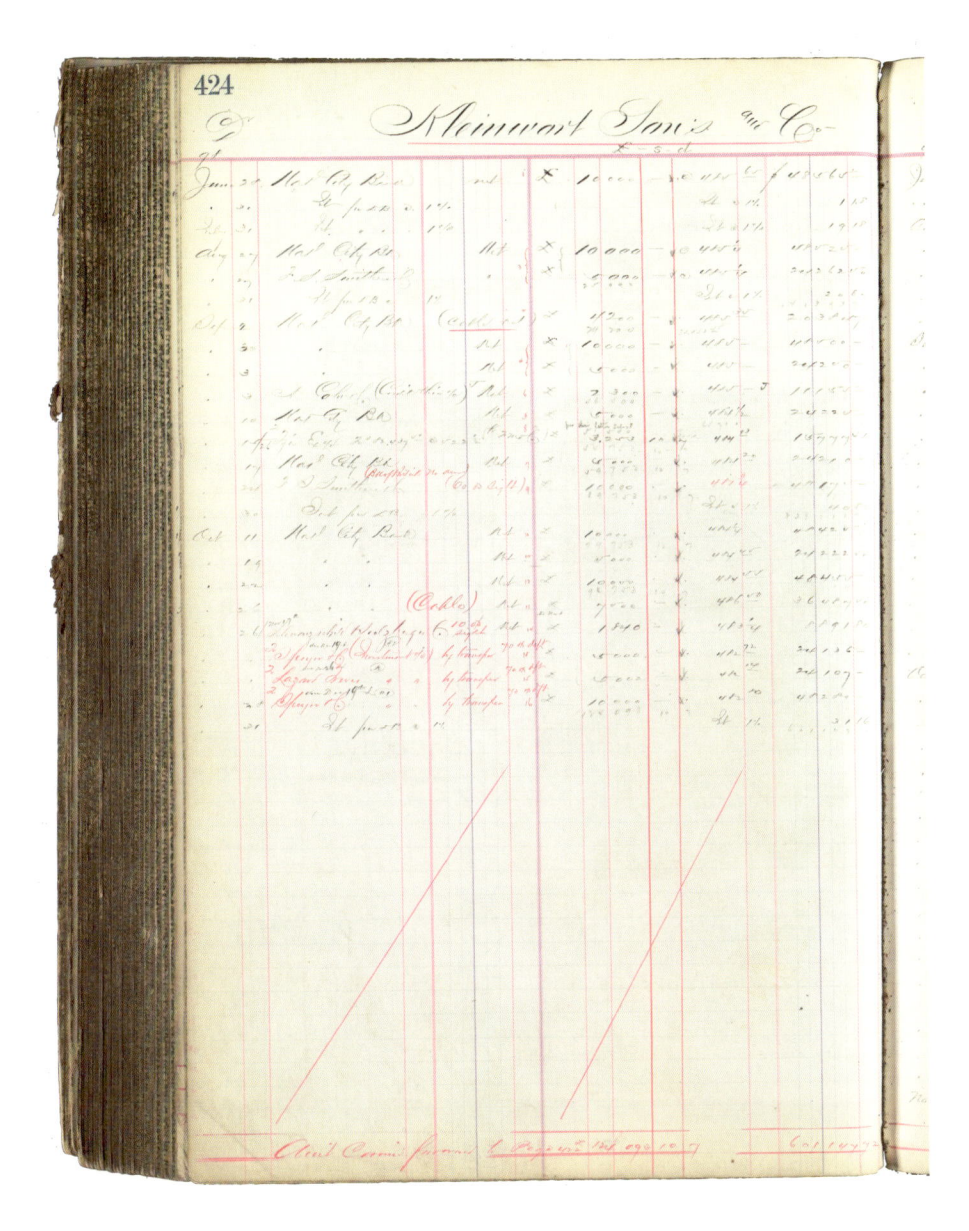

Above: Page from Kleinwort, Sons & Co. ledger, 1897.

Right: Check from Kleinwort, Sons & Co. made out to Banca Marmorosch Blank & Co., S. A., business transaction for the account of Goldman, Sachs & Co., 1926.

Adding Boston and Chicago offices, Goldman Sachs becomes a national firm

Expanding its reach to industrial New England, Goldman Sachs opened an office in Boston in 1900. Immigrants and railroads had transformed the port into a thriving factory city. Wealthy Bostonians were investing in mines, railroads and industries in the American West. The firm's first office in Boston was on State Street in the city's Financial District.

In 1900, Goldman Sachs also established an office in Chicago, in the Home Insurance Building. By then, Chicago was the second-largest city in the United States, bustling with industry and newly erected skyscrapers. The city had solidified its position as the financial capital and railroad hub of the agro-industrial Midwest.

Above: Chicago office, Home Insurance Office Building, c. 1900.

Left: Advertisement showing new Chicago address, c. 1900.

Far left: Boston office, 60 State Street, c. 1890. 60 State Street is the third building in from the far right of the photograph.

Firm's first IPO uses new earnings-based approach to valuation

In 1906, seeking a way to obtain capital for the recently formed United Cigar Manufacturers Company, Henry Goldman developed a groundbreaking approach for valuing retailers — one that ultimately became a model for future transactions and set a new industry standard for company valuation.

Unlike railroads and utilities, retailers typically had few hard assets — traditionally key inputs to underwriting. Faced with this challenge on behalf of client United Cigar, Henry Goldman innovated a new approach to valuation that would take into account a company's earning potential, not just its tangible assets.

The United Cigar IPO raised $4.5 million ($2.9 billion in 2019 dollars). The use of price-earnings ratio as a key valuation metric would eventually become common industry practice. In the near term, it was essential to Goldman Sachs' long line of successful offerings in the early twentieth century for companies that lacked significant hard assets on their balance sheets.

Top, right: United Cigar Manufacturers Company announcement, 1906.

Right: United Cigar Manufacturers Company prospectus, 1906.

Left: United Cigars store at the southwest corner of Sixth and Walnut Streets, St. Louis, Missouri, c. 1907.

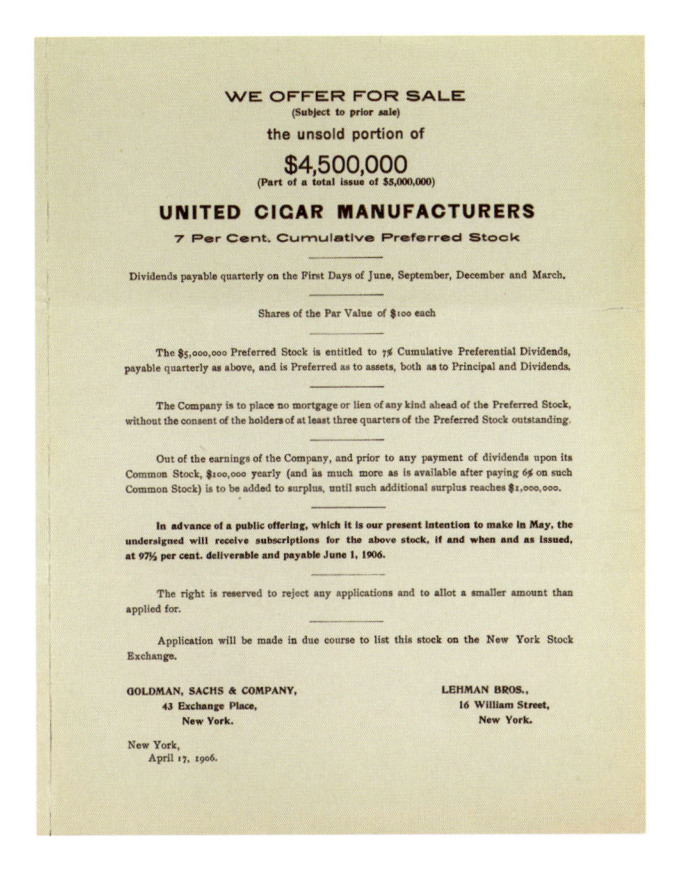

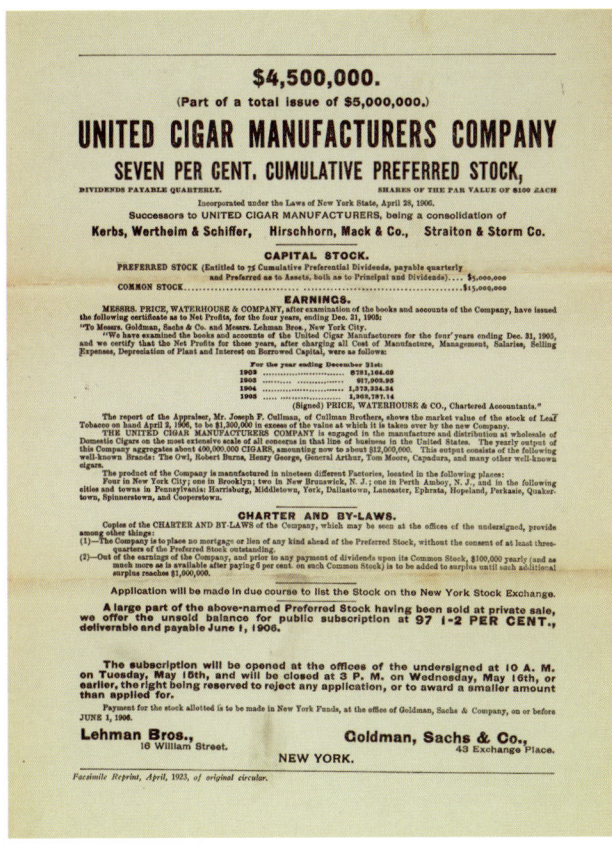

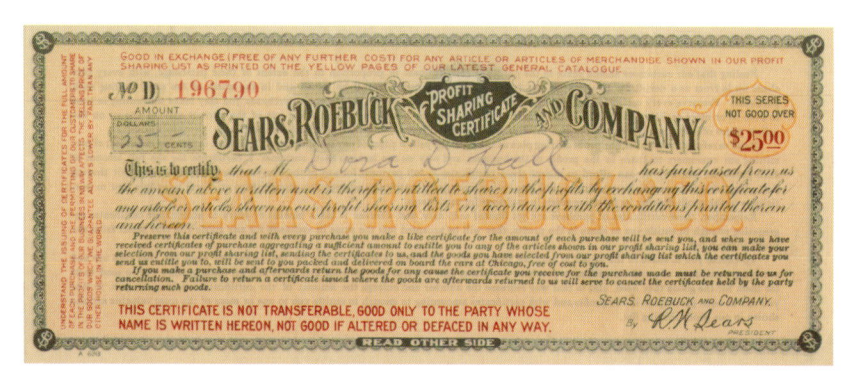

Landmark IPO helps an American retailing icon achieve the next level of growth

After publishing its first catalog in 1894, Sears, Roebuck & Co. quickly grew to become the largest mail-order house in the world. Americans could purchase everything from jewelry to sewing machines to prefabricated house kits from the pages of its catalog and have these items delivered to their doorsteps. In 1905, a Chicago clothing manufacturer named Julius Rosenwald bought into the company and helped organize a revolutionary system of distribution that dramatically increased sales.

By 1906, the retailing giant needed additional capital to finance its robust growth. A relationship between Julius Rosenwald and Henry Goldman resulted in Goldman Sachs leading Sears, Roebuck's initial public offering that year. Using the approach pioneered by Henry Goldman in the recently completed IPO of United Cigar, the firm priced the Sears, Roebuck offering based less on the company's tangible assets than on its rapidly growing sales and turnover and the stunning productivity growth of its new delivery system.

The Sears, Roebuck offering raised $40 million in preferred and common stock, the equivalent of a staggering $26.2 billion in 2019 dollars.

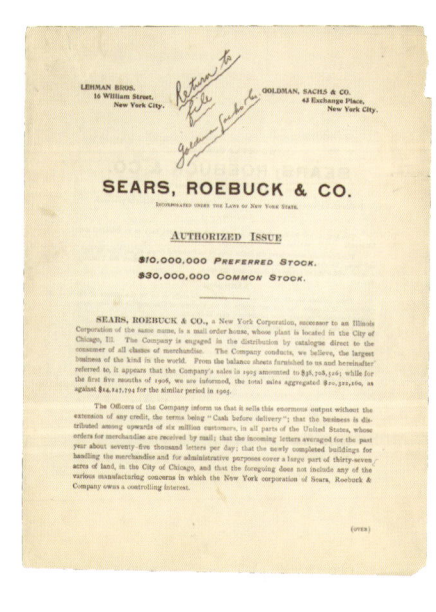

Top: Sears, Roebuck & Co. profit-sharing certificate, c. 1920.

Bottom: Cover of Sears, Roebuck & Co. catalog, 1942.

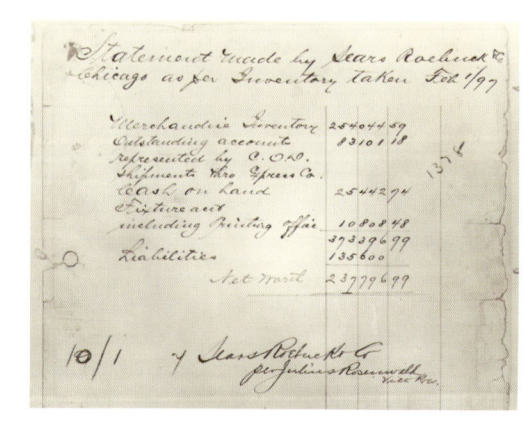

Above: On the basis of this balance sheet, Goldman, Sachs & Co. first purchased commercial paper of Sears, Roebuck & Co., 1897.

Left: Sears, Roebuck & Co. prospectus, 1906.

Sachs family legacy continues as Walter Sachs is named partner

Walter Sachs was the third son of Samuel Sachs and a grandson of Marcus Goldman. Born in New York City in 1884, Walter spent many Saturday mornings as a young man accompanying his father downtown from their home on New York's Upper East Side to the Goldman, Sachs & Co. office at 9 Pine Street. There, he would observe clerks with green eyeshades posting entries into fat ledger books. Afterward, Samuel Sachs would send his son home with pencils and pads from the office so he could practice his first lessons in basic finance, figuring interest and discount.

After graduating from Harvard University, Walter attended Harvard Law School for one year, but ultimately found himself drawn back to the family business, joining his father and two older brothers Paul and Arthur at Goldman Sachs in 1908. He was named partner in 1910.

Throughout his lifetime, Walter Sachs was active in philanthropic and civic affairs. In 1911, he became one of five incorporators of the National Association for the Advancement of Colored People (NAACP), for which he served as treasurer. He retired from Goldman Sachs in 1959 and remained a limited partner of the firm until his death in 1980 at the age of 96.

Left:
Walter Sachs, undated.

Below:
Letter from W. E. B. Du Bois to Walter Sachs, 1953.

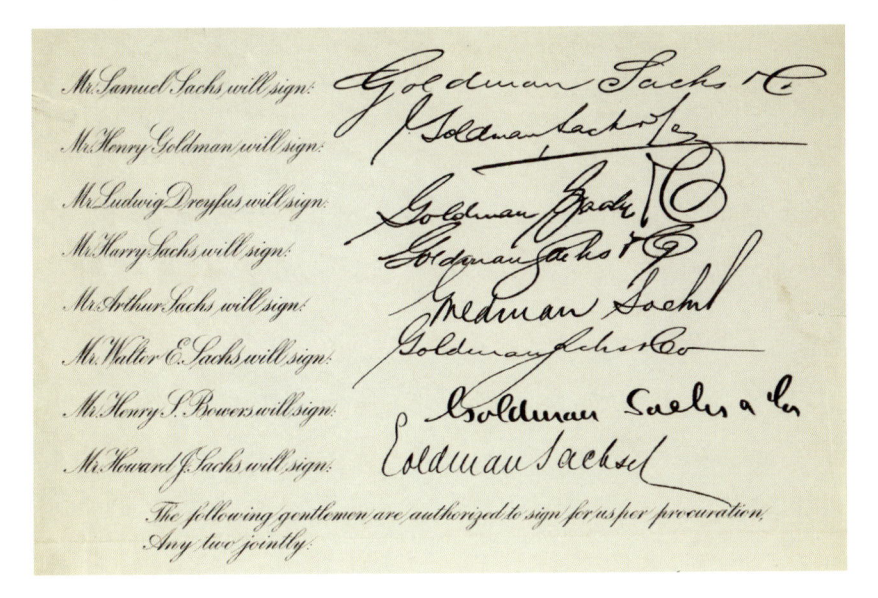

Above: Facsimiles of authorized signatures, 1914. To ensure the authenticity of correspondence, Goldman, Sachs, & Co. annually provided clients with the unique signature of each partner at the firm.

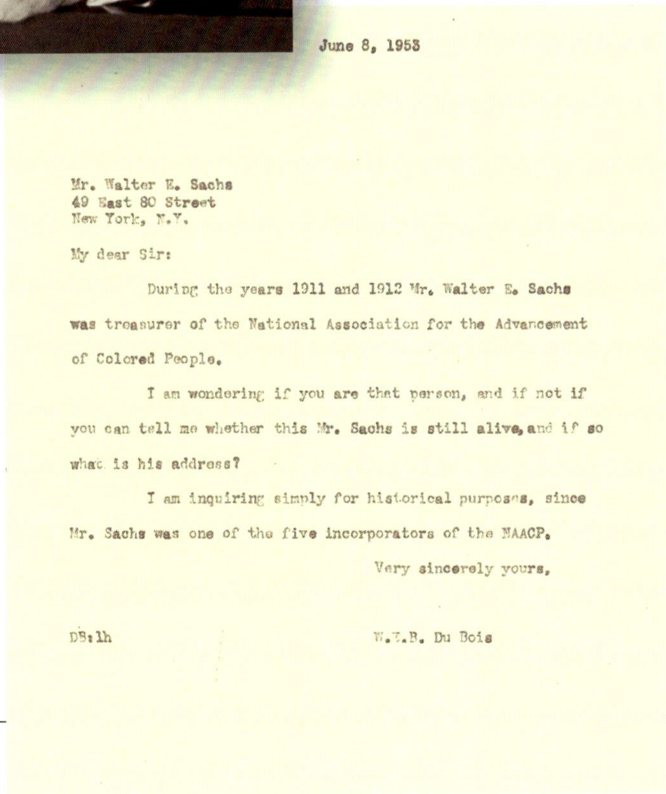

F. W. Woolworth IPO fuels the rapid growth of a retail empire

After being turned down by other underwriters who felt it somewhat undignified to be associated with a chain of five-and-ten-cent stores, Frank Winfield Woolworth sought out Goldman Sachs in 1912 to help finance the formation of F. W. Woolworth Co. with the merger of several five-and-ten-cent stores in New York, Pennsylvania, Connecticut, Massachusetts, and Canada, as well as 12 six-penny stores in England.

The Woolworth offering was a boon for Goldman Sachs; between 1906 and 1917, most of the underwritings the firm had undertaken were on behalf of existing commercial paper clients. While it had gained traction with the United Cigar and Sears, Roebuck transactions, the firm was still working hard to establish itself in the underwriting space. Henry Goldman's close friend around that time was Philip Lehman, one of five brothers running Lehman Brothers. With both firms challenged to penetrate this closed-door market, Philip and Henry agreed to target underwriting business together, with profits split fifty-fifty. Eventually they would also include the British bank Kleinwort, Sons & Co. to help underwrite deals and sell them to investors in Europe.

Above: F. W. Woolworth Co. store in Montpelier, Vermont, c. 1910.

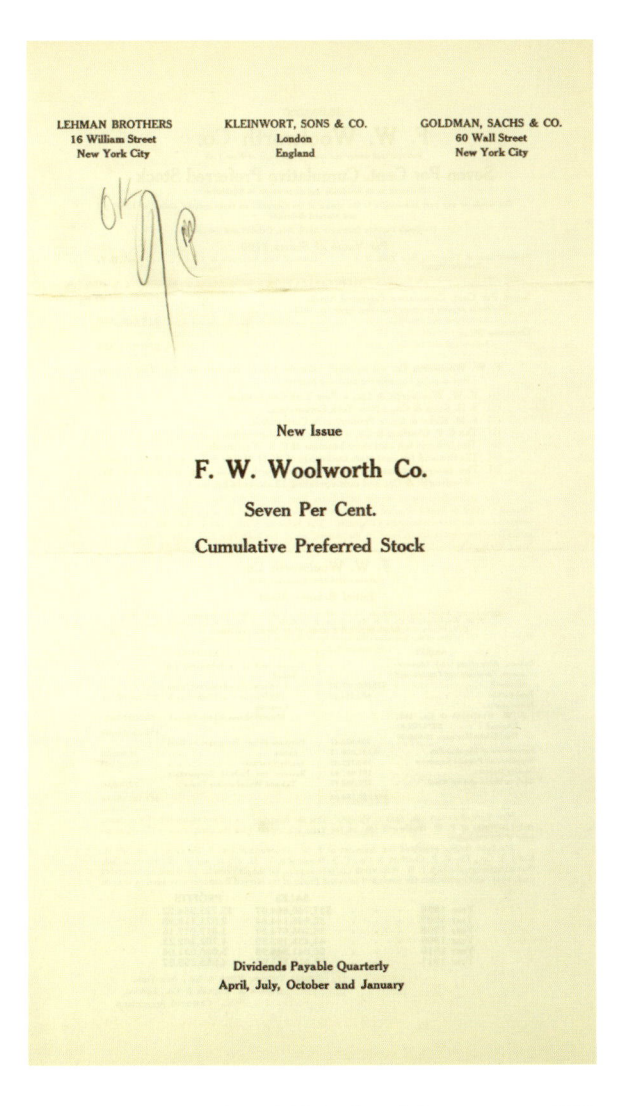

Above: F. W. Woolworth Co. prospectus, 1912.

Right: Woolworth Building, New York City, 1921.

A dream goes skyward

Among Frank W. Woolworth's ambitions was building his signature Woolworth skyscraper in Manhattan at 233 Broadway. According to Walter Sachs, at a dinner in April 1913 celebrating the building's completion, Woolworth seated its architect, Cass Gilbert, next to him on one side, with Henry Goldman seated on the other. He introduced both to those in attendance by saying, "These are the two men who made this building possible."

THE MUSIC STOPS

World War I divided not only the continent of Europe but also the ranks of Goldman, Sachs & Co., initiating a turbulent period for the firm that nearly led to its demise. Henry Goldman, Marcus Goldman's youngest son, had joined the firm in 1885. With a strong allegiance to his father's native Germany, Henry found himself at odds with his business partners, the majority of whom staunchly supported the Allies. Unable to resolve these differences, Henry resigned from the family business in 1917.

During the exuberant equity markets of the 1920s, a man named Waddill Catchings initially seemed to be the ideal outsider to bring into the fold following Henry Goldman's departure. A friend and former Harvard University classmate of Arthur Sachs (the second son of Samuel Sachs), Waddill was bright and charismatic — a dealmaker with bold vision. In 1928, he led the formation of an investment trust called Goldman Sachs Trading Corporation (GSTC), which pooled investor capital for the purchase of shares of publicly held companies. Highly leveraged, GSTC collapsed with the stock market crash of October 1929, its shares plummeting from a high of more than $300 to less than $2 by mid-1932. The failure of GSTC caused nearly irreparable damage to Goldman Sachs' balance sheet and to the reputation its partners had worked tirelessly to build for more than five decades.

Top: Front page of the Brooklyn Daily Eagle, *October 24, 1929.*

Bottom: Goldman Sachs Trading Corporation stock certificate, 1929.

Opposite: Crowds gather outside the New York Stock Exchange during the stock market crash of October 1929.

Henry Goldman leaves the firm

With the death of firm founder Marcus Goldman in 1904, Henry Goldman and his brother-in-law Samuel Sachs had become co-senior partners, presiding over substantial growth for the firm. Among their accomplishments was Goldman Sachs' partnering with Lehman Brothers (through Henry Goldman's good friend Philip Lehman) to establish inroads into the insular world of investment banking.

But the start of World War I sparked a schism among the firm's leaders. While the majority clearly backed the Allies, Henry Goldman was a vocal supporter of Germany, his ancestral home. Despite entreaties to tone down his sentiments, Henry Goldman was defiant. His sympathies posed a particular risk to the firm's business in London through Kleinwort, Sons & Co.

As the war progressed, Henry's position within the firm proved untenable. In October 1917, he retired from the partnership after 35 years, taking with him significant capital. Waddill Catchings would replace Henry as the partner in charge of industrial financings.

The departure would also lead to a rift between the Goldman and Sachs families that would last for decades. Henry Goldman and Samuel Sachs never spoke again. Henry would travel to Germany, where he witnessed firsthand the fall of the Weimar Republic and the rise of Hitler's Nazi regime. He would later return to New York City, where he died in 1937.

Above: Henry Goldman's letter to Kleinwort, Sons & Co. announcing his departure from the firm, 1917.

Waddill Catchings joins Goldman Sachs and is later named senior partner

Waddill Catchings was born in 1879 in Sewanee, Tennessee. After graduating from Harvard University and Harvard Law School, he enjoyed success restructuring bankrupt companies following the Panic of 1907.

A friend and undergraduate classmate of Arthur Sachs, Waddill was asked to join Goldman Sachs in 1918 following Henry Goldman's departure. He became partner in charge of underwriting, helping to organize offerings for General Foods and National Dairy Products (later Kraft). Waddill's drive and ambition made him an immediate firm leader.

In 1921, Waddill became the first senior partner to come from outside of the Goldman or Sachs families. By 1928, he owned the largest stake in the firm and wielded increasing power and influence. That year, he created the Goldman Sachs Trading Corporation (GSTC), a trust that pooled investors' capital in order to invest in stock. His practices brought the firm much success throughout the 1920s, but a series of overaggressive decisions ultimately led to the deterioration of his relationship with his partners. Waddill was also a prolific writer, co-authoring several influential books in parallel to his career at Goldman Sachs, including *Our Common Enterprise* (1922), *Money* (1923), *Profits* (1925), *Business without a Buyer* (1927) and *The Road to Plenty* (1928).

Following the catastrophic failure of GSTC in 1930, the firm's partners determined that Waddill should leave Goldman Sachs. After his departure, he became a director of Chrysler, Standard Packaging and Warner Brothers. Waddill would author more books, including *Progress and Plenty* (1930), *Money, Men and Machines* (1953), *Do Economists Understand Business?* (1955), *Bias Against Business* (1956) and *Are We Mismanaging Money?* (1960). He died in 1968.

Top: Waddill Catchings, 1924.

Bottom: Letter announcing Henry Goldman's retirement and Waddill Catchings' admission to the firm, 1917.

50th ANNIVERSARY

1919: Treaty of Versailles, Prohibition, and women earn the right to vote

Fifty years after its founding, Goldman Sachs continues to build its US-based stock underwriting business

Goldman Sachs turned 50 in 1919, the year World War I ended with the Treaty of Versailles. While hostilities ceased, German reparations and the question of Inter-Allied debts remained sources of conflict in the years to come.

That same year, Prohibition began in the United States, and American women earned the right to vote. In the United Kingdom, women over age 30 who met a property qualification were also granted the right to vote. As Ford Model Ts replaced horse-drawn carriages in American cities, mass production also spurred the Golden Age of Flight. New York City emerged as the preeminent center for global finance, taking the lead over London, and the dollar threatened the primacy of the pound sterling as the international reserve currency.

Fifty years after its founding, Goldman Sachs was a member of the New York and Chicago stock exchanges and had offices in Boston, Chicago and San Francisco, in addition to its location at 60 Wall Street in Manhattan. In 1919, the partnership's capital was $8.17 million ($119 million in 2019 dollars). That year, the firm underwrote several stock offerings, including the IPOs of the Goodyear Tire & Rubber Co., Merck & Co. pharmaceuticals, and the clothing company Phillips-Van Heusen Corporation.

Top: Celebration of the passage of the Nineteenth Amendment guaranteeing women nationally the right to vote, 1920.

Bottom: French Prime Minister Georges Clemenceau signing the Treaty of Versailles, France, 1919.

Postwar reconstruction bond offering modernizes French railroad

Reconstruction in Europe after World War I, particularly in Germany and France, was hampered by disputes over war reparations and repayment of war debts. In 1924, progress was made on several fronts. In particular, French government debt was restructured, helping to spur lending in Europe and around the globe.

The Paris-Lyons-Mediterranean Railroad Company, the largest railroad in France, accounted for almost one-third of all railroad receipts in the country. In September of 1924, Goldman, Sachs & Co. and the Bankers Trust Company (jointly with Lehman Brothers, Halsey, Stuart & Co., Inc. and the Union Trust Company of Pittsburgh) offered $20 million in Paris-Lyons-Mediterranean Railroad Company External Sinking Fund Gold 7% Bonds. This was the firm's first-ever bond offering for a European company. Guaranteed by the French government, this offering would fund the electrification of the lines that connected Paris with the Riviera, Marseilles, parts of Italy and, ultimately, the rest of Europe and Constantinople.

With greater access to capital via such transactions, the recovering French economy would strengthen and gain momentum throughout the latter part of the 1920s.

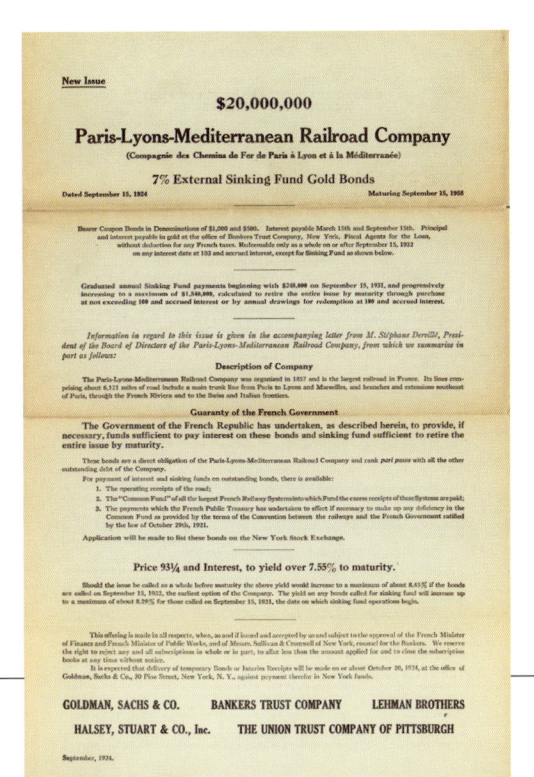

Above: Cote d'Azur Pullman Express vintage poster by artist Pierre Fix-Masseau, c. 1929.

Left: Paris-Lyons-Mediterranean Railroad Company prospectus, 1924.

Firm helps fuel the growth of Warner Brothers in an emerging industry

The early twentieth century saw the emergence and rapid growth of the motion picture industry. In 1923, in Hollywood, California, Polish immigrant brothers Albert, Sam, Harry and Jack Warner established their film studio, Warner Brothers Pictures, Inc.

Goldman Sachs partner Waddill Catchings identified early the promise of the film industry. After cultivating a relationship with Warner Brothers, the firm provided financing in 1924 to open theaters in New York and Hollywood, making Warner Brothers the first Hollywood studio to produce, print and show its own pictures.

The following year, Goldman Sachs brokered the sale of $4 million of three-year 6.5% notes for Warner Brothers to purchase the Vitagraph Company from Western Union, helping usher in the era of synchronized sound — the "talkies." Goldman Sachs became known as the banker of Warner Brothers Pictures, with Waddill on the studio's board of directors.

The firm continued to advise Warner Brothers on key initiatives throughout the 1920s, including the 1928 merger that brought Warner Brothers Pictures, the Vitaphone Corporation, the Stanley Company of America and First National Pictures into one group, combining assets of $200 million. Critically, in 1930, Goldman Sachs and Hayden Stone & Co. financed Warner Brothers' $100 million acquisition of First National Pictures, owners of the famous Burbank lot in Hollywood, where Warner Brothers would remain headquartered for decades.

Above: Warner Brothers Studios, Hollywood, California, c. 1925.

Right: Warner Brothers Pictures, Inc. prospectus, 1925.

Goldman Sachs Trading Corporation bears the full brunt of the 1929 financial crash

In December 1928, senior partner Waddill Catchings led the formation of Goldman Sachs Trading Corporation (GSTC), an investment trust to be listed on the New York Curb Exchange (later the American Stock Exchange), trading at an initial price of $104. It would be the largest investment trust yet established, with capital of $50 million ($733 million in 2019 dollars) and a cash surplus of an additional $50 million.

Following an early 1929 merger with the Financial and Industrial Securities Corporation, shares more than doubled over their initial value. The success of GSTC led to expansion for the firm, with the acquisition of American Trust Company of San Francisco. Waddill went further and formed two more trusts with an interlocking, highly leveraged ownership structure.

GSTC would bear the full brunt of the financial crash of 1929. By January 1930, its market capitalization had fallen by more than 50%. By mid-1932, adjusted for splits, the stock would ultimately fall from a high of $226 to $1.75 per share.

In May 1930, Waddill Catchings departed Goldman Sachs. Walter Sachs became the president of GSTC and, together with Sidney Weinberg, liquidated the investment trust's assets.

The consequences of the failure of GSTC were formidable, nearly causing the firm's demise and severely damaging its reputation. In the aftermath, Sidney Weinberg and his considerable financial acumen would be entrusted with the leadership of the firm. For nearly four decades, he would steadily rebuild the firm's reputation and position Goldman Sachs as a leader on Wall Street and beyond.

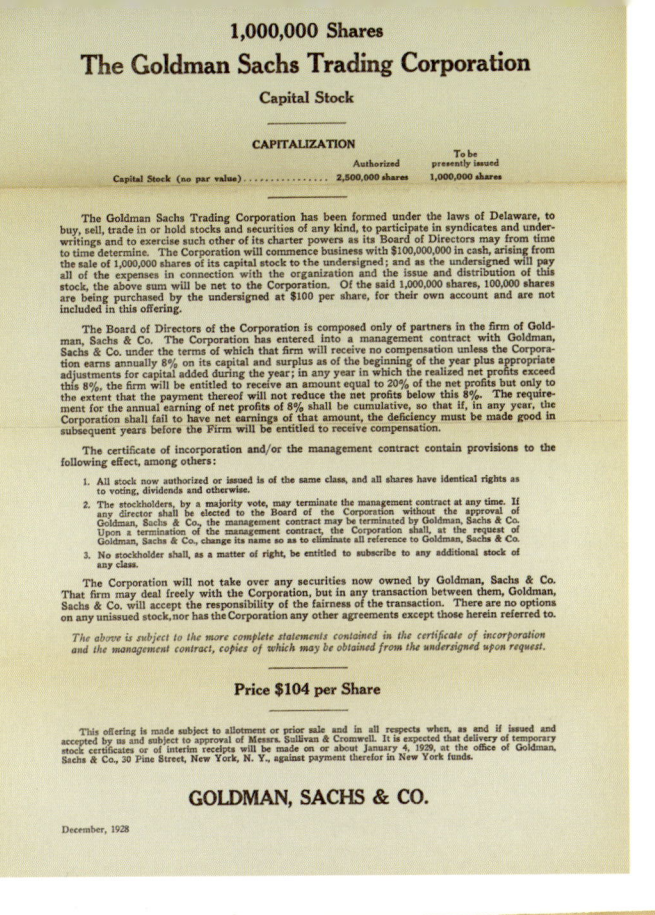

Left: Goldman Sachs Trading Corporation prospectus, 1928.

Below: Front page of The New York Times, October 29, 1929.

The Sachs family helps shape a nascent Goldman Sachs and fortify the partnership in the face of adversity

When Marcus Goldman brought his son-in-law Samuel Sachs on as his business partner in 1882, neither man could know that it would be the beginning of a partnership that would last for more than a century and a half, employing several generations of both families.

Samuel Sachs had an early and enduring impact on the firm through his measured and thoughtful approach to growing the business, his efforts to drive the firm's expansion into foreign markets and his acute client focus. Another of Samuel's key contributions would come into sharp relief after the financial crash of 1929: the strong capital base he helped create. When the Great Depression struck in the United States, the personal capital Samuel and his brother Harry had invested in the partnership played a critical role in the firm's survival.

Harry Sachs joined the family business in 1894 as a partner and was the first New York Stock Exchange (NYSE) member from Goldman Sachs. Following Henry Goldman's retirement in 1917, Harry became sole senior partner of the firm until 1921. Harry's son, Howard Sachs, was admitted as a partner of the firm in 1915.

Three of Samuel's sons would also join Goldman Sachs around the turn of the twentieth century: Arthur and Paul in 1900, and Walter in 1907. Like his father, Arthur was keenly focused on expanding the firm's international financing presence. In 1919 and 1920, he established new currency trading accounts in Amsterdam and Paris.

He also helped to fill the leadership vacuum that existed at the firm when Henry Goldman retired, acting as the key partner in virtually every major Goldman Sachs financing in the late 1910s.

Around that same time, Arthur's brother Paul was being groomed for a leadership role within the firm, handling relations with the firm's UK partner Kleinwort, Sons & Co. and key clients that included companies like the Studebaker Corporation and F. W. Woolworth Co. Yet Paul's passions lay elsewhere: in 1915 he left the firm to become an assistant director at Harvard University's Fogg Museum, where he would become a major figure in the art world.

Walter Sachs, who joined his father and brothers at Goldman Sachs in 1908, was the first employee to be trained in Europe. He was admitted to the partnership in 1910 and became co-senior partner with Arthur in 1930 upon the resignation of Waddill Catchings (who had been brought into the firm in 1918 by Arthur Sachs). Walter too, lent stability — in the form of both leadership and capital — in the wake of the financial crash of 1929 and the ensuing failure of the Goldman Sachs Trading Corporation.

The last descendant of Samuel Sachs to work at the firm retired in 1990: Peter Sachs was Howard's son and Samuel's great nephew and had worked at Goldman Sachs since 1969. While Peter's retirement marked the end of a century-plus span of Sachs family members at the firm, the legacy of this extraordinary family endures.

Right: Arthur Sachs, undated.

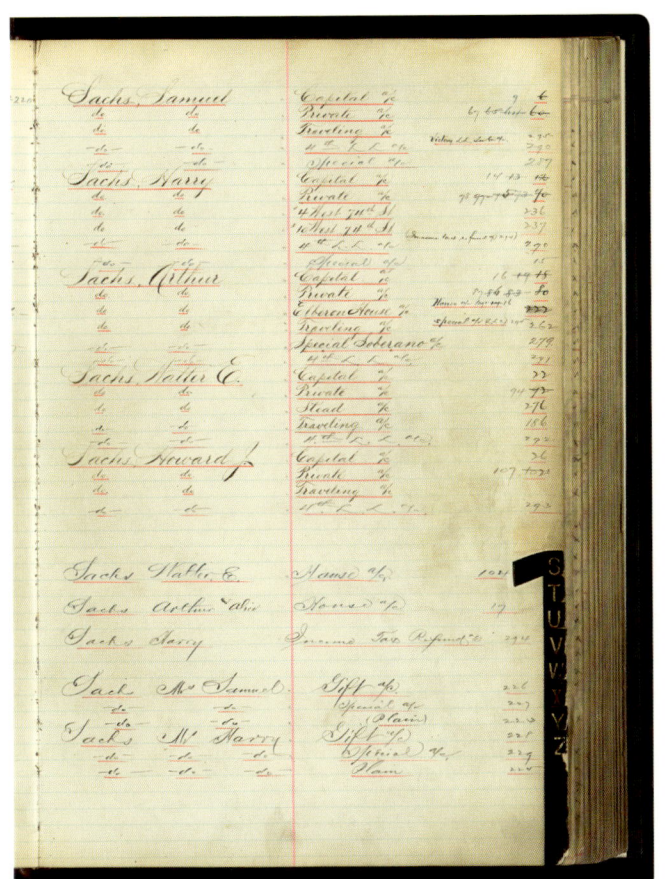

Above: Harry Sachs, c. 1915.

Top, right: Front page of the Security Dealers Daily Financial Reporter, December 19, 1935. Clockwise from upper left: Walter Sachs, Sidney Weinberg, Henry Bowers, Ernest Loveman and Howard Sachs.

Bottom, right: Paul Sachs, undated.

Bottom, left: Page from partners' accounts ledger, 1918–1919.

1ST ANNUAL OUTING OF
GOLDMAN SACHS & CO. EMPLOYEES
JUNE 1938

BACK FROM THE BRINK

Between 1930 and 1933, more than 9,000 American banks had been forced to close their doors as the country sank into the Great Depression. Against this backdrop, and as Goldman Sachs was reeling from the collapse of the Goldman Sachs Trading Corporation (GSTC), a new leader rose to the task of bringing the firm through this extraordinary period of crisis. A former newsboy from Brooklyn with an eighth-grade education, Sidney Weinberg had quietly been working his way up the Goldman Sachs ladder ever since he had joined the firm as an assistant janitor in 1907. Under Weinberg's steady and astute leadership, it became clear that Goldman Sachs would survive this unprecedented market downturn and the GSTC debacle. Not only did Weinberg salvage the firm's tattered reputation, but he also helped rebuild Goldman Sachs into the firm that, by the mid-1950s, was chosen to handle the landmark initial public offering for Ford Motor Company, then the third-largest company in the United States.

The hard lessons learned from the GSTC failure would, from that point forward, be embedded in the Goldman Sachs culture: be disciplined about risk; be patient and long-term-focused; never forget the fundamentals. With the firm on solid footing again, the 1950s and 1960s were a time of growth and innovation at Goldman Sachs. A partner named John Whitehead pioneered the concept of Investment Banking Services, a new model that dedicated teams of people solely to building and managing client relationships, with execution handled by separate groups. Gustave (Gus) Levy, named senior partner in 1969, was an industry innovator in block trading. Under his leadership, the firm grew to dominate this nascent discipline. Back from the brink of collapse, Goldman Sachs was now positioned to carve a confident and industry-leading path forward.

Opposite: First annual outing of Goldman, Sachs & Co. employees, 1938. Gus Levy, holding a bat, is seated in the front row.

Top: Page from Goldman Sachs Trading Corporation Weekly Review, a research periodical, Volume 1, September 1931–September 1932.

Bottom: Board of directors of National Dairy Products Corporation, Memphis, Tennessee, 1964. John Weinberg is fourth from right.

Goldman Sachs plans its first headquarters on the site of Marcus Goldman's original office

Above: View of construction in front of the 30 Pine Street office, looking east from Nassau Street to William Street, 1930.

On January 12, 1929, Goldman Sachs announced that it would purchase the Hanover Fire Insurance Company Building on Pine Street in Lower Manhattan, just next door to its then-current offices at 30 and 32 Pine Street. The following year, the firm would erect a new, 20-story building that would serve as its first headquarters, retaining the address of 30 Pine Street.

Goldman Sachs contracted architect Archibald F. Gilbert to design its new home, described in one 1929 press clipping as a "New Banking Skyscraper," at an estimated cost of $1.5 million ($22 million in 2019 dollars). The location was significant: in 1869, when the firm was founded, Marcus Goldman's office was located in a structure that stood on the site.

General banking offices occupied the lower floors, with the upper floors reserved for partners' offices, dining rooms and a fully equipped gymnasium, including a squash court. In the wake of the 1929 financial crash, even before the building's completion, the firm leased several floors to other firms. To save costs, the squash court became the firm's Investment Banking Department floor, where John Weinberg and John Whitehead, later co-senior partners, first worked.

Goldman Sachs would operate from 30 Pine Street until 1957.

Landmark Glass-Steagall Act separates commercial and investment banking

After the financial crash of 1929 shattered financial markets and the Great Depression began, investment banking activity in the United States ground to a halt. Recognizing that urgent reforms were needed to reestablish the public's confidence in securities trading, Congress conducted numerous hearings and passed legislation to restore investors' trust in the capital markets. As part of these efforts, the Banking Act of 1933 — also known as the Glass-Steagall Act — mandated the separation of commercial banking (the issuance of credit to households and firms) and investment banking (the issuance and trading of securities).

While historically significant, the Glass-Steagall Act had limited impact on the firm's business. In the years before the crash of 1929, Goldman Sachs accepted some funds from depositors, but the firm did not act like a deposit bank by permitting checking accounts: withdrawal of funds could only occur by written or cabled transfer instructions. After the passage of Glass-Steagall, the partnership discontinued taking depositors' money to comply with the regulation.

Above: Signing of the Glass-Steagall Act by President Franklin D. Roosevelt in the Oval Office at the White House, 1933. Behind the President are (left to right): Senator Allen Barkley, Senator Thomas Gore, Senator Carter Glass, Comptroller of Currency J. F. T. Connors, Senator William G. McAdoo, Representative Henry S. Steagall, Senator Duncan U. Fletcher, Representative Alan Goldsborough and Representative Robert Luce.

Sidney Weinberg leads a resurgent Goldman Sachs in a legendary career spanning six decades

Sidney Weinberg was born in 1891 in the Red Hook section of Brooklyn and began working at an early age, including selling newspapers and acting as a messenger for investment firms. He joined Goldman Sachs in 1907 at age 16 as an assistant to the janitor, where his responsibilities included brushing the hats of partners and cleaning spittoons. From this inauspicious beginning, Sidney Weinberg would rise to lead the firm for nearly four decades and become one of the most powerful men on Wall Street.

As young Sidney's drive and initiative gained notice within the firm, he became head of the mailroom and caught the attention of Paul Sachs with a complete plan for its reorganization. Recognizing Sidney's raw talent and charisma, Paul — son of Marcus Goldman's first partner Samuel Sachs — became an early champion of Sidney's career. In fact, he later paid the tuition for Sidney's first investment banking course at New York University and continued to mentor him in building a successful career with the firm.

After taking leave of the firm to serve in World War I, Sidney returned to resume his career at Goldman Sachs, leveraging his gregariousness and acumen in corporate finance. He was named partner in 1927.

In 1930, with the financial world in disarray and the firm's survival in question after the collapse of the Goldman Sachs Trading Corporation, Sidney was named senior partner. With a focus on integrity and an innate ability to build relationships with clients, Sidney led the rebuilding of Goldman Sachs' role as a trusted advisor, earning him the moniker "Mr. Wall Street."

Few financiers have sat on more corporate boards than Sidney Weinberg. His 35 directorships for some of America's largest, most prestigious companies included General Electric, General Foods and Ford.

Sidney epitomized the Goldman Sachs cultural tradition of service. In June 1933, he helped launch the Business Advisory Council as part of President Franklin D. Roosevelt's New Deal. A veteran of World War I, he took a leave of absence from Goldman Sachs in 1941 to serve as assistant director of purchases in the Office of Production Management (OPM), later the War Production Board (WPB) in Washington, DC. He would go on to serve as an informal advisor to five US presidents.

Near the end of his tenure at the firm, Sidney helped launch the Management Committee in 1965, which greatly eased the transition of power between Weinberg himself and Gus Levy. Over the course of his career, Sidney Weinberg displayed in his office the brass spittoon he polished in his first job at Goldman Sachs, a reminder of his, and the firm's, focus on humility. He remained a senior partner of the firm until his death in 1969, the year Goldman Sachs turned 100.

Top: *Sidney Weinberg, 1967.*

Above: *Medal for Merit Certificate, 1946.*

Right: *"Mr. Wall Street" story,* The New York Times, *November 16, 1967.*

Opposite: *Sidney Weinberg in US Navy uniform, c. 1917.*

75th ANNIVERSARY

1944: D-Day, the Bretton Woods Conference, and the dawn of the IMF and the World Bank

In the shadow of World War II, Goldman Sachs turns 75 as a leader in commercial paper and preferred stock

June 6, 1944 signaled the arrival of D-Day, the Allied invasion of Normandy, France, in what would be the largest amphibious military offensive in world history. That same year, the Bretton Woods Conference was convened to address the reorganization of the international financial and monetary system, leading to the establishment of the International Monetary Fund (IMF) and the International Bank for Reconstruction and Development (soon named the World Bank). In Washington, DC, the Dumbarton Oaks Conference resulted in a proposal for an international organization that eventually became the United Nations. And on November 7, US President Franklin D. Roosevelt was elected to an unprecedented fourth term.

Amid this sea change of world events, Goldman Sachs continued to broaden its focus, services and client base as it marked 75 years in business. True to its roots, the firm was a leader in commercial paper in the United States in 1944. As the economy moved further into the post-Depression era, the scope of the firm's services was expanding. As noted in a press release at the time, this included serving as "one of the leaders in the recently developed business of placing privately with institutional investors large blocks of industrial debentures and preferred stock."

In 1944, Goldman Sachs was led by 11 general partners: nine located in New York and two in Chicago. The partnership's capital was $8.9 million ($127 million in 2019 dollars). By then the firm had also established offices in Boston, Philadelphia and St. Louis.

Above: 75th anniversary dinner, Hotel Pierre, New York City, December 18, 1944. Clockwise from front left: Walter Sachs, David Hawkins, Jimmy Sachs, Judge Peck, Howard Sachs, Henry Ess, Sidney Weinberg, Arthur Sachs, Ed Green, Paul Sachs, Ernest Loveman, Bob Benjamin, Henry Bowers and Henry Moses.

Right: 75th anniversary dinner program, 1944.

Goldman, Sachs & Co.

SEVENTY-FIFTH ANNIVERSARY DINNER

1869-1882 M. GOLDMAN
1882-1885 M. GOLDMAN & SACHS
1885-1944 GOLDMAN, SACHS & CO.

40

Left: Photograph of signing of Ford Motor Company's initial public offering, 1956. Seated, from left: Henry Ford, II, president, Ford Motor Company (signing); H. Rowan Gaither, Jr., president, Ford Foundation; Ernest Breech, chairman of the board, Ford Motor Company. Standing are representatives of the IPO's underwriters: John Whitehead, Goldman, Sachs & Co.; J. Richardson Dilworth, Kuhn, Loeb & Co.; George J. Leness, Merrill Lynch, Pierce, Fenner & Beame; George Leib, Blyth & Co., Inc.; Milton Cross, The First Boston Corporation; John Fell, Lehman Brothers and Emery Katzenbach, White, Weld & Co.

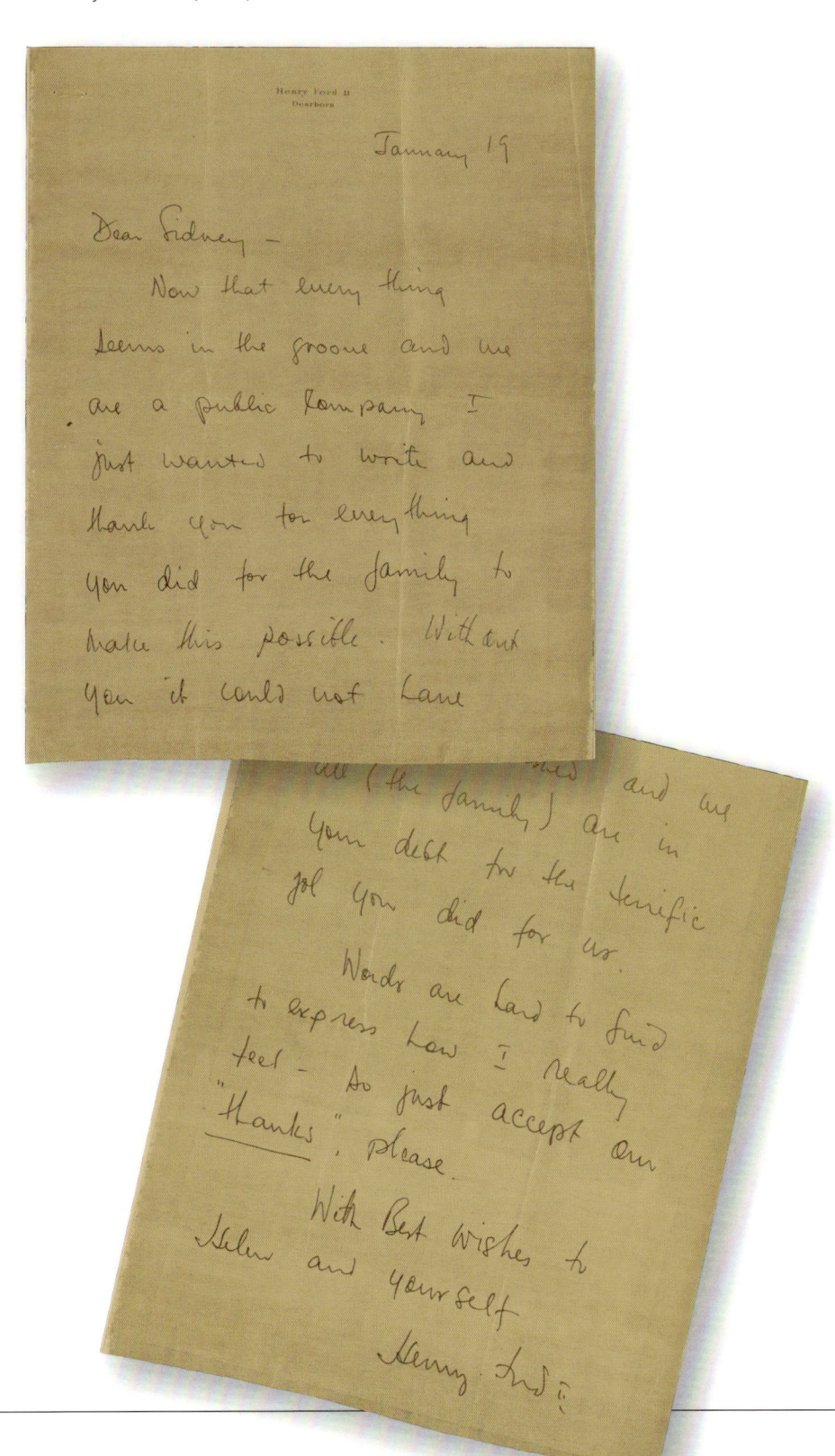

The power of relationships fuels Ford Motor Company's historic IPO

Sidney Weinberg met Henry Ford II in 1947, when the Ford heir, then just shy of 30 years old, found himself at the helm of the company founded in 1903 by his grandfather Henry. When Ford took over as president of the privately held Ford Motor Company on the death of Edsel Ford in 1945, he found the company in some financial disarray and worked to transform it into a disciplined organization with modern management systems.

Over the next several years, Weinberg and Ford's relationship deepened. Weinberg worked as an informal advisor to the Ford family and consulted closely with Henry II. In the early 1950s, Ford turned to Weinberg for counsel as he looked to restructure the company in a manner that would cede some control and voting rights to those outside of the immediate Ford family. In 1956, Weinberg formulated a plan that allowed Henry Ford II to take his company public. At $657.9 million (more than $28.5 billion in 2019 dollars) and 10.2 million shares, the 1956 Ford Motor Company IPO, led by Goldman Sachs, was the largest common stock offering to date. With Sidney Weinberg becoming one of Ford Motor's first outside directors, the Ford IPO also cemented what would be a long-standing relationship between Goldman Sachs and the Ford Motor Company.

Right: Correspondence from Henry Ford II to Sidney Weinberg, 1956.

John Whitehead memo revolutionizes investment banking

On March 14, 1956, John Whitehead submitted a memorandum to Sidney Weinberg that would revolutionize investment banking at Goldman Sachs and throughout Wall Street.

The 26-page document was created in response to a request sent by Weinberg two months earlier, on the heels of the historic Ford Motor Company IPO. Noting the firm's challenges in securing new business beyond Weinberg's own extraordinary network, he instructed Whitehead to "make a full and exhaustive study of our set-up for the solicitation of new business."

In response, what John Whitehead proposed not only changed fundamentally the new business approach at Goldman Sachs, but the firm's organizational structure itself.

Traditionally, investment banking followed a number of unwritten rules, foremost among them that clients came to the bankers; bankers did not solicit business. In addition, the same investment banker who sold the service provided the service.

Whitehead proffered a revolutionary concept: bankers would now specialize — either managing client relationships and selling banking services or providing the expertise to deliver those services. The creation of what would become Investment Banking Services was a radical new approach that many, including Sidney Weinberg, viewed with deep skepticism. But the visionary Whitehead was undaunted.

The bold decision to create distinct roles proved to be a strategic advantage that helped to increase dramatically the firm's client roster and standing. Other investment banks eventually followed suit, recasting their own approaches and changing the investment banking world forever.

Top: Memorandum from Sidney Weinberg to John Whitehead, 1956.

Bottom: Organizational chart reflecting John Whitehead's analysis of the firm's New Business Department, 1956.

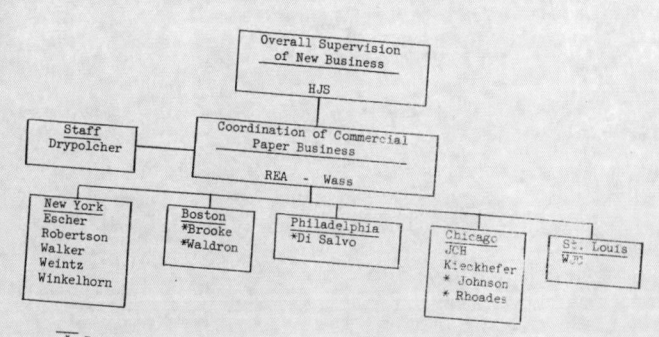

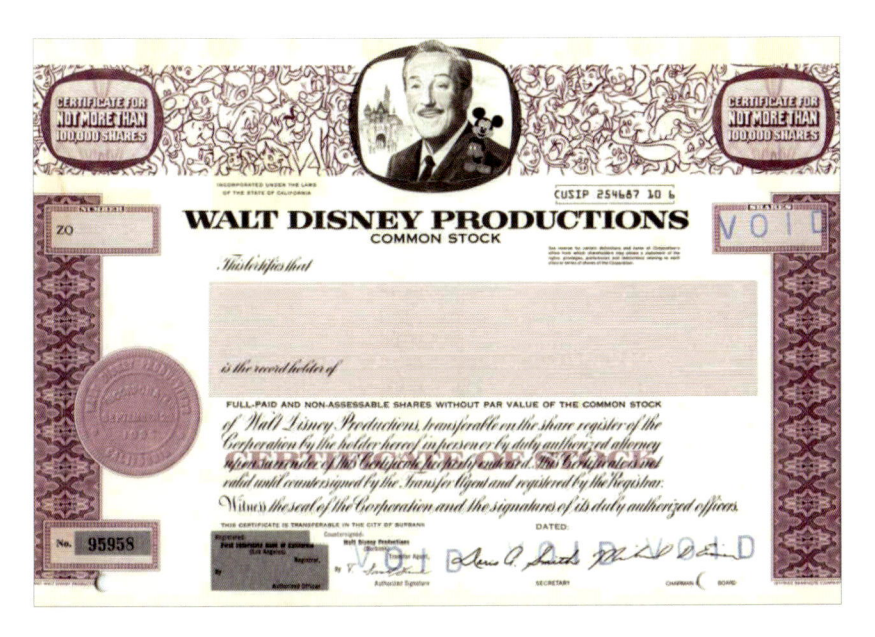

Disney magic comes to NYSE with initial public offering

Walt Disney was a creative genius who revolutionized animation and film production and virtually invented the modern theme park business. He also made astute business decisions in building the empire that is today The Walt Disney Company. In 1957, Goldman Sachs lead-managed the IPO of Walt Disney Productions on the New York Stock Exchange (NYSE), at a share price of $13.88. The timing seemed right, as Disney had opened its groundbreaking theme park Disneyland in California just two years earlier. The offering would be an important early step in what would become a long-term relationship between Disney and the firm.

Above: Walt Disney Productions prospectus, 1957.

Top left: Walt Disney Productions stock certificate, 1957.

Bottom left: Walt Disney in front of the Fantasyland castle at the opening of Disneyland, Anaheim, California, 1955.

Goldman Sachs establishes the firm's Management Committee

By the mid-1960s, Goldman Sachs senior partner Sidney Weinberg was living and working in Midtown Manhattan, and while his presence was very much still felt at Goldman Sachs' offices downtown, Weinberg was not intimately involved in the firm's day-to-day operations. These were increasingly falling to Gus Levy, a partner who headed the firm's trading business.

At the time, Goldman Sachs had hired a senior partner away from Coopers & Lybrand named George Doty. Doty had a strong background in operations and fiscal discipline and a keen focus on managing business risk. When he joined Goldman Sachs, Doty insisted that the firm establish a Management Committee — something that had not previously existed at the firm. Formed in 1965, the Committee's initial membership included Weinberg, Levy, Doty and John Whitehead.

In its early stages, the Management Committee limited its activities to new issues and other corporate finance transactions. The meetings took place in Gus Levy's office, reportedly with attendees standing because Levy, who had little patience for long meetings, thought that this would make the meetings shorter. As the Management Committee continued to serve as the firm's senior leadership group in the ensuing years, its charter expanded to encompass all issues that did not require a vote by the full partnership or a partner's individual consent.

Above: Management Committee, January 2019.

Seated, from left: Masa Mochida, Marc Nachmann, Alison Mass, Jim Esposito, Richard Gnodde, John Waldron, Stephen Scherr, Tim O' Neil, John F.W. Rogers, Stephanie Cohen, Ashok Varadhan and Steve Strongin. Standing, from left: Martin Chavez, Gregg Lemkau, Dina Powell, Dan Dees, Ken Hitchner, Laurence Stein, Sheila Patel, Michael Daffey, David Solomon, Rich Friedman, Sarah Smith, Robin Vince, Karen Seymour, Dane Holmes, Russell Horwitz (Secretary), Gwen Libstag and Julian Salisbury.

Opposite: Management Committee, 1966.

Seated, from left: John Weinberg, Walter Blaine, Sidney Weinberg, Gus Levy, George Doty and John Whitehead. Standing, from left: Howard Young and Edward Schrader.

Quarter Century Club is established to recognize long-term service

Since 1963, Goldman Sachs has honored those who have contributed to the firm's efforts for 25 years with induction into the Quarter Century Club (QCC). This achievement is celebrated as a profound reflection of commitment to the firm and to the culture of Goldman Sachs, a distinction held by more than 1,500 living members as of 2019: more than 1,000 of whom are alumni and more than 500 who currently work at the firm. In 2019 at the 56th Annual QCC dinner, 136 new members were recognized — across levels, divisions and regions of the firm.

Top: First annual meeting of the Quarter Century Club, New York City, 1964.

Bottom: 2019 inductees at the Quarter Century Club dinner, New York City, 2019.

100th ANNIVERSARY

1969: Stonewall riots, man on the Moon, Woodstock, and the rise of block trading

One hundred years after its founding, Goldman Sachs is US leader in commercial paper, block trading and arbitrage

The year 1969 would mark the final public performance of the Beatles, while the riots at the Stonewall Inn launched what would become the modern LGBTQ civil rights movement. That summer, Neil Armstrong walked on the Moon and the Woodstock music festival attracted more than 500,000 people to a farm north of New York City. The early seeds of the internet were also planted as the first communication through ARPANET, the computer network developed by the US Department of Defense, was sent.

A century after its founding, Goldman Sachs was the largest US dealer in commercial paper, yet it remained a relatively small partnership, consisting of 38 partners, with an overall workforce of 1,500 employees and $600 million in assets ($4.1 billion in 2019 dollars) and $45 million in capital ($308 million in 2019 dollars). The firm was largely still a US-based operation, with offices in ten cities but no significant presence outside the United States. The following year, however, Goldman Sachs would open its first international office in London, ushering in a period of geographical expansion for the firm.

At the same time, the 1960s marked the rise of institutional investors, bringing a growing demand for large blocks of equity shares. Led by Gus Levy, Goldman Sachs pioneered the concept of block trading, which would prove to be a strong profit center for the firm and an essential component of capital markets.

The firm had also carved out a leading position in security arbitrage and continued to expand into areas such as corporate bond trading and municipal finance, as well as trading and underwriting securities issued by federal agencies.

Right: Reception area of the 20 Broad Street office, c. 1960.

Gus Levy is appointed senior partner

Gustave "Gus" Levy was born in New Orleans in 1910. He attended Tulane University for just two months before relocating in 1928 to New York, where he worked for a brokerage firm and took courses at New York University. Gus joined Goldman Sachs in 1933 as a trader on the foreign bond desk, later moving to the arbitrage desk. His rise through the ranks heralded a new era for the firm's business. He was named partner in 1945.

Always with an eye on creating long-term value for clients, Gus transformed the sales and trading function at Goldman Sachs by popularizing the practice of block trades, making it a primary commercial focus for the firm. In 1967, Levy executed a record-breaking block trade of more than one million shares of Alcan Aluminum, worth more than $26.5 million ($199 million in 2019 dollars). Indicative of his leadership style and capital markets acumen, Gus was known for having his office in the back of the trading room, enabling him to closely monitor the tape through a window. He was appointed senior partner in 1969.

Like Sidney Weinberg before him, Gus rose to become one of the most respected men in the industry, serving as chairman of the New York Stock Exchange and director of 16 major corporations. His financial expertise was equally in demand outside of the industry, including service as a commissioner of the Port Authority of New York and New Jersey, as well as trustee for a variety of nonprofits.

A prominent philanthropist who modeled the firm's long-standing commitment to service, Gus led Goldman Sachs until he passed away in 1976 at age 66. He was succeeded by John Weinberg and John Whitehead, who served as co-senior partners.

Above: Gus Levy on the cover of Finance *magazine, May 1968.*

Right: Gus Levy and Vice President Hubert Humphrey at the 175th anniversary of the New York Stock Exchange, 1967.

Above: Gus Levy in his office, overlooking the Trading and Arbitrage Department, 1974.

TRANSFORMATION

As anti-Vietnam War demonstrations rocked college campuses across the United States and the first Boeing 747 took to the skies, change was also underway at Goldman Sachs in the late 1960s and early 1970s. Gus Levy's appointment to senior partner of Goldman Sachs upon Sidney Weinberg's death in 1969 represented a break with the firm's past and with Wall Street tradition: at the time, it was highly unusual for a trader to run an investment bank.

Considered one of the leading innovators of twentieth century American finance, Gus would lead Goldman Sachs through a period of significant growth, innovation and expansion. He would also preside over the worst crisis Goldman Sachs had faced since the Great Depression, when commercial paper client Penn Central Railroad went bankrupt in 1970. With $87 million of paper outstanding at the time of Penn Central's bankruptcy, the Goldman Sachs partnership faced a potentially devastating unlimited liability. Under Gus' leadership, the partners banded together to work through a series of litigations and settlements that ultimately secured the firm's survival. As was the case for the Goldman Sachs Trading Corporation debacle of 1930, recovery from Penn Central would take many years, but also underscored the resiliency of the partnership in the face of great adversity.

At the time, Goldman Sachs was also setting its sights abroad, opening its first non-US office in 1970, in London. With Tokyo and Zurich locations opening their doors in 1974, Goldman Sachs' global journey was officially underway. That same year, the firm became a primary dealer and market maker of US government securities, doing business directly with the Federal Reserve and the US Treasury Department.

Top: Page five of New York Post, *1974.*

Bottom: Seaboard World Airlines Boeing 747 cargo plane, 1974.

Opposite: Robert Conway, William Landreth, David Jones and Thomas Rhodes on the steps of the London International Financial Futures Exchange, 1984.

Goldman Sachs takes its first step to becoming a global firm with London office

In 1970, Goldman Sachs placed an advertisement in *The New York Times* announcing the opening of its first international office, in London. In a press clipping the prior year, senior partner Gus Levy was quoted as saying the upcoming office opening was the beginning of a "major international effort" on the part of the firm.

The new office, located on Goldsmith Street, initially focused on limited corporate finance and brokerage activities. Just three years later, with business growing and services expanding, the London team relocated to a space double in size at 40 Basinghall Street. By the mid-1970s, its activities included equities trading, corporate finance and commercial paper.

Goldman Sachs began its work in London representing the European interests of the firm's US clients, but soon local relationships would take root and flourish, and the firm increasingly advised UK and Continental European clients on a range of transactions and strategies.

In 1975, the firm co-managed a $100 million, 20-year issue of sinking fund debentures for London-based Imperial Chemical Industries Ltd., one of the largest commercial offerings to date. The following year, it executed major private placements for British pharmaceuticals company Beecham and tobacco processing machinery concern Molins Machine Company, Inc. Also active in the Eurodollar commercial paper market and in mergers and acquisitions — many of them cross-border — Goldman Sachs demonstrated that it was following through on Gus Levy's promise, rapidly solidifying its position as a global firm.

Top: Gus Levy speaking at opening of London office, 1970.

Bottom: Announcement for opening of London office, 1970.

Penn Central bankruptcy leads to turmoil in the commercial paper market

In the late 1960s, the Penn Central Transportation Company was the largest railroad in the United States, the sixth-largest firm in the country and the owner of one of the most valuable corporate real estate portfolios. The railroad controlled more than 20,000 miles of track, one-eighth of the nation's freight and a network stretching from St. Louis and Chicago to Boston and Montreal.

Penn Central had been formed in 1968 from the merger of the New York Central and the Pennsylvania Railroads, a combined entity that was plagued with integration issues and management failures. While asset rich, Penn Central was cash poor, and mounting losses forced the company — a client of Goldman Sachs — to to file for bankruptcy on June 21, 1970.

The Penn Central bankruptcy sent shock waves through the commercial paper market — a market in which the firm served nearly 300 other clients who suddenly faced widespread redemptions from panicked investors. Market liquidity vanished and companies rushed to secure funding to buy back their paper.

With $87 million in issued paper in default ($562 million in 2019 dollars), Penn Central's failure threatened the very viability of Goldman Sachs, which now faced losses exceeding the firm's capital. The firm's partners banded together and worked through a series of litigation and settlements for several years following the railroad's bankruptcy. Eventually, converted Penn Central securities enabled Goldman Sachs to recover some of its capital, but the damage to the firm and the lessons learned were costly. In the years that followed, Goldman Sachs would have to work hard to restore its reputation and market leadership.

Above: Penn Central train at Grand Central Station, New York City, 1973.

Fischer Black, future director of Quantitative Strategies at Goldman Sachs, helps to revolutionize options trading

When economists Fischer Black and Myron Scholes first met at the Massachusetts Institute of Technology (MIT) in the late 1960s, a working partnership that would last for 25 years was born. Their crowning achievement was the Black-Scholes Option Pricing model that revolutionized investing and ultimately led to a Nobel Prize.

Black and Scholes published "The Pricing of Options and Corporate Liabilities" in the May-June 1973 issue of the *Journal of Political Economy*. In it, they demonstrated how the price of a stock option could be determined from the price of the underlying stock, the volatility of the stock, the exercise price and maturity of the option and the interest rate. Bringing a new quantitative approach to option pricing, Black and Scholes' research would fuel the growth of the modern derivatives market.

Goldman Sachs would hire Fischer Black in 1984 to lead the firm's efforts in the area of quantitative risk management. During his tenure at the firm, Black leveraged his extraordinary talents to combine creative theoretical finance and market-driven strategies to develop practical financial tools. Among these were the Black-Derman-Toy model, created in collaboration with Goldman Sachs colleagues Emanuel Derman and Bill Toy in 1986 to value fixed income derivatives, and the Black-Litterman Global Asset Allocation model, developed with Bob Litterman in 1990 to help clients of the firm diversify their global bond portfolios. A year later, Black-Litterman was extended to equities, and the model was adopted by the firm's asset management arm, Goldman Sachs Asset Management (GSAM), which Black joined in 1990.

$$w(x,t) = xN(d_1) - ce^{r(t-t^*)}N(d_2)$$

$$d_1 = \frac{\ln x/c + (r + \frac{1}{2}v^2)(t^* - t)}{v\sqrt{t^* - t}}$$

$$d_2 = \frac{\ln x/c + (r - \frac{1}{2}v^2)(t^* - t)}{v\sqrt{t^* - t}}$$

Top: Robert Litterman and Fischer Black, 1994.

Center: Emanuel Derman, Brian Carrihill, Cemal Dosembet and Piotr Karasinski, 1993.

Bottom: Black-Scholes formula, 1973.

Above: Électricité de France nuclear power plant, 1978.

French utility taps the US commercial paper market

When French state-owned utility Électricité de France (EdF) sought funds for a nuclear power construction program in 1974 to lessen its dependence on foreign oil, Goldman Sachs — along with Crédit Lyonnais and Morgan Guaranty Trust Co. — privately arranged a ten-year $500 million ($2.5 billion in 2019 dollars) Eurodollar revolving credit line for the utility. A few months after the loan was underwritten, EdF began issuing commercial paper in New York. Goldman Sachs managed the commercial paper sale for EdF — the first ever in the United States on behalf of a foreign government entity. The paper, which carried French government backing, offered EdF a lower short-term borrowing cost than the prevailing Eurodollar rate. The EdF transaction not only underscored Goldman Sachs' growing profile as a trusted advisor in Europe but also the firm's commitment to developing innovative solutions to resolve client challenges.

Goldman Sachs establishes Asia presence with Tokyo office

In 1974, Goldman Sachs opened an office in Tokyo — the firm's first in Asia. Even before Goldman Sachs had an on-the-ground presence in Japan, the firm was doing significant business there. In 1971, it was tapped to handle a commercial paper issuance in the United States on behalf of centuries-old Japanese trading company Mitsui & Co., Ltd. Seeking to appeal to skeptical US investors, Goldman Sachs ultimately backed up the offering with a US letter of credit. The success of the offering elevated the firm's profile in a country that was particularly difficult for foreign firms to penetrate.

The Tokyo office, located in the Yurakucho building near the Imperial Palace in Chiyoda City, initially concentrated primarily on investment banking, international financing for Japanese corporations and external financing for Asian governments. Growth was rapid; by 1978, Goldman Sachs was forced to move to a space in the Kasumigaseki building (also in Chiyoda City) that was double the size of its initial location — a clear indication of the growing importance of the Tokyo office not only for its access to Japanese markets but also as a gateway to the broader Asian market.

By the end of the 1970s, Japan was the second-largest economy in the world, and Goldman Sachs was well on its way to establishing itself as a known and trusted name in this important market.

We take pleasure in announcing
the opening of a Representative Office in
Tokyo by our affiliate
Goldman Sachs International Corp.
704, Yurakucho Building
5, Yurakucho 1-Chome
Chiyoda-Ku
Tokyo, 100 Japan
Telephone: 03-213-1221

William H. Brown
Vice President and Far East Representative

Michael C. Bowen
Vice President

Goldman, Sachs & Co.
New York Boston Chicago Dallas
Los Angeles Philadelphia St. Louis
San Francisco Detroit Memphis
Goldman Sachs International Corp.
New York London Tokyo

Goldman Sachs

Top: Aerial view of the Marunouchi district in Chiyoda City, Tokyo, 1972. The firm's first office in Tokyo was in the Yurakucho Building, the black rectangular building in the center.

Bottom: Announcement for opening of Tokyo office, 1974.

Above: Pravin Khatau, Nicholas O'Donohue and Barton Silverman, Zurich, 1986.

Second European office opens in Zurich

Switzerland's strength as an international financial hub dates from the beginning of World War I and that conflict's disastrous economic and political aftermath. In the interwar years, the neutrality of the country, its political, fiscal and monetary stability and banking secrecy cemented the Swiss Federation's reputation as a safe haven for finance. The Bank of International Settlements, the bank for central banks, set up its headquarters in Basel in 1930. During and after World War II, the Swiss franc became one of the strongest reserve currencies in the world by virtue of its full convertibility with the dollar.

By the 1970s, Switzerland was widely considered to be the third-most important financial center in the world after New York and London. Goldman Sachs opened an office in Zurich in September 1974. By 1979, the firm provided 24-hour worldwide services in the Eurobond markets with its London, Zurich and New York offices. In the early 1980s, with the establishment of Goldman Sachs Finance AG, the firm started underwriting and trading Swiss-franc-denominated securities and providing financings via the Swiss franc/US dollar swap market.

Annual Reports

A century after its founding, Goldman Sachs published its first *Annual Review* in 1970. This overview of the firm's activities and financial performance spoke to a narrow audience of partners, clients and industry professionals. Over time, as the firm grew, so too did its audience. When Goldman Sachs went public in 1999, there emerged an even greater urgency to communicate the firm's work, results and insight. In 2012, a digital version of the *Annual Report* was first made available, increasing its reach to an expanding audience of stakeholders. The *Annual Report* remains an important part of the cumulative Goldman Sachs voice, addressing not only recent performance but a vision for the future as well.

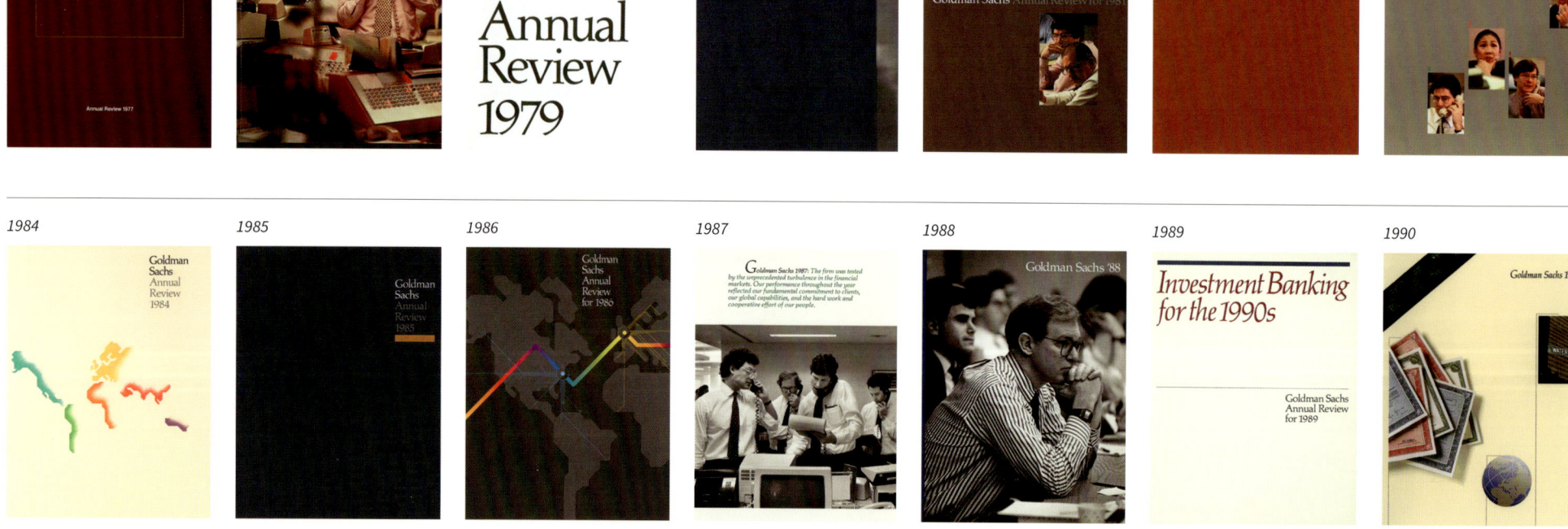

1970   *1971*   *1972*   *1973*   *1974*   *1975*   *1976*

1977   *1978*   *1979*   *1980*   *1981*   *1982*   *1983*

1984   *1985*   *1986*   *1987*   *1988*   *1989*   *1990*

1991 *1992* 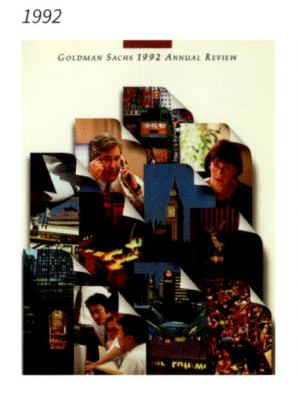 *1993* 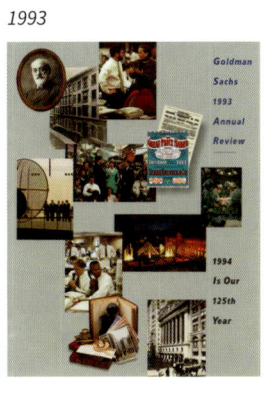 *1994*  *1995* 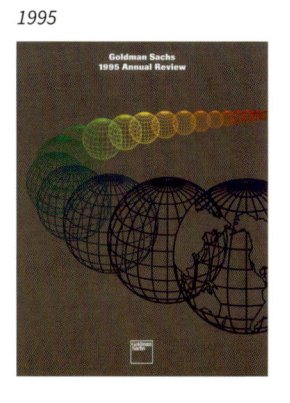 *1996* 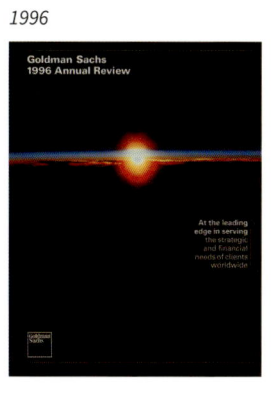 *1997*

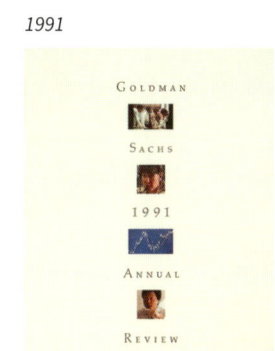

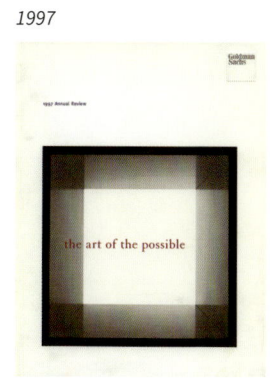

1998 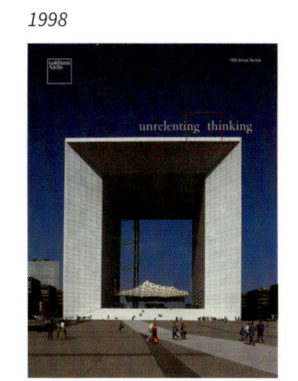 *1999*  *2000*  *2001* 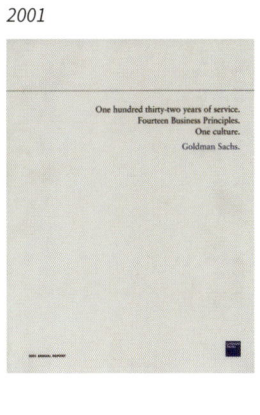 *2002* 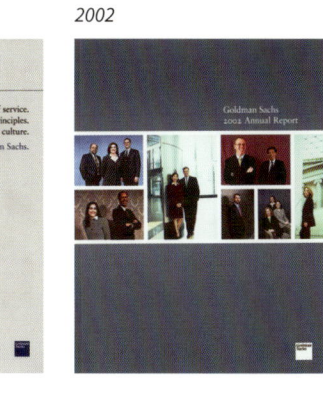 *2003*  *2004*

2005 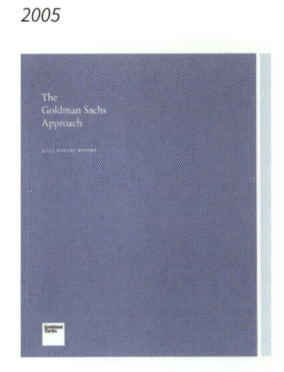 *2006* 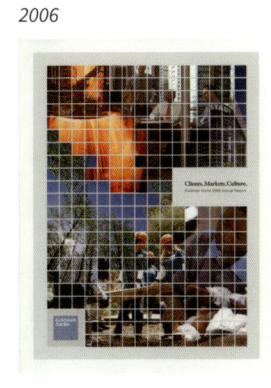 *2007* 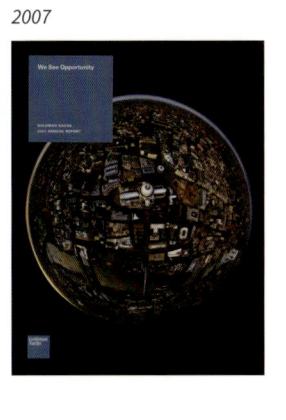 *2008*  *2009*  *2010*  *2011*

2012 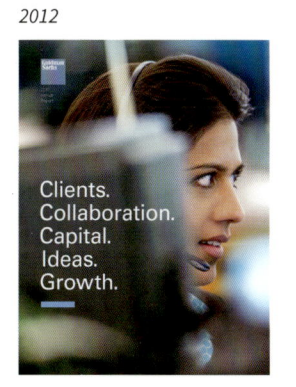 *2013*  *2014* 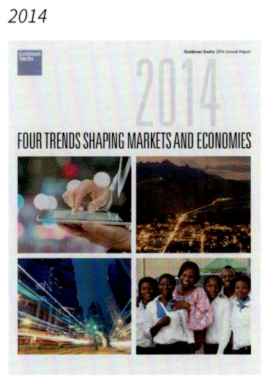 *2015* 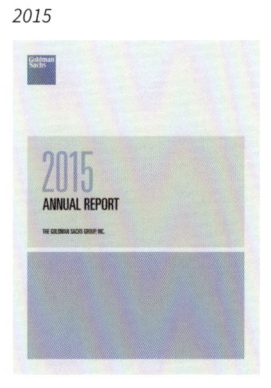 *2016* 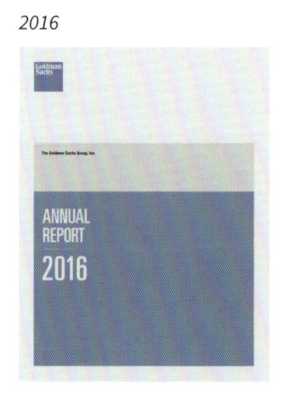 *2017* 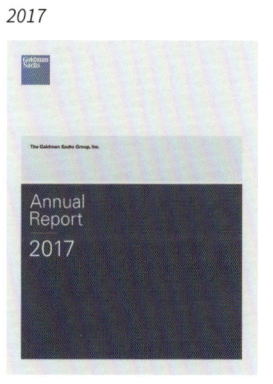 *2018*

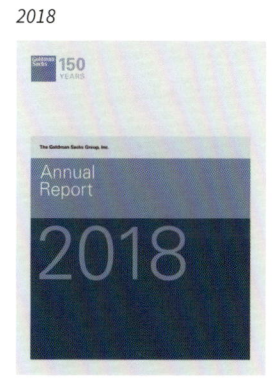

59

Clients

Goldman Sachs' first Business Principle states, "Our experience shows that if we serve our clients well, our own success will follow." Through the years, the firm has assumed many roles on behalf of its diverse clients, including advisor, financier, market maker, asset manager and co-investor. From Sydney to São Paulo, from Miami to Milan, Goldman Sachs teams bridge time zones and miles to offer clients access to the information, insight and capital they need to grow and seek out opportunity wherever it may exist.

61

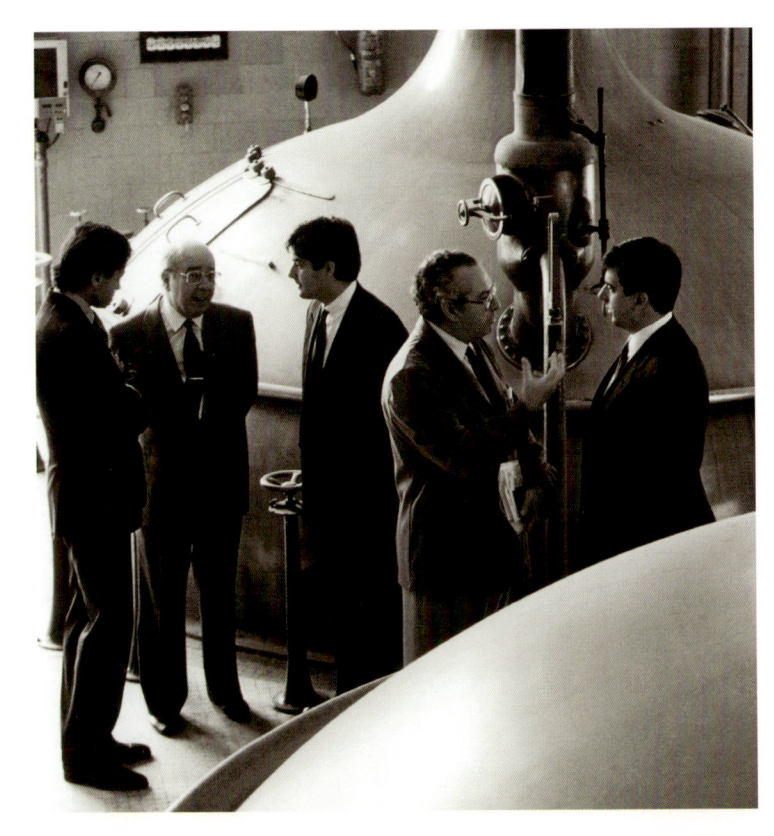

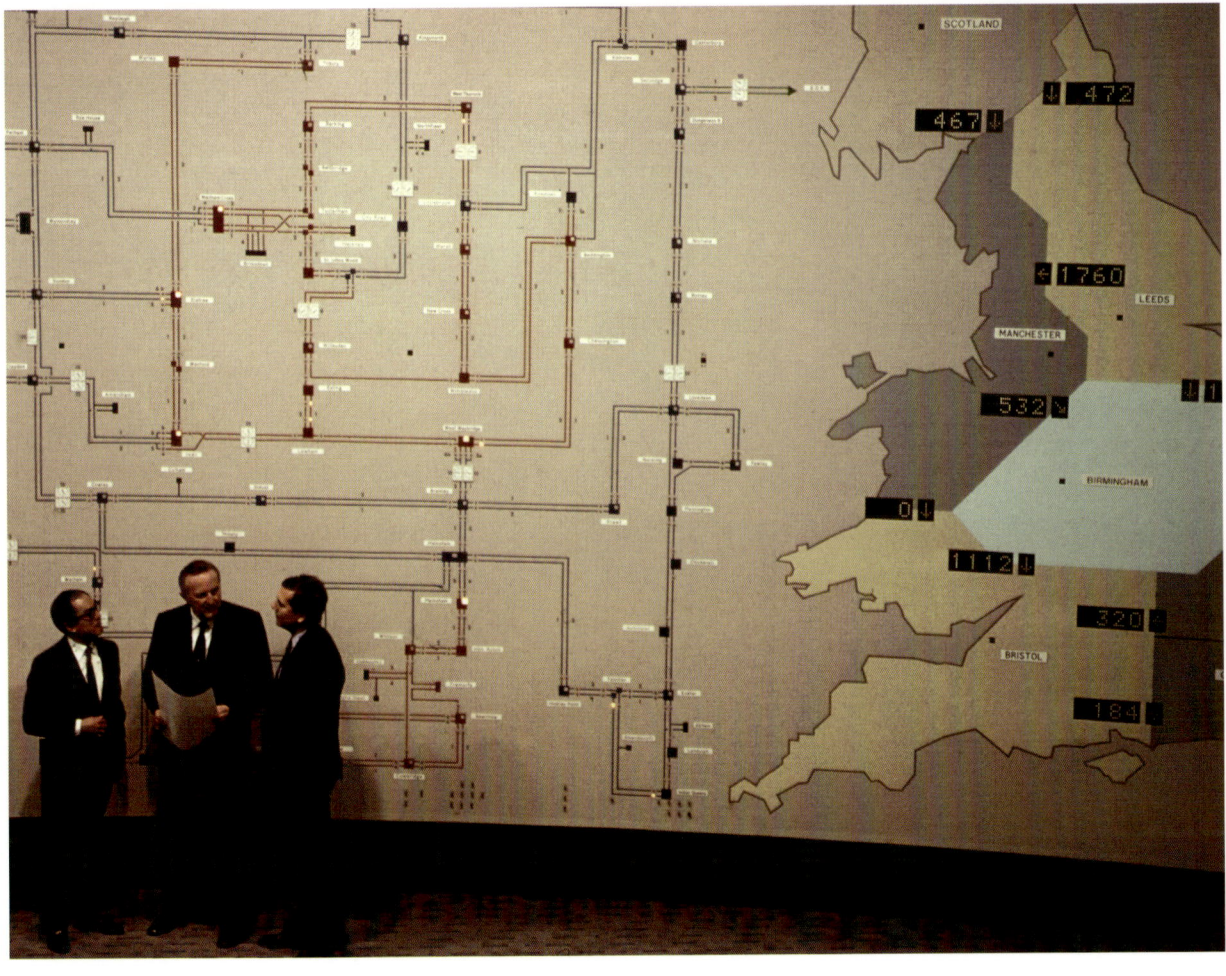

Clients

63

Institutional Investor
January 1984

The 1984 pensions directory
Favorite stocks for 1984

How CFOs make interest rate calls
Pensions: What went wrong at Wells Fargo?
Research: The perils of saying "sell"

Co-chairman John Whitehead

Co-chairman John Weinberg

Inside the Goldman Sachs culture

PRINCIPLED LEADERSHIP

The 1970s were a time of rapid growth for Goldman Sachs. In 1976, the firm elected its first co-senior partners, an unusual leadership structure in the industry at the time but one under which the the firm's Management Committee would flourish. John Weinberg, son of Sidney Weinberg, joined Goldman Sachs in 1950 after serving in combat overseas as a second lieutenant with the US Marine Corps in World War II and earning an MBA at Harvard University. John Whitehead had joined the firm in 1947 after serving in the US Navy and attending Harvard for his MBA.

As he settled into his new senior leadership role, Whitehead calculated that if the firm continued on its current trajectory, in a matter of just a few years, fully half of Goldman Sachs' employees would be new to the firm. Whitehead saw growth, while necessary, as a potential threat to the firm's carefully nurtured culture. The time had come to work toward institutionalizing one of the most singular, and yet amorphous, attributes of Goldman Sachs. One Sunday afternoon in the late 1970s, Whitehead sat down with a yellow legal pad and sketched out the business principles that defined Goldman Sachs and what it stood for. After the incorporation of feedback from his fellow partners, the 14 Business Principles were approved and codified in 1979. From putting clients' interests above all else to stressing creativity and teamwork in every endeavor, the Business Principles remain the bedrock of Goldman Sachs' distinct culture four decades later.

The 1980s brought sweeping industrial deregulation to many developed economies ("Reaganomics" in the United States and the United Kingdom's "Big Bang") and ushered in the heyday of the hostile takeover. Knowing that it meant sacrificing opportunities for meaningful near-term profit, Goldman Sachs made the strategic decision to represent only the targets of hostile takeovers, a move that only deepened client trust over the long term. The firm's successes during this period of changing markets, new challenges and rapid growth underlined the timelessness of Goldman Sachs' Business Principles, reinforcing that if the firm held fast to these values, it would make the best decisions for both its clients and itself.

Top: Floor of the International Stock Exchange, London, 1990.

Bottom: "Unrelenting Thinking" advertisement, c. 1999.

Opposite: Cover of Institutional Investor *magazine, January 1984.*

John Whitehead and John Weinberg are named co-senior partners

As young associates at Goldman Sachs in the early 1950s, John Weinberg (born in 1925 in Scarsdale, New York) and John Whitehead (born in 1922 in Evanston, Illinois) ate lunch daily at Scotty's, a local sandwich shop, exchanging ideas about the firm and their vision for its future growth. Decades later, those conversations took on greater significance when the two men were named co-senior partners and co-chairmen of the firm's Management Committee in 1976.

There were many parallels between Weinberg and Whitehead. Both had served in the military during World War II: Weinberg in the US Marine Corps and Whitehead in the US Navy, where he piloted a landing craft on Omaha Beach on D-Day and served in the Pacific theater of the war. Later, Weinberg would take leave from the firm to serve as a captain during the Korean War. Both men joined the firm after receiving MBAs from Harvard Business School (Whitehead in 1947 and Weinberg in 1950). Weinberg and Whitehead started their careers in the Buying Department of Goldman Sachs (later called the Corporate Finance Department and, ultimately, the Investment Banking Division), and both were named partners in 1956.

In the early 1970s, Weinberg ran the firm's Fixed Income Division and Whitehead the Investment Banking Division. Following the death of Gus Levy in 1976, the two were named co-senior partners. Many predicted that a joint leadership structure would fail, but Weinberg and Whitehead proved to be a formidable combination. With an unwavering commitment to clients, an innate modesty and a candid leadership style, Weinberg played a critical role in forging some of the firm's most important and enduring client relationships in the 1950s, '60s and '70s. These strengths were complemented by Whitehead's strategic, organizationally oriented mindset. Often referred to as the "Two Johns," they embodied the firm's ethos of teamwork and cooperation and would go on to jointly lead Goldman Sachs for nearly eight years.

Above: John Whitehead and John Weinberg, 1981.

When Whitehead retired in 1984, Weinberg, then 59 years old, remained on as sole senior partner for an additional six years. Whitehead was asked to become deputy secretary of state under President Ronald Reagan, a position he held from 1985 to 1989; in 2005, he published his memoir *A Life in Leadership: From D-Day to Ground Zero*. John Weinberg retired from Goldman Sachs in 1990. He was a member of the firm's first board of directors after Goldman Sachs' 1999 IPO. He died in 2006 at the age of 81. John Whitehead died in 2015 at the age of 92.

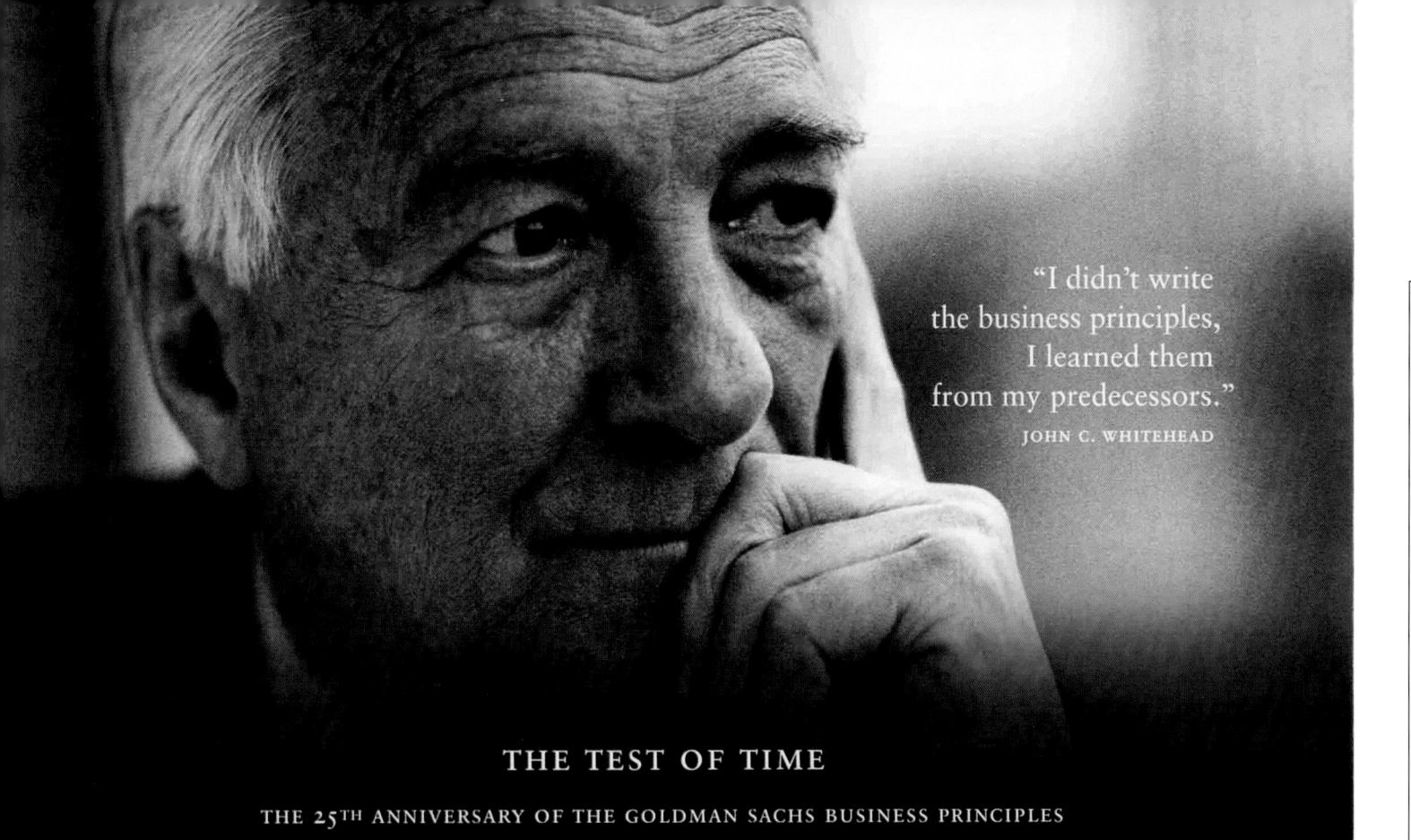

"I didn't write the business principles, I learned them from my predecessors."
— JOHN C. WHITEHEAD

THE TEST OF TIME

THE 25TH ANNIVERSARY OF THE GOLDMAN SACHS BUSINESS PRINCIPLES

1. Our clients' interests always come first. Our experience shows that if we serve our clients well, our own success will follow.

2. Our assets are our people, capital and reputation. If any of these is ever diminished, the last is the most difficult to restore. We are dedicated to complying fully with the letter and spirit of the laws, rules and ethical principles that govern us. Our continued success depends upon unswerving adherence to this standard.

3. Our goal is to provide superior returns to our shareholders. Profitability is critical to achieving superior returns, building our capital, and attracting and keeping our best people. Significant employee stock ownership aligns the interests of our employees and our shareholders.

4. We take great pride in the professional quality of our work. We have an uncompromising determination to achieve excellence in everything we undertake. Though we may be involved in a wide variety and heavy volume of activity, we would, if it came to a choice, rather be best than biggest.

5. We stress creativity and imagination in everything we do. While recognizing that the old way may still be the best way, we constantly strive to find a better solution to a client's problems. We pride ourselves on having pioneered many of the practices and techniques that have become standard in the industry.

6. We make an unusual effort to identify and recruit the very best person for every job. Although our activities are measured in billions of dollars, we select our people one by one. In a service business, we know that without the best people, we cannot be the best firm.

7. We offer our people the opportunity to move ahead more rapidly than is possible at most other places. Advancement depends on merit and we have yet to find the limits to the responsibility our best people are able to assume. For us to be successful, our men and women must reflect the diversity of the communities and cultures in which we operate. That means we must attract, retain and motivate people from many backgrounds and perspectives. Being diverse is not optional; it is what we must be.

8. We stress teamwork in everything we do. While individual creativity is always encouraged, we have found that team effort often produces the best results. We have no room for those who put their personal interests ahead of the interests of the firm and its clients.

9. The dedication of our people to the firm and the intense effort they give their jobs are greater than one finds in most other organizations. We think that this is an important part of our success.

10. We consider our size an asset that we try hard to preserve. We want to be big enough to undertake the largest project that any of our clients could contemplate, yet small enough to maintain the loyalty, the intimacy and the esprit de corps that we all treasure and that contribute greatly to our success.

11. We constantly strive to anticipate the rapidly changing needs of our clients and to develop new services to meet those needs. We know that the world of finance will not stand still and that complacency can lead to extinction.

12. We regularly receive confidential information as part of our normal client relationships. To breach a confidence or to use confidential information improperly or carelessly would be unthinkable.

13. Our business is highly competitive, and we aggressively seek to expand our client relationships. However, we must always be fair competitors and must never denigrate other firms.

14. Integrity and honesty are at the heart of our business. We expect our people to maintain high ethical standards in everything they do, both in their work for the firm and in their personal lives.

28 GOLDMAN SACHS 2004 ANNUAL REPORT

Fourteen Business Principles define the firm and reflect its culture

The culture of Goldman Sachs is as enduring as it is distinct. Over the past century and a half, the firm has navigated periods of significant change and challenges — economic, geopolitical and societal — while staying true to a shared set of values that are the product of the firm's rich history. The Goldman Sachs Business Principles, first codified in 1979 by John Whitehead, have formed the foundation of a lasting culture rooted in integrity, excellence, innovation and teamwork.

Left: 25th anniversary of the Business Principles, page from Goldman Sachs Annual Report, 2004.

67

Above: J. Aron employees tasting coffee, c. 1982.

Goldman Sachs adds strength in commodities and foreign exchange with J. Aron acquisition

In 1898, Jacob Aron established a small, family-owned coffee trading company in New Orleans called J. Aron & Company. Over the years, J. Aron moved to New York and expanded into other agricultural commodities and, in the 1960s, precious metals. Goldman Sachs served as the company's investment banker and acted as one of its futures brokers. In 1981, when the J. Aron partners decided they had grown their firm as much as they could as an independent concern, they asked Goldman Sachs to find them a buyer.

After presenting at least one offer that J. Aron rejected, and recognizing that the company treasured its privately held status, Goldman Sachs' senior management proposed what they thought would be a more palatable buyer and a better fit for J. Aron: Goldman Sachs itself. After a long stagnation in the securities market, the firm saw an opportunity to expand trading in commodities and to deepen its international presence through those markets. The offer was accepted, and in 1981, Goldman Sachs acquired J. Aron & Company for an undisclosed amount.

The J. Aron acquisition would prove to be a powerful strategic decision for Goldman Sachs. In the decades that followed, the talent, technical expertise and trading capabilities of J. Aron reinforced Goldman Sachs' position as a leading provider of truly integrated financial and risk management solutions to its clients around the globe.

International Advisory Board is formed to provide global insight

In 1982, Goldman Sachs formed its International Advisory Board to assist the firm in monitoring political and economic developments worldwide. The first chairman of the board was Henry "Joe" Fowler, former secretary of the treasury under President Lyndon B. Johnson and a limited partner of the firm. Senior partners John Weinberg and John Whitehead observed that this new board would "contribute greatly to the further development of [the] firm's international activities" and "broaden the scope of services and advice on international matters which we are able to offer to our clients." To this day, the firm maintains a global network of regional advisors providing market and industry insights both to the firm and its expansive client base.

Above: Members of the inaugural International Advisory Board, 1983. Standing, from left: Robert McNamara, Maurice Perouse, Otmar Emminger. Seated, from left: Sir David Orr, Henry Kissinger, Henry Fowler.

Left: Henry Kissinger visits the 55 Water Street office in New York City, 1982. Standing, from left: Steve Goldenberg, Henry Kissinger, Nick Caporale and Jonathan Cohen. Sitting at desk: James Halloran.

New global headquarters opens at 85 Broad Street

In 1983, Goldman Sachs opened a newly constructed headquarters building at 85 Broad Street in New York City's Financial District. The building site was historically significant as it was the location of the official Stadt Huys, or Town Hall, of the City of New Amsterdam in the mid-1600s. Goldman Sachs cooperated with New York City's Landmarks Preservation Commission as it conducted a year-long archaeological excavation of the site — the most ambitious dig in the city's history — before construction could begin. Located just blocks from the Pine Street location where Marcus Goldman first set up shop in a basement office, 85 Broad Street would serve as Goldman Sachs' global headquarters until late 2009.

Top: New York Mayor Ed Koch speaks during the dedication of the 85 Broad Street construction site, New York City, 1980.

Bottom: 85 Broad Street, New York City, 1983.

Looking to expand in Asia, Goldman Sachs establishes a Hong Kong presence

Goldman Sachs opened an office in Hong Kong in October of 1983, appreciating the vital role the port territory played as a bridge to other Asian markets. The office initially focused on investment banking activities, with the overarching objective of establishing the Goldman Sachs name in the region.

Within a year, and with only two employees, Goldman Sachs reaped the benefits of an on-the-ground presence in Hong Kong. The firm led the first US commercial paper issuance by a Hong Kong corporation on behalf of the Mass Transit Railway Corporation in 1984, the same year it was asked to assist two of the most important organizations in Hong Kong at the time: the Hongkong and Shanghai Banking Corporation (HSBC) and Hongkong Land.

By late 1989, the office had grown to 15 people. A year later, the Equities Division was established and investment banking activities expanded. In 1992, both research and principal investment activities were initiated, and in 1993, a specialized Capital Markets Group was formed, and substantial commodities, currency and derivatives operations began.

Within a decade of its opening, Goldman Sachs' Hong Kong office had grown to become the regional hub for the firm's rapidly growing presence in other parts of Asia.

Above: Sung-June Hwang, Janice Wallace and Jan Lee, Hong Kong, 1993.

Left: Hong Kong office interior view, c. 2003.

Goldman Sachs joins the Tokyo Stock Exchange

In the mid-1980s, the Tokyo Stock Exchange was the world's largest after New York, with one-third of total global equity trading volume — yet it was entirely closed to non-Japanese firms.

In 1982, a year after Japanese firms first became members of the New York Stock Exchange, the Tokyo Stock Exchange modified its constitution to allow foreign members. However, membership was limited, vacancies were rare and the price for a seat was prohibitive for many firms. In 1985, the Exchange announced it would increase its membership by ten seats, selecting new members after examining their management and financial strength. For foreign securities firms, the Exchange would also consider their volume of Japanese business and length of time conducting business in Japan.

After a highly competitive process, in late 1985 the Tokyo Stock Exchange announced that it would grant seats to six foreign firms — three British and three American. Goldman Sachs was one of the three US firms selected. In addition to further elevating its profile in Japan, this accomplishment greatly strengthened the firm's ability to provide expanded trading and investment banking services to clients in the Pacific Basin.

Left: Floor of the Tokyo Stock Exchange, 1988.

Amid London's "Big Bang" deregulation, the firm joins the newly formed International Stock Exchange

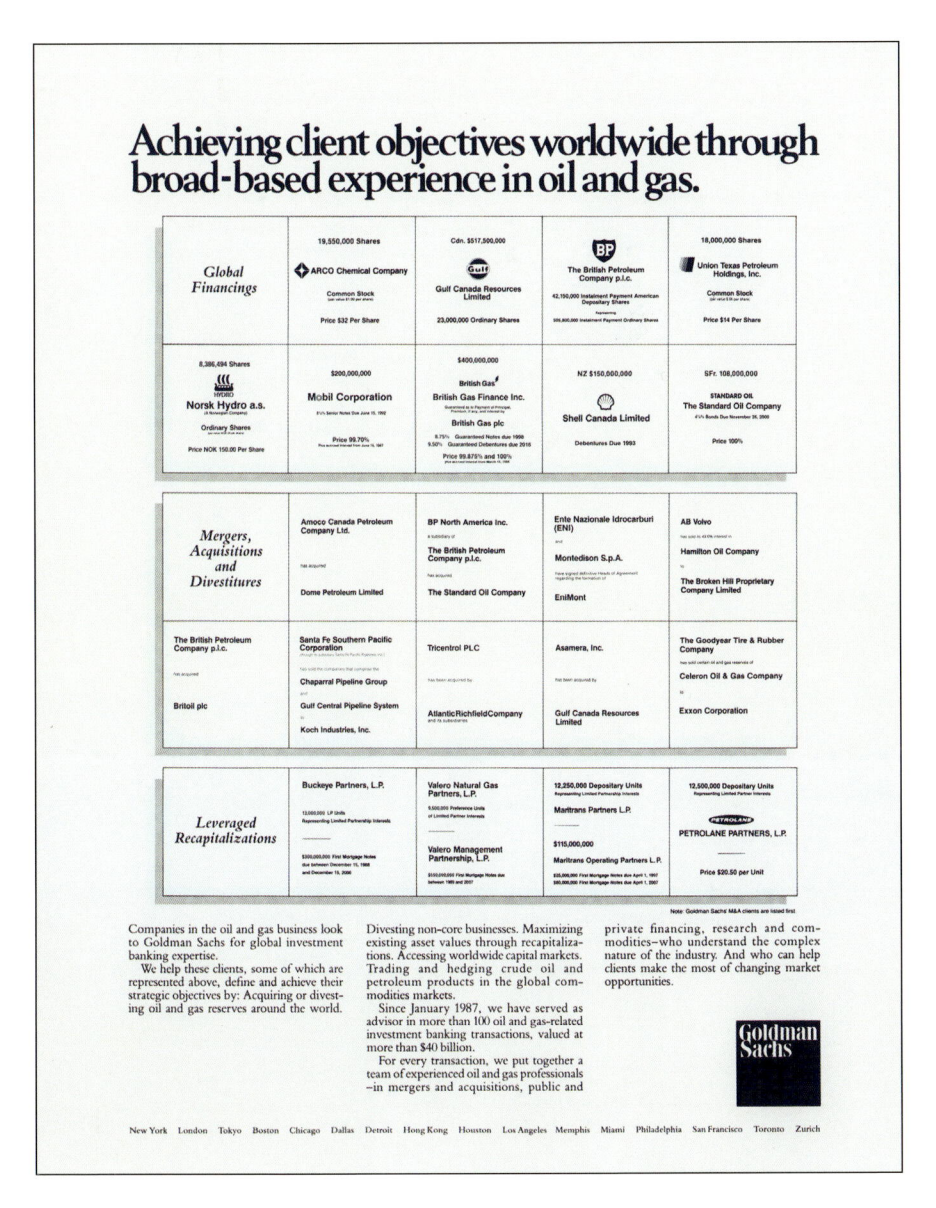

On October 27, 1986, London's stock market was deregulated in what is referred to as the "Big Bang." The event — which included the automation of price quotes, the removal of fixed commission charges and the allowance of foreign firms to own UK brokers — revolutionized European capital markets and reinforced London's position as a leading center for international finance.

In December of that year, the London Stock Exchange merged with a 187-member global trade group to become the International Stock Exchange (ISE). The ISE would change its name back to the London Stock Exchange (LSE) in 1995. Goldman Sachs joined the ISE that year and became a primary dealer in UK government securities.

By 1987, Goldman Sachs made markets in securities issued by more than 200 non-US corporations, had trading desks in New York, London and Tokyo and served more than 5,000 institutional clients globally. The firm's activities in the mid-1980s in the United Kingdom underscored Goldman Sachs' ability to evolve and remain nimble in an ever-changing market and regulatory landscape, and to act as an integral participant in global financial markets.

Above: Goldman Sachs corporate advertisement, 1988.

Right: Floor of the International Stock Exchange, London, 1986.

"IPO of the year" puts Goldman Sachs on the map with tech companies

Microsoft Corporation was founded in 1975 by childhood friends and fellow college dropouts William H. Gates (age 19) and Paul Allen (age 22). By the mid-1980s, the company was one of the three giants in the personal software industry, and the only one of the three that was not publicly traded. Gates would have preferred to keep the company private, but an expansive employee stock options policy meant that Microsoft was fast approaching 500 private stockholders, which would trigger the need to register with the SEC.

When Microsoft ultimately made the decision to pursue a public stock offering, Goldman Sachs and Alex. Brown & Sons were selected as co-managing underwriters following an extensive vetting process. Goldman Sachs was book running manager of the IPO, whose underwriting syndicate would ultimately include 103 firms.

The highly successful 1986 offering (dubbed "the IPO of the year" by many analysts) generated $61 million for Microsoft ($140 million in 2019 dollars) and a market capitalization of $777 million ($1.78 billion in 2019 dollars). The Microsoft IPO strengthened Goldman Sachs' position as a leading banker to software and other technology companies. In the years and decades to follow, the firm would continue to further its reputation as a strategic and trusted adviser for innovative technology companies in markets around the world.

Right: Bill Gates, co-founder, chairman and CEO, Microsoft Corporation, 1985.

Left: Tombstone advertisement, Microsoft Corporation initial public offering, The Wall Street Journal, 1986.

Left: British Gas roadshow, 1986.

Goldman Sachs advises the British government in the country's largest privatization yet

The 1980s saw a wave of privatization across many sectors of the economy in the United Kingdom. The first large-scale privatization, that of British Telecom, took place in 1984 under the leadership of the government's advising merchant bank at the time, Kleinwort Benson. British Gas was next on the government's list, and as it reviewed options for bankers, it was willing to also consider American firms, believing that they might be able to contribute fresh thinking and techniques to structuring such transactions. Goldman Sachs was selected as the US book running manager for the British Gas common stock issue — the largest-ever global equity offering at the time at $8 billion ($19.3 billion in 2019 dollars). The success of this high-profile assignment helped the firm later win roles in other significant transactions in the United Kingdom, including selling British Gas' first bond market issue and the 1987 sale of the government's remaining interest in British Petroleum, which, at $12.4 billion ($27.4 billion in 2019 dollars), would surpass British Gas as Britain's largest privatization to date.

The Weinberg family contributes a legacy of leadership and service

From its earliest days, Goldman Sachs was a family business. Several generations of the Goldman family and even more branches of the Sachs family tree are reflected in its history.

One other family has also left its lasting mark on the firm and its culture. Spanning more than 100 years, members of the Weinberg family have served in key leadership positions at Goldman Sachs, playing pivotal roles in some of the signature moments in the firm's history.

The Weinberg family's connection to Goldman Sachs began with the humble origins of Sidney J. Weinberg, joining the firm as a teenager in 1907. He would serve as senior partner from 1930 until his death in 1969, in an extraordinary career as a leader on Wall Street and in public service.

His son John L. Weinberg joined the firm in 1950, after serving as a US Marine during World War II and graduating from Harvard Business School. Soon after he joined the partnership, he took leave during the Korean War for a year and a half. John would rise to be named co-senior partner and ultimately sole senior partner, a role he held until 1990. John was a member of the firm's first board of directors after Goldman Sachs' 1999 IPO. He passed away in 2006.

John's brother, Sidney J. "Jim" Weinberg, Jr., would also serve in senior leadership at Goldman Sachs during his 45-year tenure with the firm. Jim also earned an MBA from Harvard and served as a first lieutenant in the US Army during World War II. He joined the firm in 1965 and was an early member of the Investment Banking Services Department, which he led from 1978 to 1988. He was named a senior director after the firm's initial public offering in 1999 and maintained his office at the firm until his death in 2010.

The Weinberg family's legacy would continue with Jim's son, Peter A. Weinberg, who joined Goldman Sachs in 1988. Peter was a member of the firm for 17 years.

He began in investment banking, eventually serving as co-head of Investment Banking Services. In 1999, Peter moved to Europe, becoming co-chief executive officer of Goldman Sachs International. He retired from the firm in 2005.

John S. Weinberg, son of John L. Weinberg, joined the firm in 1983 and would serve for more than 32 years, including 13 years as co-head of the Investment Banking Division (IBD). In 2006, he was named vice chairman. His retirement from the firm in 2015 would come more than 100 years after his grandfather Sidney Weinberg began work as an assistant janitor.

Throughout more than two-thirds of the firm's existence, members of the Weinberg family have worked to further its mission and strengthen its culture. Their collective legacy of diligence, professional achievement and service is unparalleled in the history of Goldman Sachs.

Above, from left: Peter Weinberg, Jim Weinberg, John L. Weinberg and John S. Weinberg at a dinner honoring John L. Weinberg's 50th anniversary with the firm, 2000.

Right: John S. Weinberg presenting the John L. Weinberg Award at the Investment Banking Division (IBD) Global Conference, 2006.

Opposite, from left: John L. Weinberg, Sidney Weinberg and Jim Weinberg at a Harvard Business School dinner, 1958.

Deal Toys

A time-honored practice in financial services has been the commemoration of successful transactions via the "deal toy," a small gift to the client and key members of a deal team to memorialize a successfully completed merger, security issuance or other transaction. The 1950s saw the introduction and broad-based adoption of the lucite "tombstone," a typically rectangular or square block of clear plastic that encased a piece of paper with pertinent details of the transaction. In the ensuing decades, more three-dimensional, often whimsical objects increasingly replaced the tombstone on the desks of clients and bankers, as firms sought more creative and innovative ways to celebrate their accomplishments and capture the spirit of specific deals.

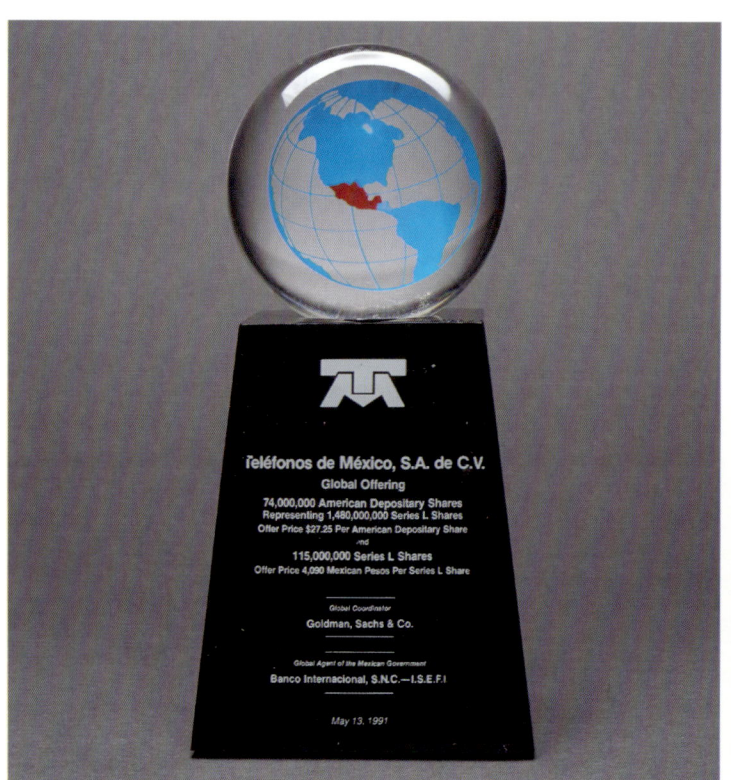

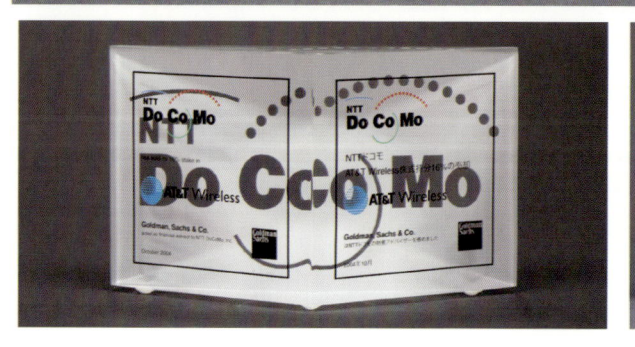

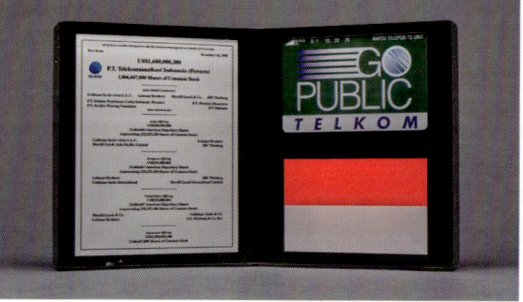

79

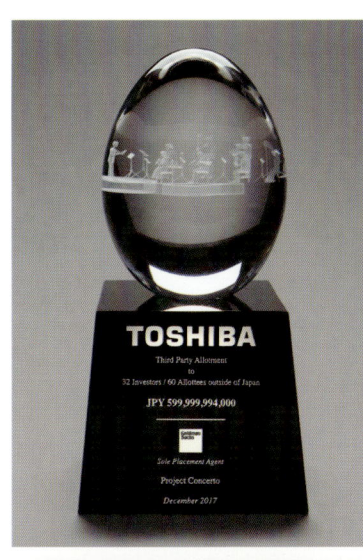

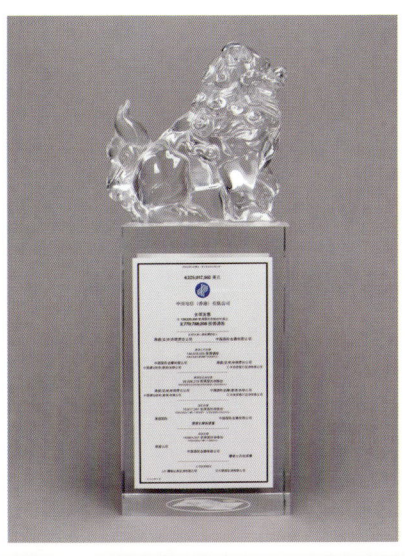

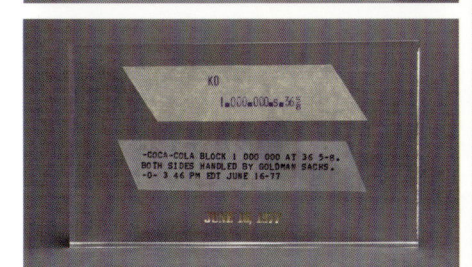

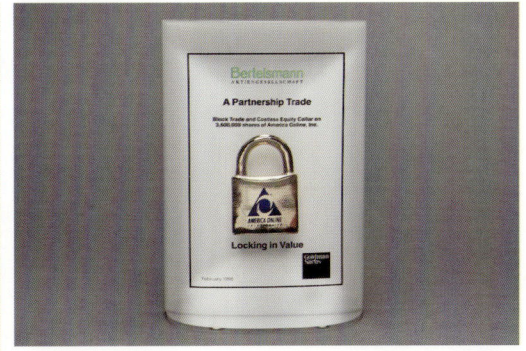

The Changing Workplace

As the breadth of expertise and services provided to clients evolves at Goldman Sachs, so too does the work environment. Advanced digital communication facilitates real-time collaboration among teams around the globe, with video conferencing that can convene a face-to-face meeting across several continents. Work-from-anywhere solutions enable teams to be flexible, mobile and productive. Today's Goldman Sachs makes overall wellness a priority for its people and invests in the resources that support that goal. This includes community hubs for a relaxed work environment, fitness programs, onsite healthy dining options and much more — resources brought to bear to promote a resilient workforce.

81

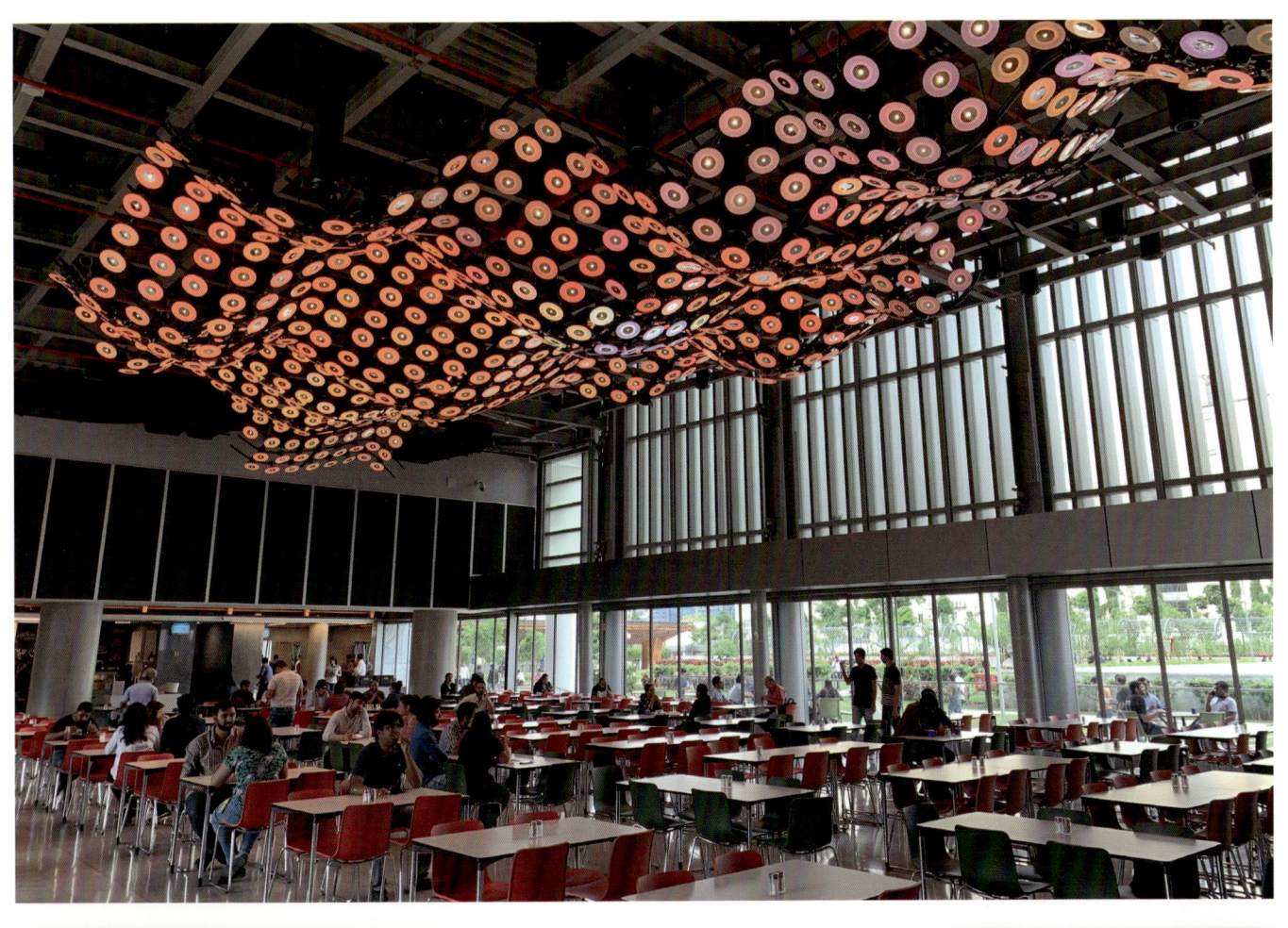

Research

For nearly a century, Goldman Sachs has provided clients with critical analysis of markets and economies around the globe. Today, an essential source of this insight is proprietary research from the firm's Global Investment Research Division (GIR). The GIR team provides original, fundamental analysis that helps investors better understand issues, trends and opportunities. This includes dedicated teams covering a wide range of markets and economies — by industry, sector, country and region. The Global Markets Institute, the research think tank of Goldman Sachs launched in 2004, provides unique insights to its global client base of policy makers, regulators, business leaders, investors and the public regarding issues that affect public policy, corporate strategy and society.

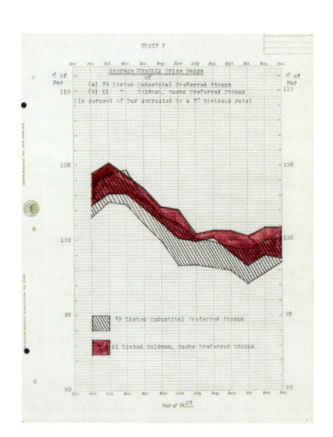

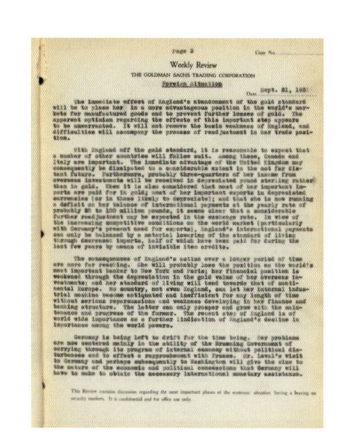

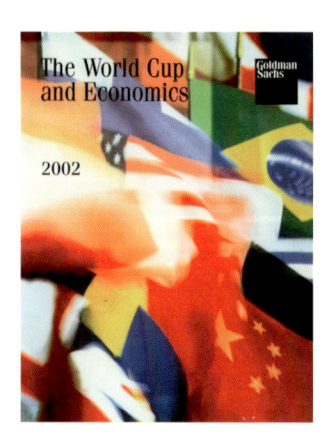

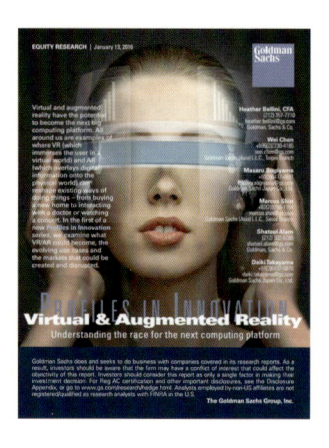

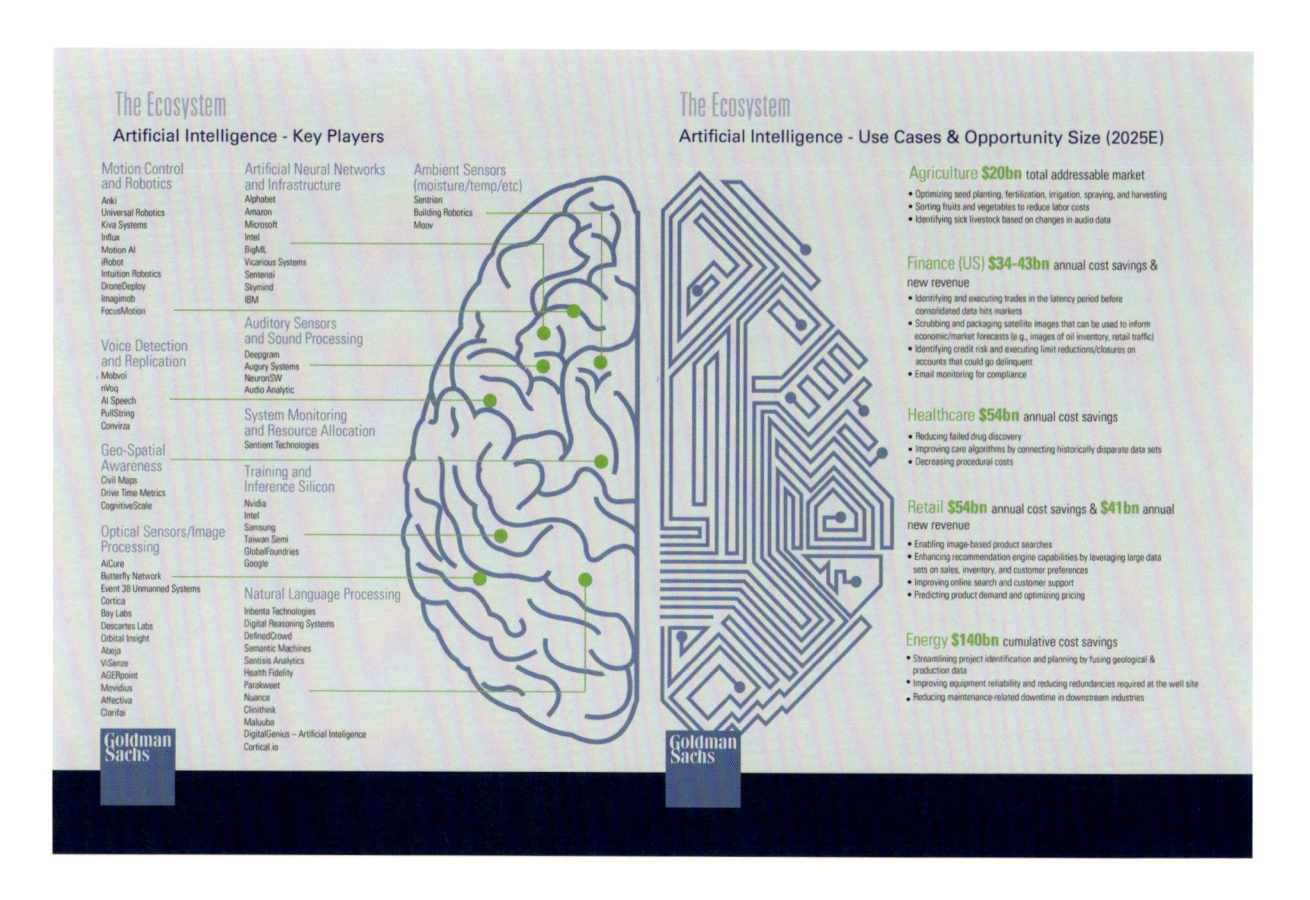

82

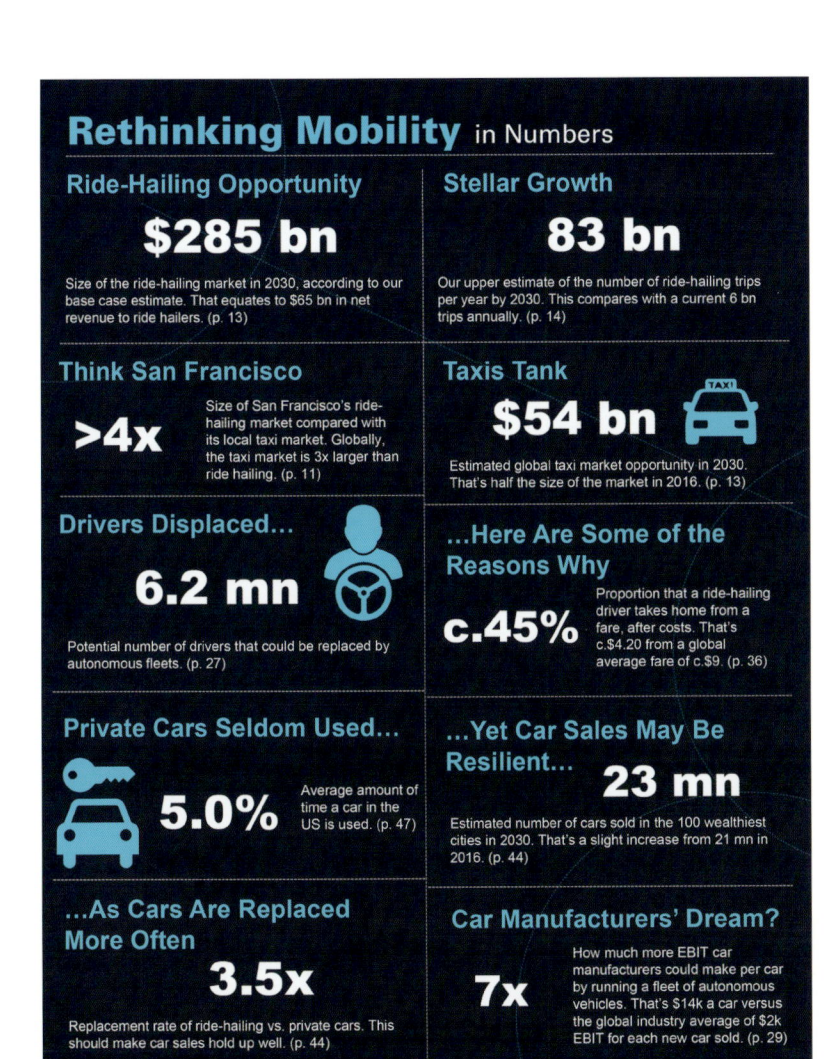

Rethinking Mobility in Numbers

Ride-Hailing Opportunity
$285 bn
Size of the ride-hailing market in 2030, according to our base case estimate. That equates to $65 bn in net revenue to ride hailers. (p. 13)

Stellar Growth
83 bn
Our upper estimate of the number of ride-hailing trips per year by 2030. This compares with a current 6 bn trips annually. (p. 14)

Think San Francisco
>4x
Size of San Francisco's ride-hailing market compared with its local taxi market. Globally, the taxi market is 3x larger than ride hailing. (p. 11)

Taxis Tank
$54 bn
Estimated global taxi market opportunity in 2030. That's half the size of the market in 2016. (p. 13)

Drivers Displaced...
6.2 mn
Potential number of drivers that could be replaced by autonomous fleets. (p. 27)

...Here Are Some of the Reasons Why
c.45%
Proportion that a ride-hailing driver takes home from a fare, after costs. That's c.$4.20 from a global average fare of c.$9. (p. 36)

Private Cars Seldom Used...
5.0%
Average amount of time a car in the US is used. (p. 47)

...Yet Car Sales May Be Resilient...
23 mn
Estimated number of cars sold in the 100 wealthiest cities in 2030. That's a slight increase from 21 mn in 2016. (p. 44)

...As Cars Are Replaced More Often
3.5x
Replacement rate of ride-hailing vs. private cars. This should make car sales hold up well. (p. 44)

Car Manufacturers' Dream?
7x
How much more EBIT car manufacturers could make per car by running a fleet of autonomous vehicles. That's $14k a car versus the global industry average of $2k EBIT for each new car sold. (p. 29)

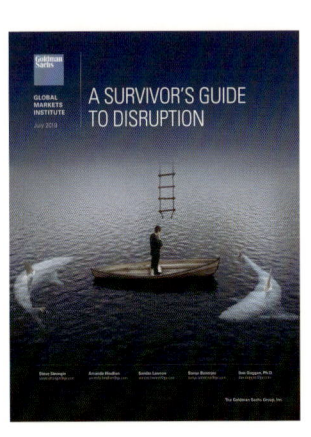

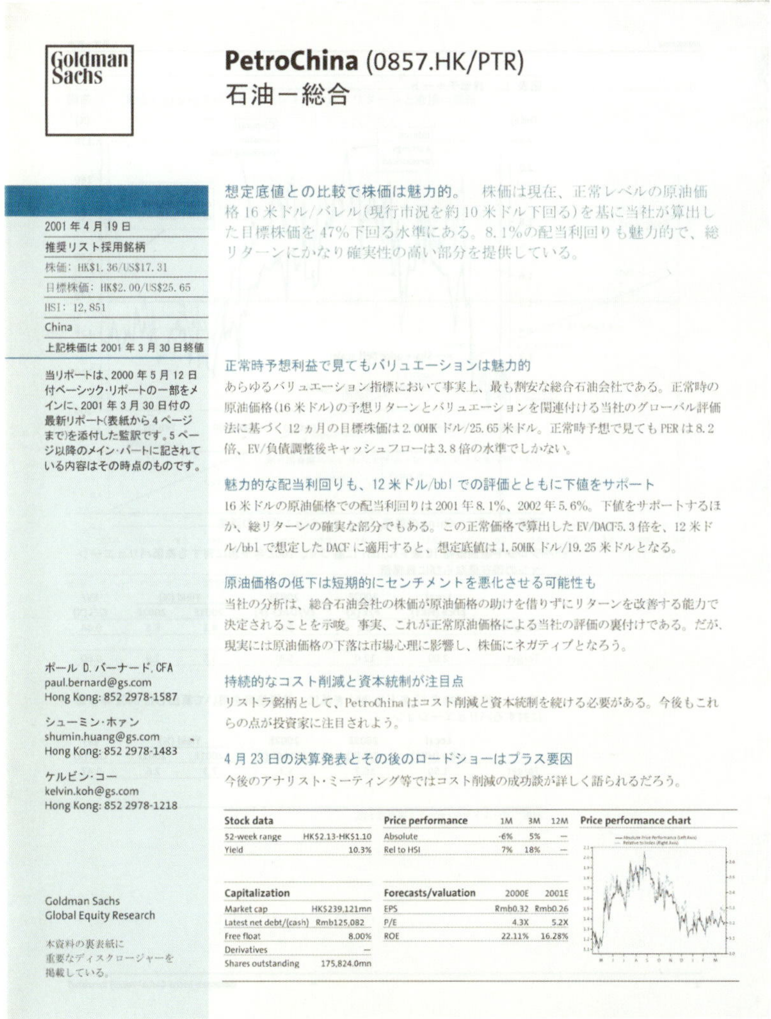

83

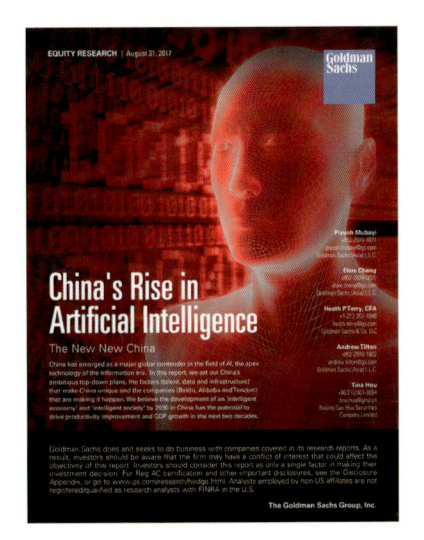

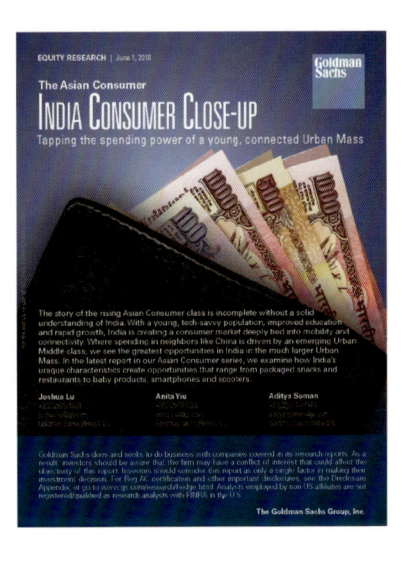

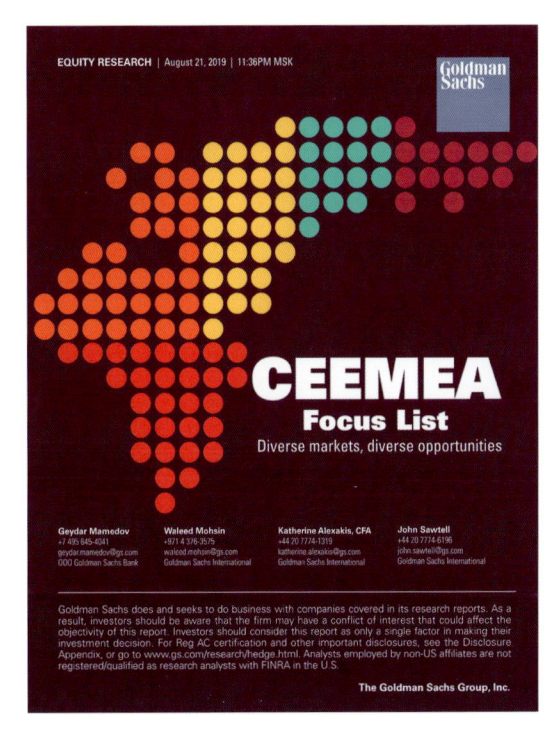

WALLS COME DOWN

The fall of the Berlin Wall in 1989 was a powerful and tangible symbol of the dramatic changes transforming the world in the late 1980s and early 1990s. Boundaries — physical and otherwise — were shifting and, in some cases, melting away entirely. The Soviet Union was dissolved in 1991, allowing self-governance for the 15 separate republics that had made up the USSR since 1922. A treaty signed in Maastricht established the European Union in 1993, allowing for the free movement of people, goods, services and capital among member nations. Widespread deregulation in the mid-1980s had vastly grown and globalized the financial services sector. The same year that the Berlin Wall crumbled, the World Wide Web was born, forever transforming the way people and businesses would communicate and transact.

Walls were coming down at Goldman Sachs too — in 1986 the firm named its first woman partner and its first partner of color, a step toward building a more diverse workforce. The firm continued to deepen its roots outside of the United States during this period, recognizing the importance of having a physical presence and a local team in the many markets around the world in which the firm operated. Under the leadership of co-senior partners Robert Rubin and Stephen Friedman, Goldman Sachs' new European headquarters, Peterborough Court, was inaugurated by former Prime Minister Margaret Thatcher in 1991. The firm's first mainland China offices, in Beijing and Shanghai, opened their doors in 1994. With the Mexican financial crisis that erupted in 1994 and the turmoil that followed in Asia in 1997 and Russia in 1998, Goldman Sachs would experience firsthand how interconnected the global financial system had become, and would intensify its focus on evaluating and managing risk in this "new normal" of global capital markets.

Top: *Fall of the Berlin Wall, 1989.*

Bottom: *Stephen Friedman and Robert Rubin, New York City, 1986.*

Opposite: *Former Prime Minister Margaret Thatcher at the opening of Peterborough Court, London, 1991.*

86

New partners reflect the firm's evolving partnership

On October 16, 1986, Goldman Sachs named 37 new partners, the most ever in the firm's history.

Among those named partner was Jeanette Loeb, the firm's first woman partner. Jeanette joined Goldman Sachs on a full-time basis in 1977 after receiving an MBA from Harvard Business School. She had worked in Investment Research during the summer of 1976. Jeanette began in the firm's Private Finance Department and spent her career there and in its successor, the Structured Finance Group. Among her key accomplishments, Jeanette served as the lead banker financing one of the first continuous casters for the US steel industry and developed the supplier financing product.

Also in the 1986 partner class was Garland Wood, the firm's first black partner. Garland had joined the firm in 1972 after receiving his MBA from Columbia Business School. He began his career in the Municipal Bond Department, which had fewer than ten professionals at the time. By his retirement in 1994, it had grown to more than a hundred. Garland was an innovator in public finance, instrumental in leading advance refunding efforts in the late 1970s and early 1980s. He also played a significant role in the firm's early work financing single-family housing, which helped make Goldman Sachs a leader in the tax-exempt business.

Another member of the 1986 partner class was economist Fischer Black, whose innovative financial models would revolutionize option pricing, fixed income derivative valuation and global portfolio diversification. A leading voice in both academia and the business of finance, Fischer Black served as director of the Quantitative Strategies Group at Goldman Sachs, spearheading the firm's efforts in quantitative risk management.

Opposite, top: Partner Class of 1986 with John Weinberg.

Opposite, bottom: Garland Wood, Robin Wiessmann and Robert Downey, Municipal Bonds meeting, 1987.

Top: Kevin Kennedy, Jeanette Loeb and Peter Fahey, Global Finance meeting, 1986.

Bottom: Jeanette Loeb with David Solomon and current and former partners at the dedication of the Jeanette Winter Loeb Reception Room at 200 West Street headquarters, New York City, 2019.

Sumitomo Bank makes a landmark investment in Goldman Sachs

In August 1986, Goldman Sachs announced a deal with Sumitomo Bank, Ltd., whereby the Japanese conglomerate would invest $500 million in the firm ($1.15 billion in 2019 dollars) and become a limited partner. While Sumitomo's initial holdings would be predominantly debt, they would convert eventually into a 12.5% equity stake and allow Sumitomo to share in the annual profits of Goldman Sachs.

With the Sumitomo investment, Goldman Sachs increased its capital by more than a third, from $1.33 billion to $1.83 billion ($3.05 billion to $4.19 billion in 2019 dollars). The innovative deal secured for the firm the capital that was essential to remain competitive in an increasingly global market while maintaining its autonomy and partnership structure. While many of the firm's competitors raised money by going public, the partners of Goldman Sachs had thus far resisted this path.

The firm had ended 1985 as the sixth-largest Wall Street firm by capitalization. With the Sumitomo investment, it jumped to fourth in a deal that surprised many on Wall Street. While seen as a big win for Goldman Sachs, Sumitomo was equally contented, as the investment helped fulfill the Japanese firm's commitment to become a global financial enterprise.

Top: John Weinberg and Koh Komatsu, president of Sumitomo Bank, signing investment agreement, 1986.

Bottom: John Weinberg with Ichiro Isoda, chairman of Sumitomo Bank, 1986.

Above: Goldman Sachs office at 6, rue Newton, Paris, c. 1990.

Reinforcing its commitment to Europe, Goldman Sachs opens Paris office

In the mid-1980s, French credit markets were liberalized and financial innovation gained momentum with the creation of the financial futures market (MATIF) in 1986. In April 1987, Goldman Sachs was one of five US financial organizations admitted to MATIF. That same year, the firm started operations in Paris on rue Halévy — its third European office — to facilitate clients' futures trading in that market. Highlighting its commitment to France, Goldman Sachs expanded its Paris operations between late 1991 and early 1992, with Investment Banking joining the Fixed Income Futures Department.

By spring 1994, when it relocated to rue de Thann on the edge of the Parc Monceau, the Paris office had a staff of more than 60, with expertise in investment banking, capital markets, operations, technology and fixed income sales and trading. Goldman Sachs was present throughout the European process of convergence toward the single market, providing strategic advice to French firms through domestic Franco-French and cross-border deals, and joined the Paris Stock Exchange in 1998. The Paris office moved to its Avenue Kléber office near the Arc de Triomphe in the fall of 2013.

Client offerings are broadened to include asset management

On September 16, 1988, the Management Committee of Goldman Sachs announced the establishment of a new division: Goldman Sachs Asset Management (GSAM). GSAM would focus on fixed income separate account management and on the expansion of the firm's money market mutual funds. In addition to providing a valued new service to the firm's clients, the recurring, fee-based revenues of the new division could help offset the variability of profits from other areas of the firm. From its initially narrow focus, GSAM grew to serve pension funds, endowments, foundations, unions, financial institutions, corporations and governments, as well as individuals and family offices. Through a combination of in-house development and selective acquisitions, its offerings expanded to encompass virtually all asset classes, including fundamental and quantitative equity, alternatives, and multi-manager strategies.

Top: Michael Armellino, Marcia Beck, Alan Shuch and others at a Goldman Sachs Asset Management meeting, 1992.

Bottom: Robert Jones, David Ford and Sharmin Mossavar-Rahmani, Goldman Sachs Asset Management, 1994.

British Petroleum's privatization is completed amid the chaos of Black Monday

Amid the wave of privatization sweeping the United Kingdom in the 1980s, Goldman Sachs was tapped in 1987 to act as lead underwriter in the United States for the sale of the UK government's remaining 31.5% stake in British Petroleum (BP) — the largest sale ever by the British Treasury.

Per British underwriting standards, the share price was agreed upon two weeks before the stock would begin trading. The first day of trading was to be Friday, October 30, 1987. Over that two-week waiting period, the deal's underwriters assumed market risk. On October 19, the "Black Monday" market crash occurred in the United States, triggering a chain reaction of equity market declines around the world. As a result, Goldman Sachs and other underwriters of the BP deal faced massive prospective losses.

Several firms, Goldman Sachs included, sought to persuade the British government to trigger a force majeure clause that would allow the offering to be suspended until market conditions normalized. When the banks' case was rejected, rather than attempting to extricate itself from the deal, Goldman Sachs made the decision to move forward — and absorb the largest underwriting loss in the firm's history.

The firm's resolve to not only assume this loss but also to continue to seek participation in future UK privatization deals — which would be subject to the same underwriting standards that put the firm's capital at risk — led to its growing status as a leading advisor and banker to British government and industry in the years to come.

Right: British Petroleum logo, c. 1989.

Far right: Front page of The New York Times, October 20, 1987.

Historic Conrail IPO is the largest-ever public offering

By the late 1960s and early 1970s, railroads in the northeastern and midwestern United States were struggling to survive amid reduced passenger and freight traffic, escalating costs, heightened regulation and competition from air and truck transport. By 1972, several northeastern railroads were bankrupt. In response, President Richard Nixon signed into law the Regional Rail Reorganization Act in 1974, providing temporary funding to keep the railroads operating in anticipation of a more permanent plan for their survival.

With 17,000 miles of track in 15 states in the Northeast and Midwest, Consolidated Rail Corporation, commonly known as Conrail, was the second-largest railroad in the United States. After Congress approved Conrail's operation plan in 1976, the railroad continued to operate with massive losses despite billions of dollars in improvements and assistance from the federal government. Following the enactment of additional legislative reforms and under new corporate leadership, Conrail had turned profitable by 1981. As it sought to return the railroads to private ownership, the US government weighed selling Conrail to a variety of bidders, ultimately deciding to dispose of its interest in Conrail through what would become the largest initial public offering in US history.

Having served as an advisor to the US Transportation Department regarding Conrail, Goldman Sachs was selected as the book running manager for the historic 1987 public offering, in which the US government's 85% stake in the company sold for $1.65 billion ($3.65 billion in 2019 dollars). With the addition of Conrail's cash reserves, the government received $1.875 billion from the IPO ($4.14 billion in 2019 dollars) — funds that were used to reduce the federal deficit.

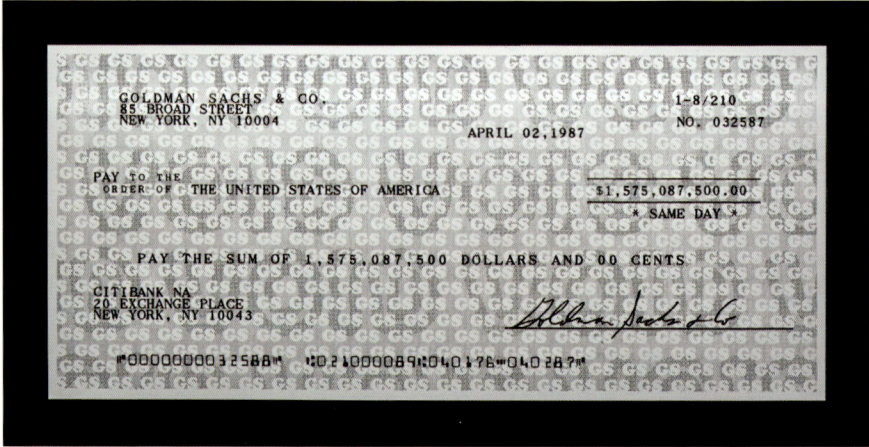

Top: President Ronald Reagan and Secretary of Transportation Elizabeth Dole hold a presentation check during an announcement of the privatization and sale of Conrail in the Roosevelt Room at the White House, 1987.

Bottom: Conrail initial public offering deal toy, 1987.

Telmex privatization is the first international equity offering from a Mexican corporation

During the late 1980s and early 1990s, Mexican policy makers adopted an ambitious program of economic modernization, free trade and the privatization of telecommunication companies and banks. The Mexican government chose Goldman Sachs as advisor in the 1990 sale of a 20.4% stake and a controlling interest in the state-owned telecommunications enterprise Telmex to a group led by Carlos Slim's Grupo Carso for $1.76 billion ($3.38 billion in 2019 dollars). In a May 1991 secondary offering, Goldman Sachs served as the global coordinator for a $2.17 billion issue ($4 billion in 2019 dollars) of 79.75 million American Depositary Shares, equivalent to 15% of the Mexican government's stake in Telmex. This was the first international equity offering from a Mexican corporation, the largest offering for a Latin American company to date and the largest equity offering in the Mexican markets.

Right: Thomas Tuft, Equity Capital Markets; Dr. Jacques Rogozinski Schtulman, director in chief, Office for Privatization, Secretariat of Finance (Mexico) and Guy Erb, Investment Banking Services, Mexico City, 1991.

Stephen Friedman and Robert Rubin are named co-senior partners

When John Weinberg retired in 1990, Stephen Friedman and Robert Rubin, who for the past three years had served as the firm's vice chairmen and co-chief operating officers, became co-senior partners of Goldman Sachs.

Born in New York City in 1937, Steve Friedman joined the Investment Banking Division (IBD) of Goldman Sachs in 1966 after earning a BA from Cornell University in 1959 and an LLB from Columbia Law School in 1962. He was named partner in 1973 and became a member of the firm's Management Committee in 1982. During his tenure at the firm, Steve acted as co-head of both the Investment Banking and Fixed Income Divisions and head of Mergers and Acquisitions. Notably, Goldman Sachs took the stance in the takeover frenzy of the mid-1980s to represent only the targets of hostile bids, further strengthening its client relationships and reputation as a trusted advisor.

Between 1985 and 1988, Steve's co-head of Fixed Income was Bob Rubin. Born in New York City in 1938, Bob had also joined Goldman Sachs in 1966, as an Associate in Risk Arbitrage. He held an AB from Harvard College (1960) and had earned an LLB from Yale School of Law in 1964. He was named partner in 1971 and was tapped to become co-head of the Trading and Arbitrage Division in 1977. Appointed to the Management Committee in 1980, Bob was the committee member responsible for the firm's J. Aron Division, which focused on currencies and commodities. In 1984, Bob asked financial economist Fischer Black to join the Trading and Arbitrage Division and lead the firm's ongoing efforts in quantitative trading and model-based risk management.

Top: Robert Rubin (seated) and Stephen Friedman, New York City, 1990.

Bottom: Stephen Friedman and Robert Rubin, New York City, 1986.

Steve and Bob were another example of a dynamic and highly complementary team of co-heads. Trained as lawyers, they were known among colleagues for their propensity to ask questions and probe problems from many angles. Both brought a deep understanding of trading risk to their leadership roles, and Bob pushed the firm to explore — and in some cases pioneer — new opportunities in the area of trading. Steve helped vastly extend the firm's global reach, seeking to elevate Goldman Sachs' status in markets outside the United States to the same leading level it enjoyed domestically. He would also lead a push for new initiatives in the area of principal investments. Under Steve and Bob's leadership, the firm expanded and reinforced the back-office operations that were growing increasingly critical to supporting the firm's complex global businesses.

Steve and Bob's dual leadership would last only two years, however. In 1992, Bob Rubin departed the firm to serve as President-elect Bill Clinton's special assistant on economic affairs and director of the newly created National Economic Council. Steve Friedman was named sole senior partner, a role in which he would serve until his retirement in 1994.

Both Steve and Bob would go on to have careers in public service after leaving the firm. Among the many roles they held, Bob was appointed as the United States' 70th secretary of the treasury under President Clinton in 1995, a position he held for four and a half years. Bob wrote a memoir, *In An Uncertain World: Tough Choices from Wall Street to Washington*, published in 2003. Steve served as assistant to President George W. Bush for economic policy as well as director of the National Economic Council in the early 2000s and would go on to be appointed chairman of the Federal Reserve Bank of New York in 2008.

Top: Robert Rubin, New York City, 1976.

Bottom: Stephen Friedman, New York City, 1987.

Above: Peterborough Court office opening with Eugene Fife, unidentified man, former Prime Minister Margaret Thatcher, Robert Rubin and Stephen Friedman, 1991.

Margaret Thatcher presides over the opening of Goldman Sachs' new European headquarters

Goldman Sachs' physical presence in the United Kingdom dated to 1970, when its small office on Goldsmith Street in London focused on limited corporate finance and brokerage activities. Over the next two decades, the firm would intensify its efforts to build lasting client relationships in the United Kingdom and broaden the services it offered clients in the United Kingdom and continental Europe.

By the late 1980s, the firm repeatedly earned top rankings in international equity underwritings, American Depositary Receipts, privatizations and worldwide mergers and acquisitions, consolidating its position as a preeminent global investment bank. With staff growing to meet expanding business activities, the firm soon faced a situation where its people were spread across three separate buildings in London. Thus began an ambitious, three-year-long project to build a new European headquarters for the firm.

Goldman Sachs' own Real Estate department acted as developer and project manager for the 565,000-square-foot, 12-story office building designed by the firm Kohn Pederson Fox, appointing 145 construction companies representing 13 countries to build it. Mixing functionality, the latest technology and aesthetic integrity, the new building, named Peterborough Court, was inaugurated on June 6, 1991, by former British Prime Minister Margaret Thatcher. It would continue to serve as Goldman Sachs' European headquarters for nearly three decades.

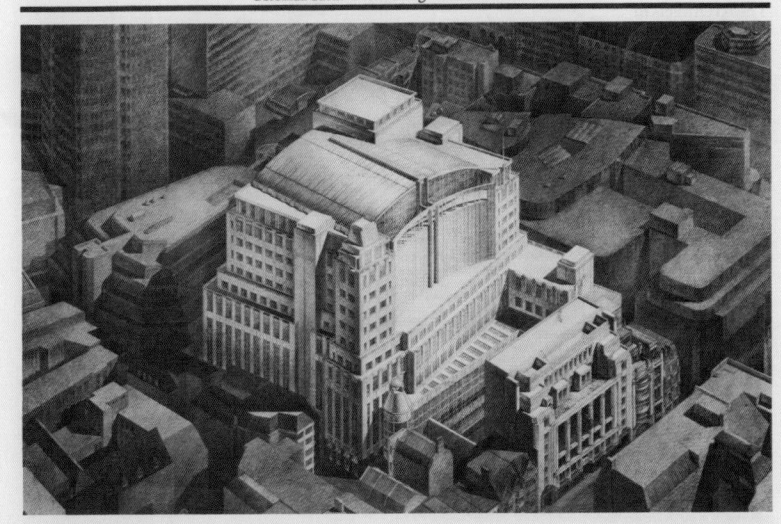

Above: Front page of Moving Times, *Goldman Sachs' Peterborough Court newsletter, 1990.*

A groundbreaking risk management system is born

The year 1993 marked a significant milestone in Goldman Sachs' technological history, with the development of a proprietary software system called Securities Database (SecDB), a platform to price trades and assess risk for trading positions. The system was spearheaded by a distinguished team of Goldman Sachs "strats," multidisciplinary specialists who blend quantitative finance, engineering and technology to design solutions across many areas of the business. SecDB was originally conceived as a risk management platform for the firm's currencies and commodities business, but soon after its launch, was applied to other businesses within the firm, allowing traders to price securities, analyze potential trades and monitor risk.

Above: Diagram from the notebook of Michael Dubno, one of the original members of the SecDB team, c. 1992.

Below: Former members of the SecDB development team during "SecDB – Celebrating 25 Years" event, New York City, 2019. From left: Derek Yi, Danielle Davidian, Rui Lopes Viana, Nick Sedlet, Jeremy Glick, Dan Sharfman, Scott Weinstein, Elisha Wiesel and Michael Turok.

Above: Stephen Friedman during ribbon-cutting ceremony for the opening of The Children's Center at 85 Broad Street, New York City, 1993.

Below: Children of employees at The Children's Center, New York City, 1993.

First on-site childcare center opens at Goldman Sachs' New York headquarters

In 1993, Goldman Sachs opened the firm's first on-site backup childcare facility at its 85 Broad Street headquarters in New York City, recognizing the challenges that many of its employees face when their primary childcare arrangements become unexpectedly unavailable. Embraced by many of the firm's working parents, the program was instituted in other global offices in the years to follow. Backup childcare centers opened in London in 2003 and Jersey City in 2004. Later, full-time childcare centers opened in Tokyo in 2009, Bengaluru in 2011 and Salt Lake City in 2017. Ten years after it opened, the Bengaluru childcare center had tripled in capacity, making it one of India's top corporate childcare offerings in both quality and capacity.

Above: The beginning of trading of Daimler-Benz stock at the New York Stock Exchange, 1993. Included in photo are: Eric Dobkin; Richard Grasso, executive vice president and president, NYSE; Edzard Reuter, chairman, Daimler-Benz; William Donaldson, chairman and chief executive officer, NYSE; Dr. Gerhard Liener, chief financial officer, Daimler-Benz; Edward Jankowski, Jr., senior floor broker; Eugene Maio, NYSE reporter and George Diaz, NYSE reporter.

Daimler-Benz becomes first German company to list on NYSE

In 1991, one year after opening its Frankfurt office, Goldman Sachs became a member of the Frankfurt Stock Exchange, signifying its commitment to the German marketplace after the reunification of the country. On October 5, 1993, Daimler-Benz became the first German company to list on the New York Stock Exchange (NYSE). Goldman Sachs served as lead advisor, along with Deutsche Bank, in the listing. The move reflected the automaker's increased international focus and desire to establish a financial presence in its largest market outside of Germany. Less than a year later, Goldman Sachs was also a member of the underwriting group, international marketing coordinator and member of the international selling group of a global rights offering for Daimler-Benz.

125th ANNIVERSARY

1994: Nelson Mandela assumes South African presidency, "Chunnel" opens, and General Motors tops Fortune 500

As Goldman Sachs marks its 125th anniversary, the firm is a truly global enterprise, with 34 offices around the world and a team of 9,000 people from 91 countries

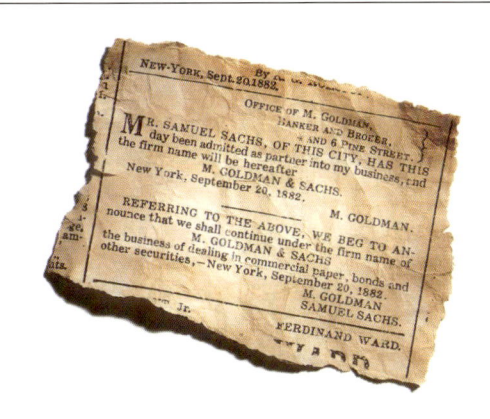

In 1994, Nelson Mandela was elected president of South Africa, just four years after his release from more than 27 years in captivity. The Channel Tunnel, commonly known as the Chunnel, would open, connecting England and France. BMW purchased British vehicle manufacturer Rover from British Aerospace, and the Dow Jones Industrial Average would close the year at 3,834 units.

The Fortune 500 list featured General Motors at the top with revenues of $1.33 billion. Ford Motor, Exxon Mobil, IBM and General Electric rounded out the top five. US real GDP totaled $10.51 trillion in 2019 dollars.

In September of that year, Steve Friedman would resign as chairman and senior partner, succeeded by Jon Corzine. Hank Paulson was named vice chairman and chief operating officer. The prior year, the firm had turned in a particularly strong performance, earning $2.3 billion ($4 billion in 2019 dollars), up 75% from 1992, making it the most profitable firm on Wall Street. 1994 would, however, prove to be an extremely challenging year for Goldman Sachs. Amid steep fixed income trading losses, the firm saw an unusually large number of partners retire, taking their capital along with them and triggering a reexamination of the firm's governance and capital structure.

Above: Advertisement marking Goldman Sachs' 125th anniversary, 1994.

Above: The Velaro E 320 train being tested during the inauguration of a new Eurotunnel freight line in the Channel Tunnel, Coquelles, France, 2015.

Expanding its commitment to China, Goldman Sachs opens offices in Beijing and Shanghai

On February 28, 1994, Goldman Sachs opened its first representative office in China, in Beijing. In August, the People's Bank of China granted the firm a special seat on the Shanghai Stock Exchange, with a license to trade B share issues reserved for foreign investors. On November 18, the firm opened a second mainland China office, in Shanghai.

Goldman Sachs also made its first principal investment in the country that year when it purchased a combined stake, along with Morgan Stanley, of 10% in Ping An Insurance Company. The deal, among the first private equity investments in a Chinese company, was also the largest foreign investment in a Chinese financial institution at the time.

In the years that followed, the firm took on ever larger and more significant transactions in China, including advising the government on the partial privatization of China Telecom (now China Mobile) in 1997 — at more than $4 billion ($6.26 billion in 2019 dollars), the largest privatization of a Chinese company to date — and successfully managing a $1 billion ($1.54 billion in 2019 dollars) Chinese sovereign bond issue in 1998 amid turbulent Asian markets.

Establishing offices in mainland China was a critical step in the evolution of Goldman Sachs' Asia journey — one that reinforced the firm's belief in the country's economic promise and demonstrated its commitment to best serving its clients around the globe.

Top: Bob Hurst speaking at the Shanghai office opening, 1994.

Bottom: Beijing office opening, 1994. From left: Li Xiaopeng, Huaneng International Power Development Corporation; John Thornton, Lord Brian Griffiths and Hang Xu.

Above: Ralph Lauren and Stephen Friedman, 1994.

The firm helps iconic fashion brand achieve strategic objectives

In 1994, Goldman Sachs acquired a minority interest in the iconic fashion brand Polo/Ralph Lauren. Goldman Sachs affiliates became the first outside investors in the company, acquiring a 28% stake for $135 million ($229 million in 2019 dollars). The investment enabled the fashion design company to achieve two prime objectives: remain private and fund its global growth. The transaction represented the firm's continued growth as a principal investor in corporate equity and debt, real estate and infrastructure.

In 1997, Goldman Sachs lead-managed Polo/Ralph Lauren's $882 million IPO ($1.38 billion in 2019 dollars). In 1998, to further coordinate investment banking and long-term principal investment activities, Goldman Sachs announced the formation of the Merchant Banking Division (MBD).

Left: Jon Corzine, New York City, 1994.

Jon Corzine is named senior partner

Born in Willey's Station in central Illinois in 1947, Jon Corzine joined Goldman Sachs' Fixed Income division in 1975 after earning his BA from the University of Illinois and his MBA from the University of Chicago. Quick to develop strong relationships throughout the firm, he was named partner just five years after joining Goldman Sachs' Fixed Income Division. In 1985, Jon became a member of the Management Committee. He was named co-head of Fixed Income in 1988, a role in which he served for six years before being named senior partner in 1994.

Jon was known throughout the firm as someone with an intuitive and expert understanding of capital markets and who was committed to solidifying the firm's best-in-class reputation in the financial services industry. An informal leader with a common touch, Jon enjoyed a wide base of support at the firm. As senior partner, he worked hard to convince the partnership that an initial public offering would give the firm a strong capital base from which it could invest in technology and fund long-term principal investments. Under his leadership, the firm's signature community outreach effort, Community TeamWorks, was launched in 1997.

One day after the firm's successful IPO in 1999, Jon retired after 24 years at Goldman Sachs to pursue a career in public service. He served as US senator for New Jersey from 2001 to 2006 and as the 54th governor of New Jersey from 2006 to 2010.

Above: Jon Corzine was senior partner when Goldman Sachs joint lead-managed a $750 million bond offering for the Republic of South Africa in 1994. From left: Carlos Cordeiro; Chris Stals, governor, South African Reserve Bank; Tito Mboweni, minister of labour; Jon Corzine; Richard Gnodde; Chris Liebenberg, minister of finance; Alec Erwin, deputy minister of finance and James Cross, general manager, South African Reserve Bank.

Right: Mark Winkelman and Jon Corzine on the Fixed Income Division trading floor, New York City, 1990.

GS Financial Workbench™ breaks new ground in firm's digital offerings to clients

At the same time that Goldman Sachs was deploying innovative information technology across internal functions, the firm also recognized the value of sharing information and ideas with clients electronically. The firm's first major initiative in this area was the launch in 1995 of GS Financial Workbench™, one of the first sophisticated financial analysis websites. Accessible online by both employees and institutional clients, the *GS Financial Workbench* website was a central resource for downloading research reports, accessing earnings and valuation models, submitting trades, monitoring accounts, building and viewing presentations, calculating derivative prices and viewing market data. The *GS Financial Workbench* website represented an important milestone in Goldman Sachs' digital journey, laying the groundwork for a series of robust client-facing tools, applications and services to follow.

Above: Graphics on mouse pad from original GS Financial Workbench development team, c. 1995.

Left: Global Economics portal on GS Financial Workbench website, undated.

Above: The Goldman Sachs team that worked with Rockefeller Center, New York City, 1985. From left, Charlie Hoffmann, P. Sheridan Schechner, Thomas Healey, Robin Neustein, Kenneth Brody, Brian Maier and Jun Makihara.

Goldman Sachs adds iconic NYC property to its real estate portfolio

Believing that it could increase the value of Rockefeller Center, an iconic complex of ten major buildings and home of Radio City Music Hall in Midtown Manhattan, Goldman Sachs led a team of investors in a successful bid to buy Rockefeller Center from Rockefeller Center Properties (RCP) in 1995. RCP was a real estate investment trust formed to make a $1.3 billion ($2.14 billion in 2019 dollars) mortgage on the property after the Mitsubishi Estate Company and the Rockefeller family trusts filed for bankruptcy, as the building struggled financially in the difficult mid-1990s US commercial real estate market. The consortium of buyers led by Goldman Sachs included David Rockefeller, whose father, John D. Rockefeller, Jr., had built the iconic New York property in the middle of the Great Depression. The offer totaled $1.15 billion ($1.89 billion in 2019 dollars). This significant investment in what David Rockefeller called "a treasured asset of our city and our nation" would pave the way for the firm's growing involvement in real estate investment.

$13 billion privatization of Deutsche Telekom is the largest IPO ever

To grow its presence in Europe through the 1980s and 1990s, Goldman Sachs employed a country-by-country strategy of building relationships with key decision makers. While each local market had its challenges, the barriers to entry for a non-German investment bank in Germany were particularly high.

By the 1990s, however, the firm had established a presence in the country, serving as the leading advisor to the Treuhandanstalt, the agency established to privatize significant sectors of the East German economy. It also had advised Deutsche Telekom AG, then Europe's largest telecommunications provider, on that company's largest acquisition, a 30% stake in Hungarian telecommunications company Matav, as well as a joint investment with France Télécom to form the Global One Alliance with Sprint America.

With this strong track record in German telecom deals, Goldman Sachs was selected in 1996 to serve as joint global coordinator and US book running manager on Deutsche Telekom's privatization. The $13 billion — DM20 billion — IPO ($20.8 billion in 2019 dollars), was the largest ever and the capstone of years of intense effort by the firm to build its investment banking franchise in Germany.

Top: Deutsche Telekom initial public offering's launch on the New York Stock Exchange, 1996.

Bottom: Deutsche Telekom initial public offering deal toy, 1996.

Left: Keiji Tachikawa, NTT DoCoMo, center, visiting a Goldman Sachs Equities Division trading floor, Tokyo, 1998. Pictured from Goldman Sachs, from left: Mark Schwartz, Masa Mochida, Tadanori Matsumura and Johnny Yoo.

NTT DoCoMo IPO cements Goldman Sachs' leadership position in Japan

In 1992, Japan's national telco, Nippon Telegraph & Telephone Corp. (NTT), established a new cellular service provider called NTT DoCoMo from a carve-out of its mobile communications operations. The new company derived the name "DoCoMo" from the phrase "DO COmmunications over the MObile network." By 1998, it served 57% of Japan's 36.5 million wireless subscribers.

Even amid the worst recession Japan had experienced since World War II, the cellular phone business had proven to be growing and profitable, and in 1998, NTT DoCoMo announced plans for a massive stock offering. Goldman Sachs International and Nikko Securities Co. were joint global coordinators and joint book runners for the offering, which turned DoCoMo into Japan's third-largest company by market capitalization. Demand for the offering was strong; DoCoMo stock traded up 19% in its first day of trading and raised just over $18 billion ($27.7 billion in 2019 dollars), nearly $5 billion more than the then-record IPO of its parent company, NTT, in 1986.

The DoCoMo IPO was a bright spot during a turbulent time for global financial markets, lifting Japan's Nikkei Index and restoring confidence in global capital markets at a critical time. For Goldman Sachs, the historic offering reinforced the firm's status as a major distributor of equities with institutional investors in Japan at a time when distribution was still largely in the hands of domestic firms.

Goldman Sachs launches Community TeamWorks

In 1997, senior partner Jon Corzine supported the creation of Community TeamWorks (CTW), a program that embodies Goldman Sachs' culture of service and that has become the firm's flagship volunteering initiative. CTW encourages Goldman Sachs people to take a day away from work to volunteer in team-based projects to help local nonprofit organizations achieve their missions, while promoting teamwork and a culture of service.

Since its launch, Community TeamWorks has become a prized component of the Goldman Sachs experience, with thousands of employees — from more than 50 offices — volunteering alongside their friends and families each year to benefit nonprofit organizations around the world. From 1997 to 2018, more than 426,000 employees, family members and friends volunteered through CTW, assisting more than 4,000 community partners around the world. In honor of the firm's 150th anniversary, CTW provided more than 150,000 hours of service to local communities throughout 2019.

By revitalizing public spaces, mentoring future leaders, protecting the environment and more, Community TeamWorks strengthens and supports communities around the globe while providing Goldman Sachs employees with access to new and innovative ways to have an impact in the communities in which they work and live.

Left: Yokohama, Japan, 2003.
Top: London, 2016.
Bottom: Bengaluru, 2018.

Opposite, clockwise from top: Bengaluru, 2007; Hong Kong, 2013; New York, 1998; London, 2018; New York, 1997.

111

Our People

As Goldman Sachs has grown over the years, the firm has worked hard to retain the spirit of its origins. Central to this effort is the recruitment, training and development of individuals who exemplify the firm's key values, including teamwork and collaboration, innovation, integrity and excellence. Along with a commitment to these ideals, the people of Goldman Sachs bring a diversity of backgrounds, thought and perspective that both enriches the firm's culture and leads to better solutions for the clients and communities they serve around the globe.

113

Evolution of Trading

Stock exchanges date back centuries, providing a means for buyers and sellers to trade securities and for investors to participate in the growth opportunities those securities offer. Today's exchanges have come a long way from the simple open outcry auctions of old, and the trading floors of Goldman Sachs reflect this. While electronic trading may have accelerated transaction speeds from minutes to nanoseconds, the essential function of exchanges endures: providing a critical forum for buyers and sellers to put capital to work on behalf of shareholders and investors.

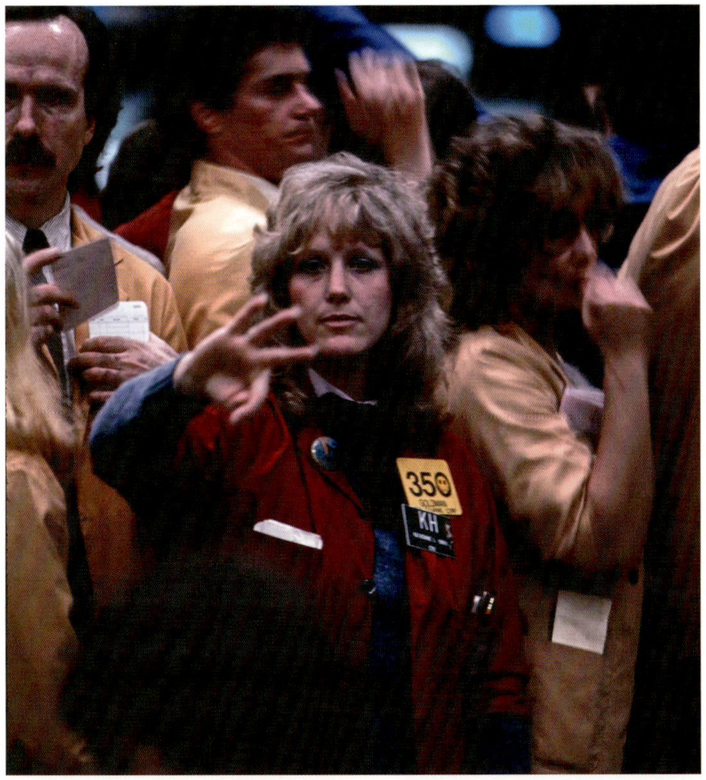
350
KH

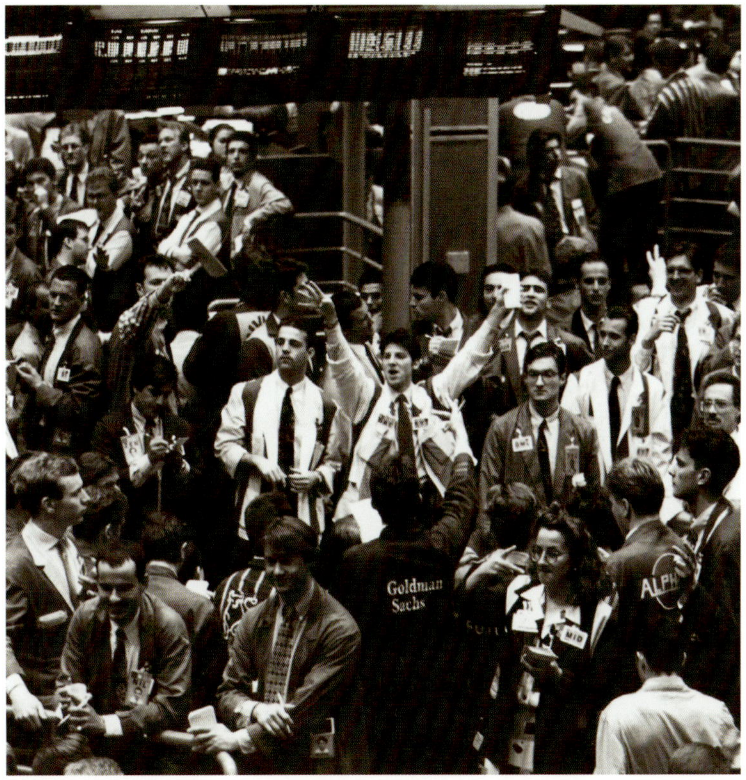
Goldman Sachs

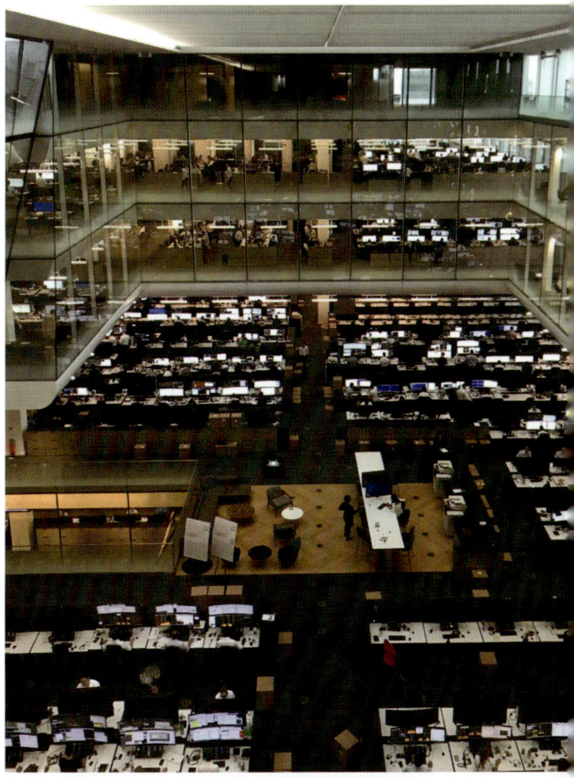

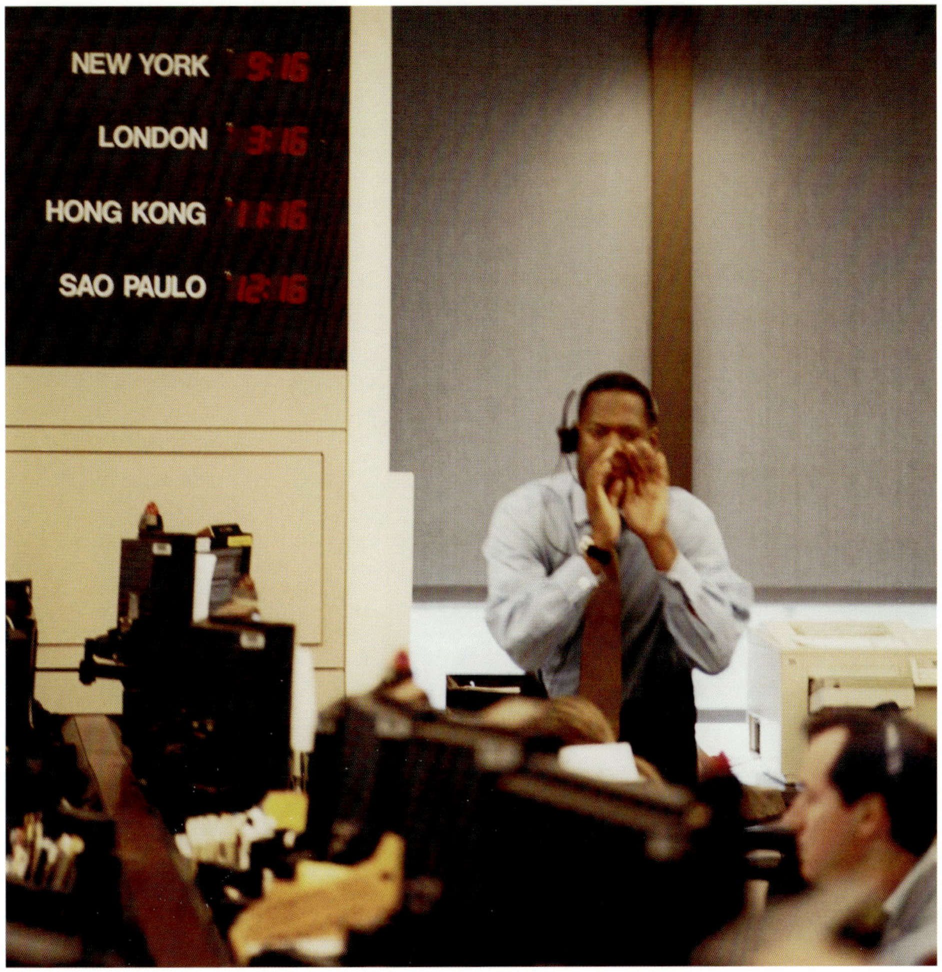
NEW YORK
LONDON
HONG KONG
SAO PAULO

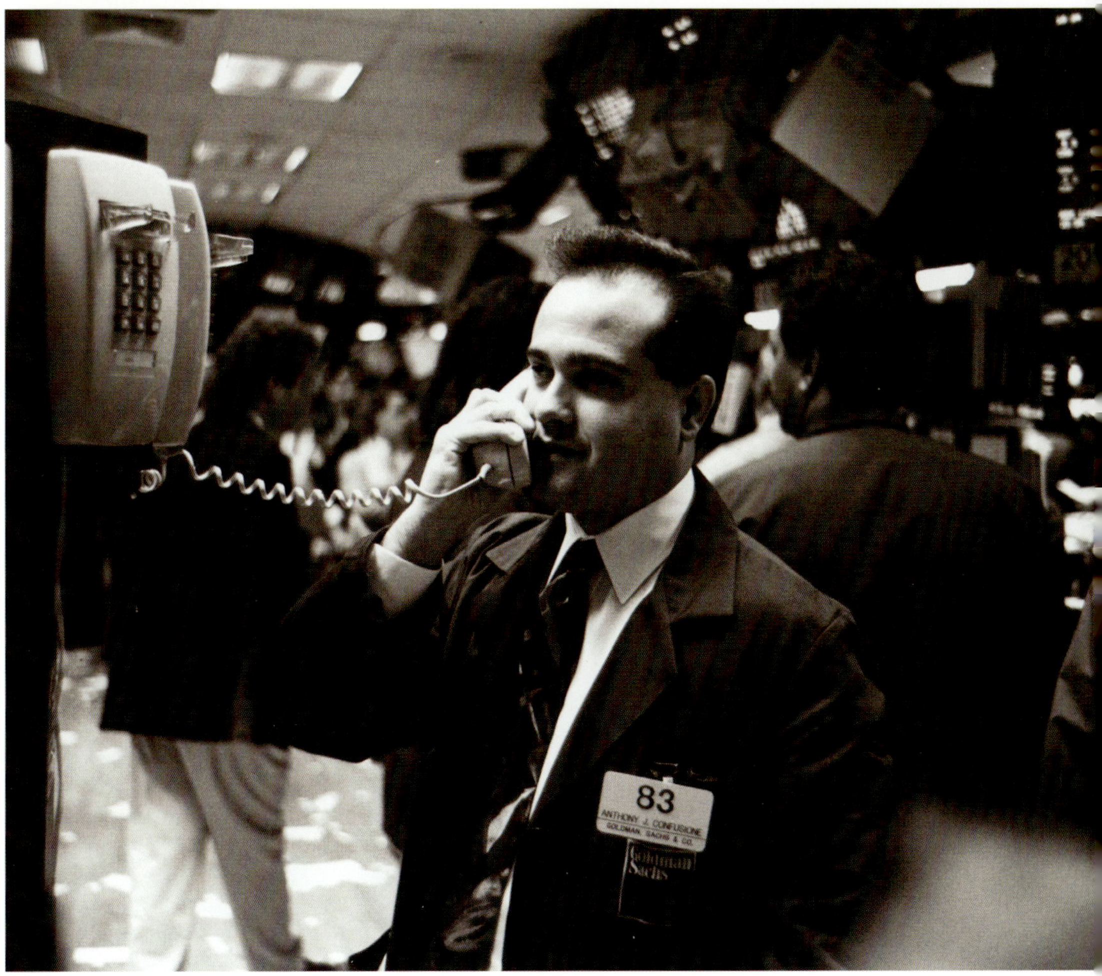
83

TURNING POINT

By the late 1990s, Goldman Sachs was one of the last of the investment banks — and certainly the largest — in the United States to be privately held. The firm's partnership structure was so closely intertwined with its distinct culture that it was not until 1986 that a solid proposal for an initial public offering was even debated among senior leaders (it did not come to a vote). A confluence of events in the following decade, however, infused the issue with a renewed sense of urgency. In 1994, the firm's Fixed Income Division experienced steep trading losses on the back of rising global interest rates. Amid the carnage, a record number of partners departed, further depleting the firm's already strained capital base. That same year, leadership of the firm passed from Stephen Friedman to Jon Corzine. As Friedman had been, Corzine was a proponent of the firm going public.

Over the next four years, the senior leaders of Goldman Sachs passionately debated all aspects of a potential public offering: financial, strategic and cultural. A strong and flexible balance sheet would allow the firm to survive and thrive in increasingly competitive global financial markets. From a strategic standpoint, equity capital would now be at its disposal for future acquisitions. And while some feared that departing from the private partnership structure that had defined the firm since its inception would fundamentally alter its ethos, others maintained that broadening ownership would in fact deepen the culture of partnership — and could also help the firm continue to attract and retain top talent. Thus, in 1999, as a new millennium dawned, Goldman Sachs became a public company in what was, at the time, the second-largest IPO in the history of finance.

Opposite: Goldman Sachs' initial public offering on the New York Stock Exchange, May 4, 1999. From left: John Thain; David Viniar; Richard Grasso, chairman, NYSE; Dan Jester; John Thornton; Hank Paulson; Greg Palm; Bob Hurst; Mike Evans; William Johnston, president, NYSE; Jim Johnson and John Weinberg.

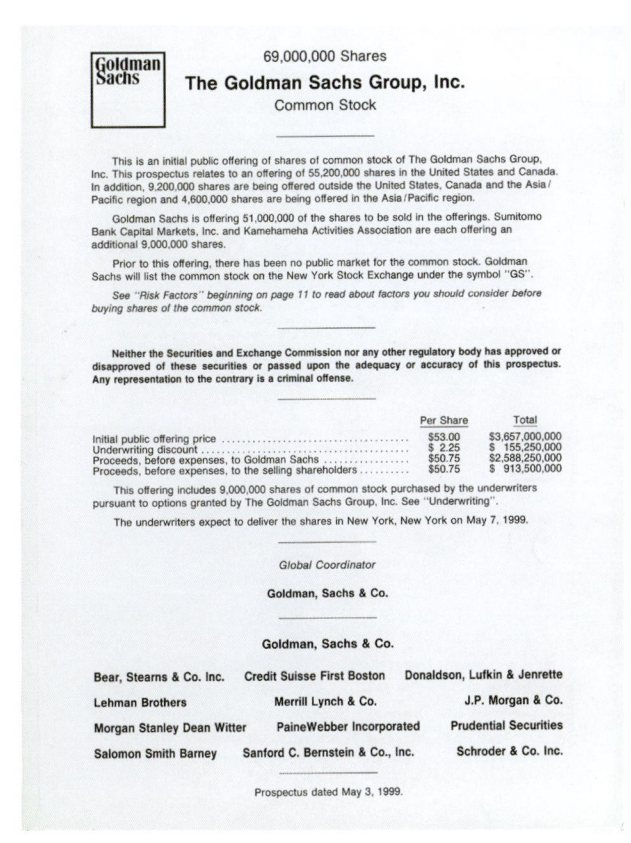

Top: The Goldman Sachs Group, Inc. commemorative stock certificate, 1999.

Bottom: The Goldman Sachs Group, Inc. prospectus, 1999.

Hank Paulson is named chairman and CEO as Goldman Sachs transitions to a public company

Born in Palm Beach, Florida in 1946, and raised in Barrington, Illinois, Henry "Hank" Paulson, Jr. graduated from Dartmouth College where he was named Phi Beta Kappa. He received an MBA from Harvard Business School. Prior to joining the firm, he was a member of the White House Domestic Council, serving as staff assistant to President Richard Nixon from 1972 to 1973 and as staff assistant to the assistant secretary of defense (comptroller) at the Pentagon from 1970 to 1972.

Hank joined Goldman Sachs in 1974 in the Chicago office, then headed by Jim Gorter, as an investment banker. Initially focusing on clients in the Midwest, he would go on to develop strong relationships in Asia, particularly in China. Noted for his intense dedication to his clients and his candor, he became a partner in 1982. Hank served as co-head of the Investment Banking Division from 1990 to 1994, vice chairman and chief operating officer (1994–1998) and president (1998–1999), after Stephen Friedman retired and Jon Corzine became senior partner.

In June 1998, Hank was named co-chairman and co-chief executive officer, serving along with Jon Corzine and continuing the firm's long tradition of joint leadership. He would be named sole chairman and CEO in January 1999, leading the firm during its pivotal transition from a private partnership to a publicly held company.

During his tenure as head of Goldman Sachs, Hank worked to preserve the partnership culture while continuing the firm's global expansion, ultimately presiding over the greatest period of growth and change in the firm's history since Sidney Weinberg led the firm. He helped to gain a foothold in China's domestic financial markets, traveling there frequently. Under Hank's watch, new language was added to the Business Principles underscoring the importance of a diverse and inclusive workforce. Among the challenges he would face were the terrorist attacks of September 11, 2001, their disruption of markets and the devastation of parts of Lower Manhattan.

Hank retired from the firm in 2006 after being confirmed to serve as 74th secretary of the treasury of the United States under President George W. Bush from June 2006 to January 2009. During that time, Hank would play a central role in the efforts to stabilize financial markets in the aftermath of the 2008 global financial crisis, the subject of his 2010 memoir, *On the Brink: Inside the Race to Stop the Collapse of the Global Financial System*. Hank has also authored *Dealing with China: An Insider Unmasks the New Economic Superpower*, published in 2015, and is a co-author of *Firefighting. The Financial Crisis and Its Lessons*, published in 2019.

Above: Hank Paulson participating in Community TeamWorks, Prospect Park, Brooklyn, 1998.

Above: Hank Paulson and Jim Gorter, 2004.

Left: Hank Paulson speaking at a Goldman Sachs press briefing in Beijing, 2003.

In a paradigm shift, Goldman Sachs goes public

The journey to becoming a public company was a long and introspective one for Goldman Sachs. In the late 1960s, Sidney Weinberg first weighed the possibility, asking Gus Levy to survey partners for their opinions about incorporation. The idea lacked support at the time.

In 1971, recognizing the value of additional capital to grow the firm, the Management Committee again considered incorporating, going as far as printing new business cards before deciding that the existing partnership structure continued to be most advantageous. Another proposal by Steve Friedman and Bob Rubin to take the firm public in 1986 generated heated conversations among the partners, but in the end, no vote was taken.

In 1998, Goldman Sachs was the last big private investment bank in the United States. By then, the business advantages of going public became undeniable to most, and the firm's partners voted to undertake the same institutional transformation through which Goldman Sachs had guided hundreds of clients. The firm's prospectus listed three principal reasons for going public: "to secure permanent capital to grow; to share ownership broadly among our employees now and through future compensation; and to permit us to use publicly traded securities to finance strategic acquisitions that we may elect to make in the future."

One of the largest financial services initial public offerings in US history at the time, Goldman Sachs' IPO on May 4, 1999, involved 69 million shares (a stake of 15%) and raised $3.657 billion. Shares in The Goldman Sachs Group, Inc. were offered at $53 dollars on the New York Stock Exchange under the symbol GS and rose 33%, closing at $70.375.

Top: Goldman Sachs' initial public offering roadshow, Hong Kong, 1999. From left, David Viniar, John Thain, John Thorton and Hank Paulson.

Bottom: London staff awaiting the release of Goldman Sachs' initial public offering, May 4, 1999.

Left: Members of the initial public offering team at Goldman Sachs' New York office, May 1999. From left: Dan Jester, Chris Cole, Rose Shabet, Greg Palm, Hank Paulson, Mike Evans, John Weinberg, John Thornton, David Viniar, Thomas Tuft, Elizabeth Beshel Robinson and John Thain.

Above: Attendees at a dinner commemorating the 20th anniversary of Goldman Sachs' initial public offering, New York City, May 2, 2019. First row, from left: Michele M. Burns, Eric Dobkin, Robin Neustein, Alan Beller, Stephen Friedman, Megan Kenney, Esta Stecher, Suzanne Donohoe, Greg Palm, Stephen Scherr and John F.W. Rogers. Second row, from left: Bill George, Adebayo Ogunlesi, Elizabeth Beshel Robinson, Mark Winkelman, Bob Hurst, Chris Austin, John Waldron, Doug Feagin, Rose Shabet, Steve Bunson, Sarah Smith, Jan Tighe, John Andrews, Jim McHugh and John Mead. Third row, from left: Randy Fort, Bob Reeder, Ken Josselyn, Jon Winkelried, Thomas Tuft, David Viniar, Bob Katz, Drew Faust, Hank Paulson, David Solomon, Dan Jester, Lakshmi Mittal, Ellen Kullman, Bruce Larson and Zaid Alsikafi.

Goldman Sachs Foundation invests in global education and entrepreneurship

In 1999, Goldman Sachs set aside $200 million from the proceeds of the firm's initial public offering to fund the Goldman Sachs Foundation. Building on the firm's long-standing tradition of leadership and public service, the foundation was established with the mission of promoting excellence and innovation in education by making grants in three principal areas: developing high-potential youth; promoting entrepreneurship, business education and leadership; and advancing academic achievement. Former co-senior partner John Whitehead was the founding chairman of the Goldman Sachs Foundation from 1999 until he passed away in 2015.

At the time of its formation, the Goldman Sachs Foundation was the sixth-largest corporate foundation in the country. It enjoyed close ties with Goldman Sachs early on: three of the foundation's initial seven trustees were executives of the firm, and within five years of its establishment, more than 500 Goldman Sachs professionals had stepped forward to serve as coaches, mentors, board members and judges at competitions for foundation-related initiatives.

In 2007, the Goldman Sachs Foundation refined its focus to align further with the mission of the firm by dedicating 100% of its programming to local economic growth, specifically through investing in entrepreneurship. All programming was designed under the following principles: address a proven whitespace where innovation can address unmet needs; set a scalable, ambitious goal (e.g., 10,000 people served); measure results to ensure maximum success; ensure CEO and executive-level sponsorship; and engage the time and talent of the people of Goldman Sachs.

Initiatives such as 10,000 Women® and 10,000 Small Businesses® would soon follow — both designed to grow local economies by providing thousands of underserved entrepreneurs with greater access to a business and management education, financial capital and business support services.

In 2014, the Goldman Sachs Foundation partnered with the International Finance Corporation (IFC) to create The Women Entrepreneurs Opportunity Facility® (WEOF), the first-ever global finance facility for women-owned small- and medium-sized businesses.

Looking ahead, the Goldman Sachs Foundation is focused on building on its proven model while continuing to innovate and extend its impact and convening power to help foster economic growth, stability and opportunity to communities around the world.

Top: Global Leadership Institute Class, 2008.

Bottom: Winners from Aston Business School entrepreneurship competition with Glenn Earle, c. 2006

Left: Cover of Goldman Sachs Foundation report, "Developing High-Potential Youth," 2005.

PINE STREET
GOLDMAN SACHS

Pine Street launches to develop the next generations of exceptional leaders

In 1999, Goldman Sachs selected a diverse group of senior professionals from within the firm to form the Leadership Development Advisory Committee. This group's official charter was to "assess the future training and development needs of Goldman Sachs, with particular focus on the need for a more systematic and effective approach to developing leaders." The task was especially critical given that Goldman Sachs had recently completed its IPO, transitioning from a closely held partnership to a public company that was growing rapidly.

After extensive research, including interviewing employees and outside experts, the committee presented its recommendation, the cornerstone of which was a dedicated leadership development practice for senior-level employees. The group was named Pine Street, a nod to the location in Lower Manhattan where Marcus Goldman began his business in 1869.

Pine Street was built from the ground up: while the committee borrowed key learnings from its extensive research, the group molded them to fit the firm and its own standards regarding leadership in an intensely teamwork-oriented culture. Similar to the way the firm's 14 Business Principles had established a shared vision and vernacular, Pine Street established a common leadership language and skill set across the firm globally. This was particularly important considering that, in 2001, of Goldman Sachs' then more than 20,000 employees, nearly half had been with the firm for less than two years.

The first Pine Street Leadership Program was held in New York on March 22, 2001. Through the years, Pine Street also moved in the direction of offering fewer, more experiential programs targeted at critical points in a partner's career, with a strengthened focus on executive coaching. While necessarily evolving with the needs of the business and the marketplace, since its inception, Pine Street has remained true to its core objectives: to advance the culture of Goldman Sachs and to develop world-class leaders.

Today, Pine Street continues to prepare partners and select managing directors to lead the firm's next generation of people and businesses. In pursuit of this mission, Pine Street aims to be a world-class leadership development organization that enhances the reputation of Goldman Sachs as an institution committed to leadership excellence, cultivating leaders who help the firm capitalize on opportunity.

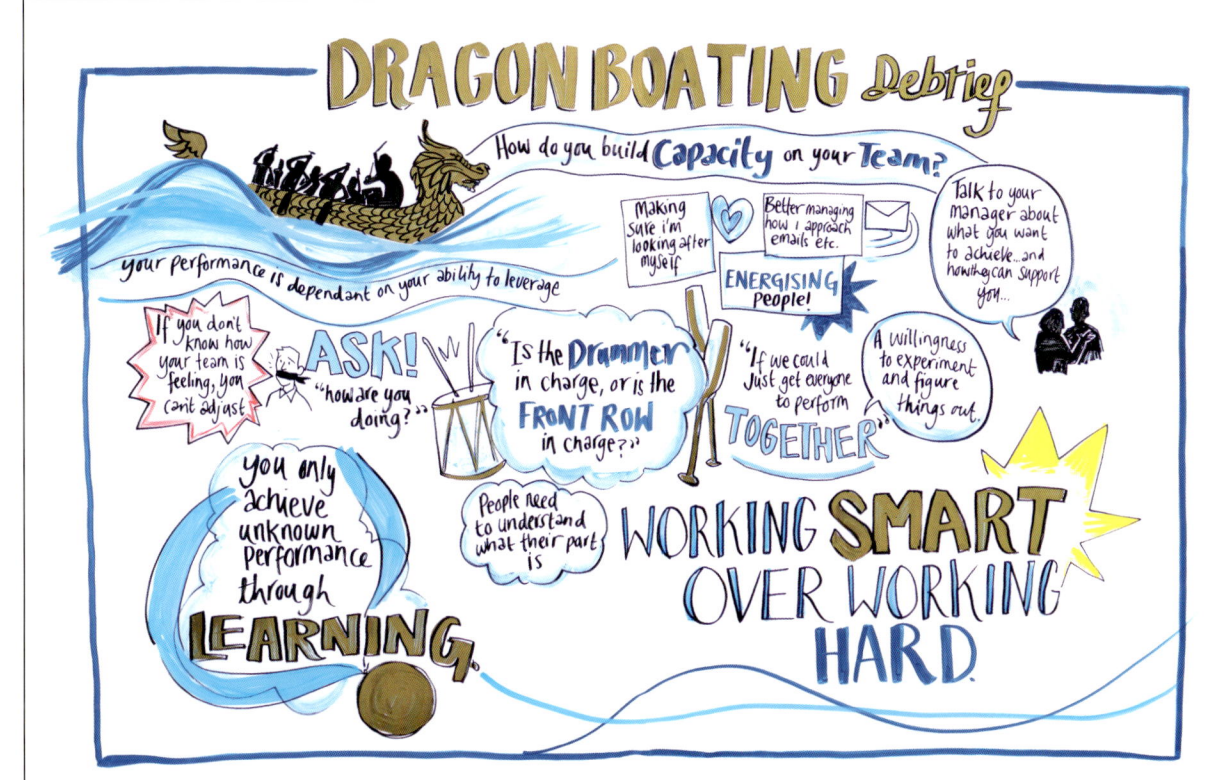

Above: Members of the Partner Class of 2018 during Pine Street Partner Orientation, New York City, 2019.

Right: Artwork representing participants' debrief from a team-building activity, Pine Street Third-Year Partner Program, 2017.

Opposite: Pine Street logo, 2019.

125

Corporate Advertising

The history of advertising at Goldman Sachs has mirrored the evolution of the firm itself. In its early days as a closely held partnership, public pronouncements were largely limited to simple declarations of newly named partners or office openings. Over time, messages from Goldman Sachs have been shared on a broader scale, addressing key constituencies and strategic aims. This includes highlighting the firm's wide-ranging insights and expertise, its positive impact on global communities and markets, and its distinct culture, as exemplified by its people — all while keeping up with the evolving media landscape.

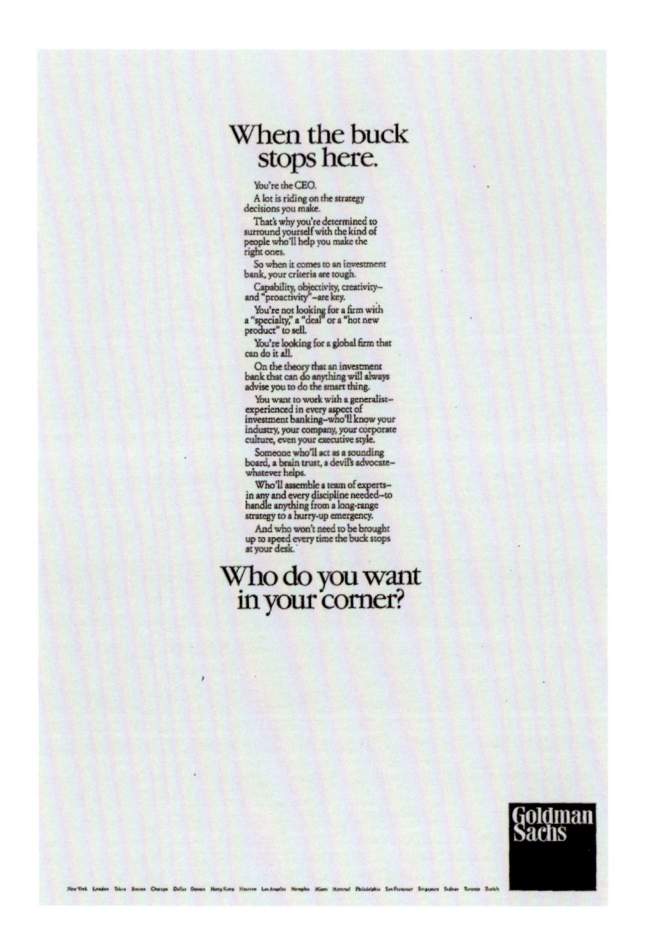

"Who do you want in your corner?," 1988

"Unrelenting Thinking," 1999

"What Matters," 2001

"Matrix," 2007

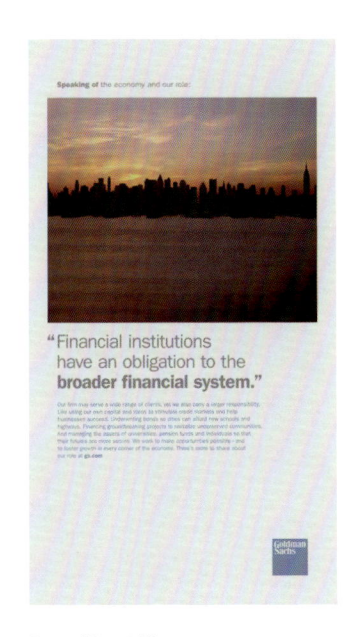

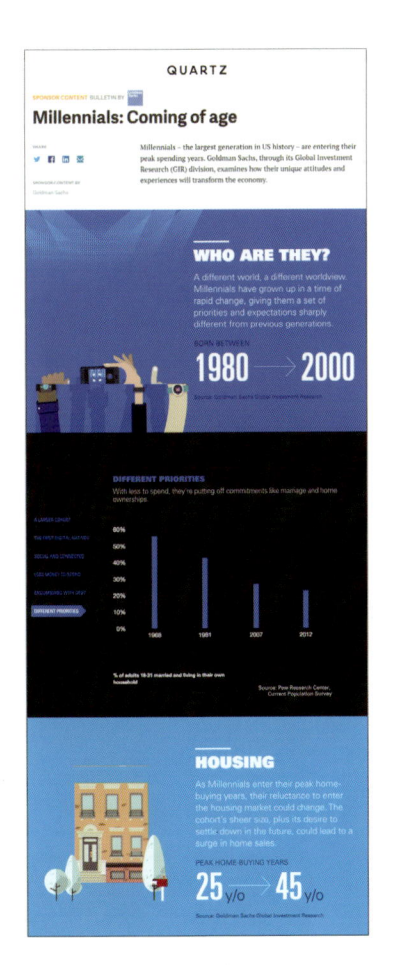

"Millennials: Coming of Age," 2015

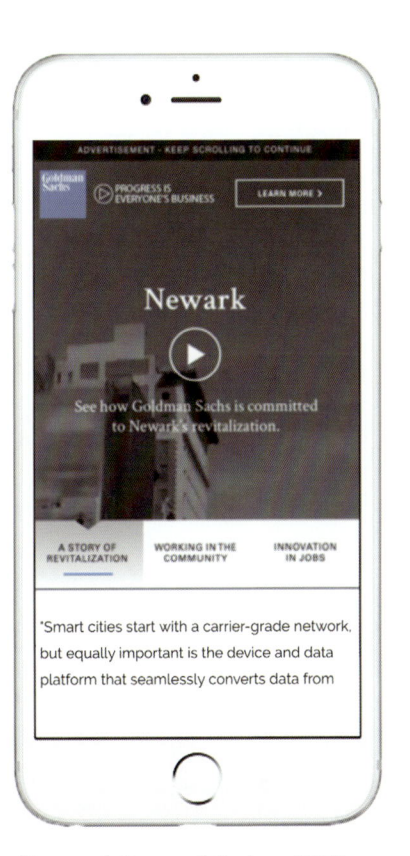

"Progress is Everyone's Business," 2017

"eSports Joins the Big Leagues," 2019

Twitter

"Speaking Of," 2009

LinkedIn

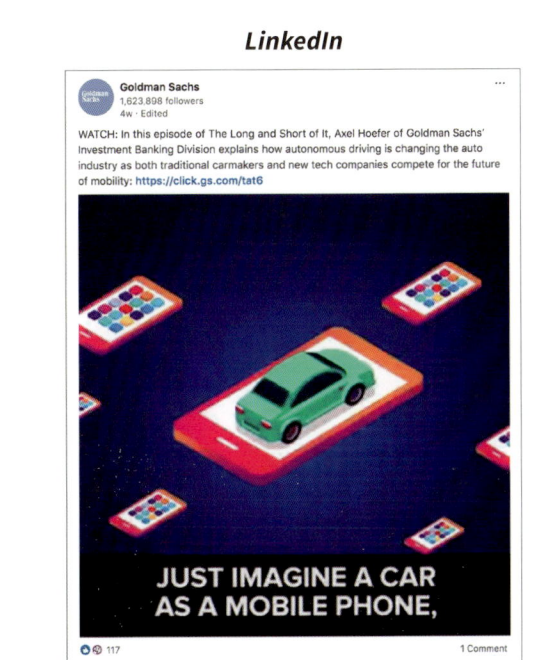

"The Long & Short of It," 2019

Instagram

"3 Things," 2019

"Womenomics 5.0," 2019

127

Leaders in Action

Leadership at Goldman Sachs is an active enterprise. Throughout the firm's history, its leaders have demonstrated an unwavering focus on its clients and a deep commitment to its team around the world. Also essential to the success of the leaders of Goldman Sachs has been the vision and courage to chart the future course of the firm, positioning it to make the most of the opportunities yet to materialize.

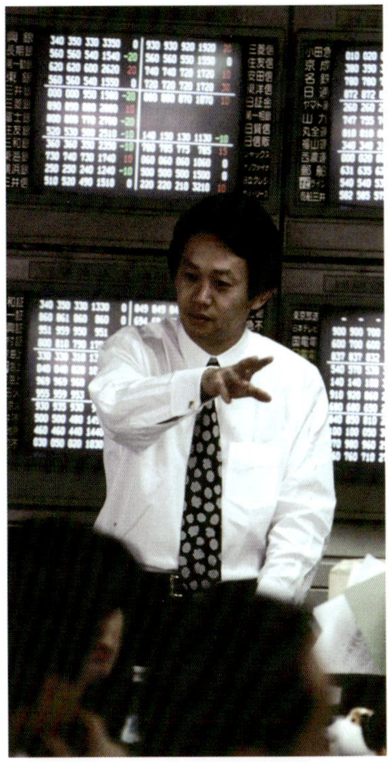

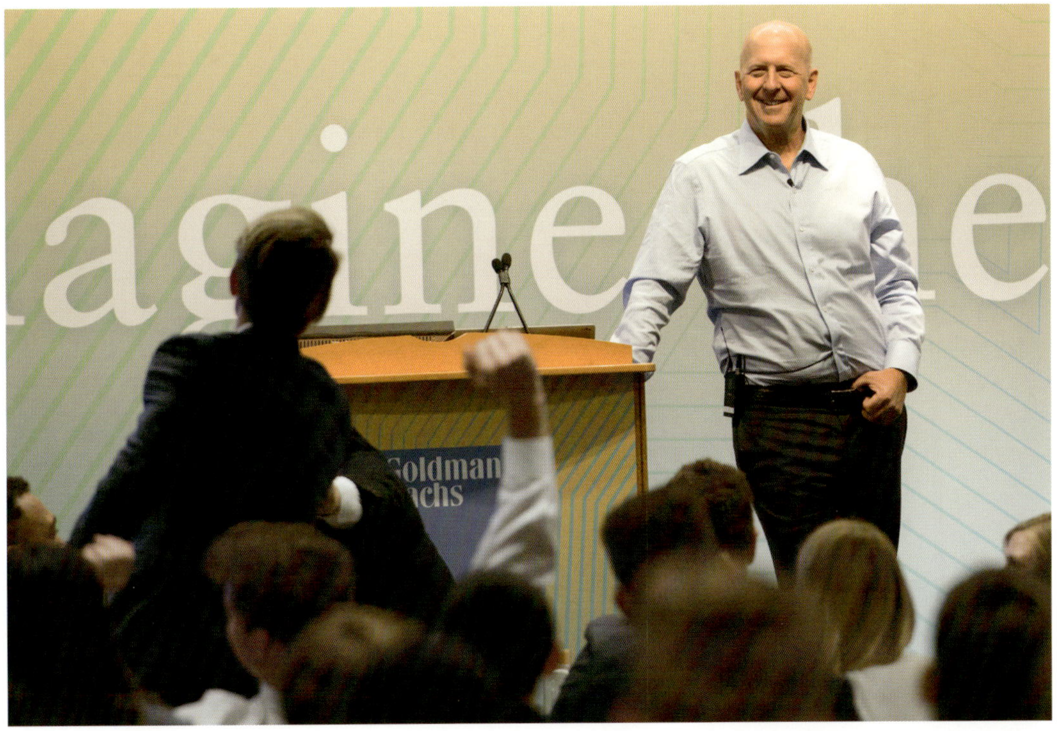
Goldman

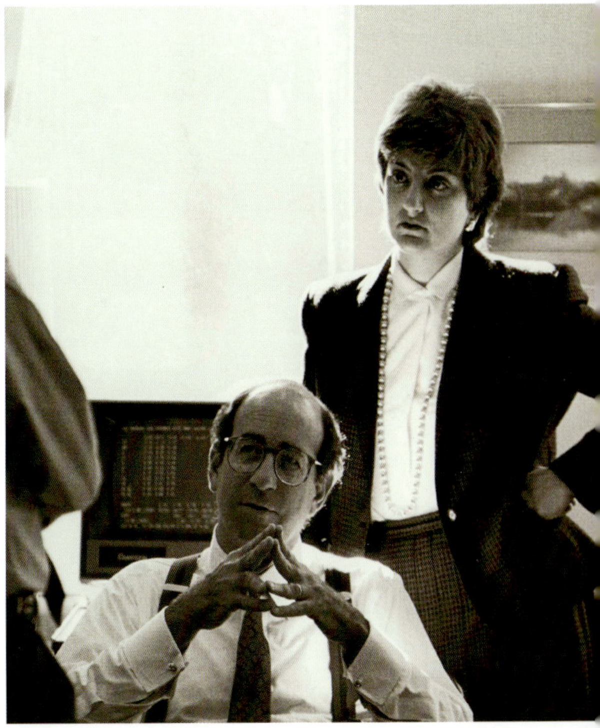

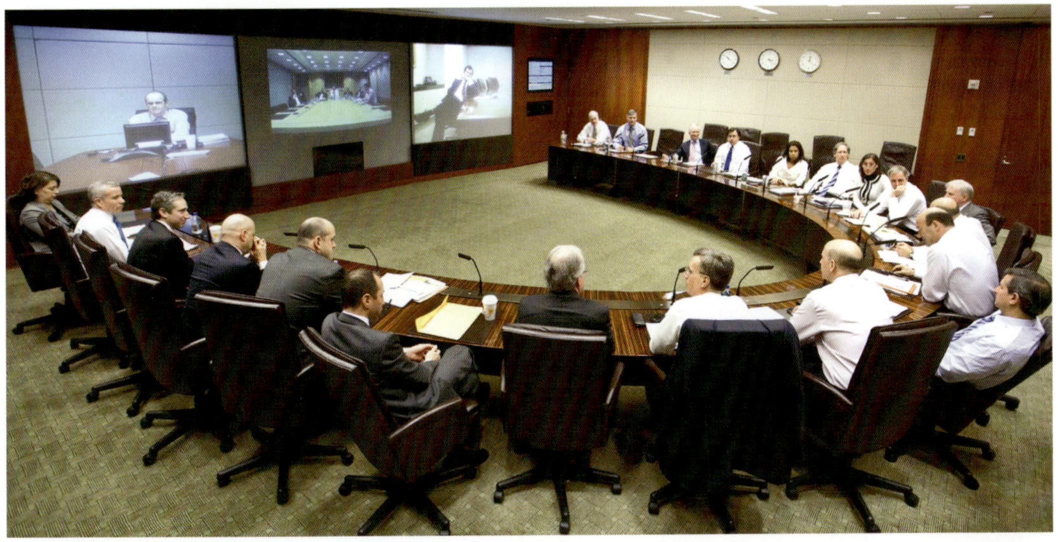

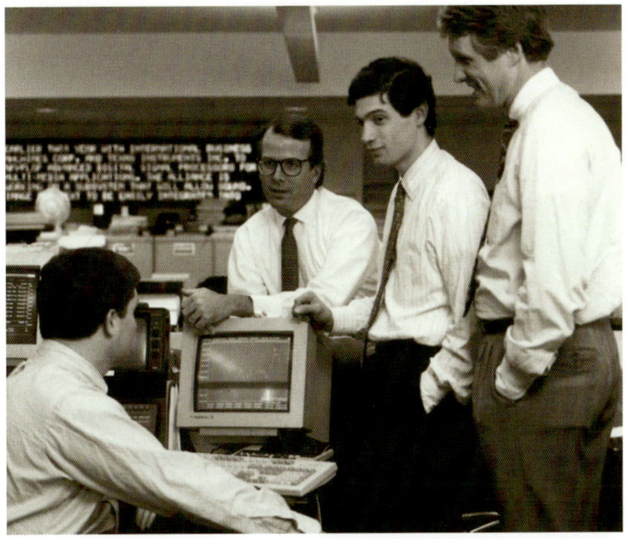

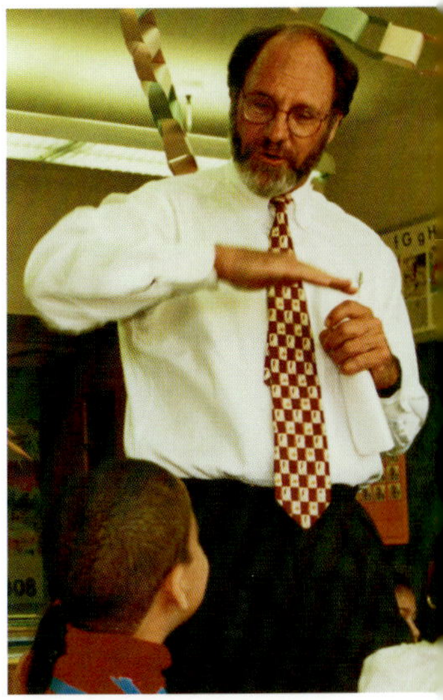

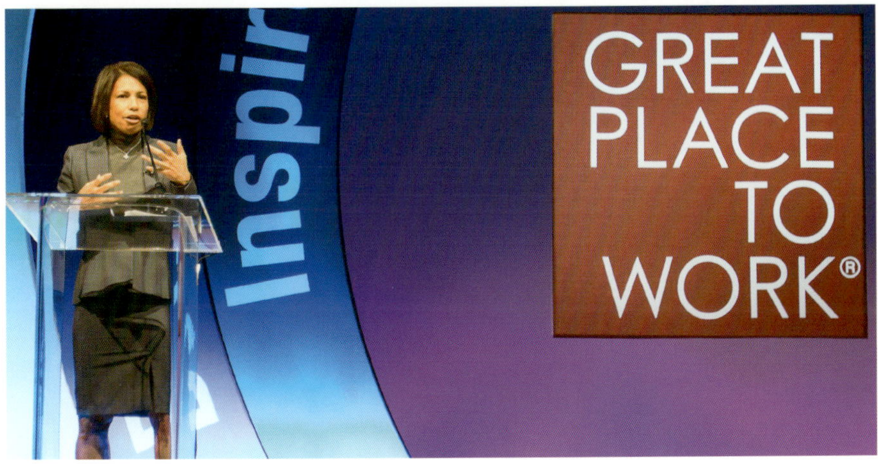
GREAT
PLACE
TO
WORK®

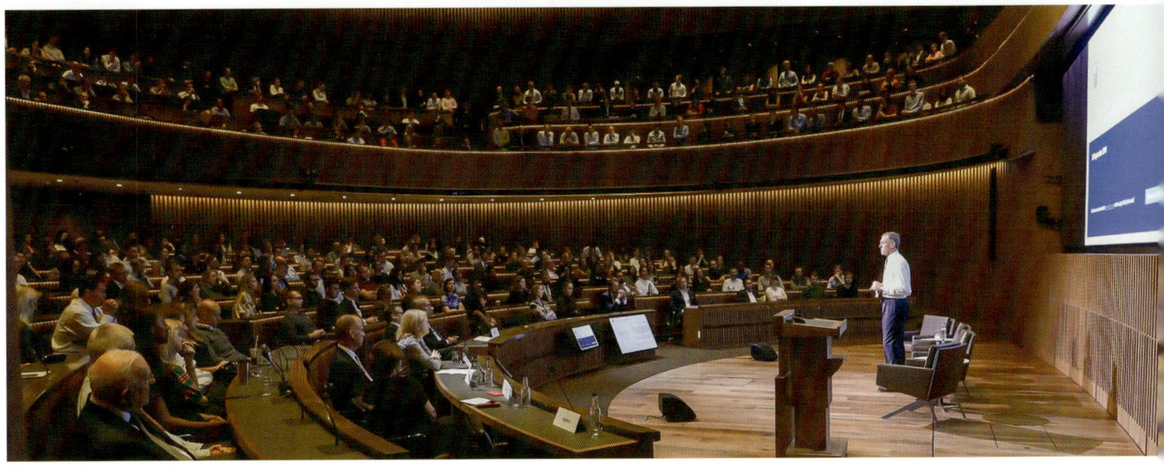

Leaders in Action

145 Years.
Honoring our past. Building our fu

The Goldman Sachs Logo

The original Goldman Sachs logo was designed in 1921 and has continued to evolve over the years. In 1968, Goldman Sachs created a unified logo to reflect the firm's shift from an investment bank to a broader financial services firm. First used in 1969, the box logo, originally black, has undergone subtle modifications over the years. By 1999, it had become the "blue box" that is known and used today.

M. GOLDMAN & SACHS

Goldman, Sachs & Co.
60 Wall Street

1880s

1900s

1890s

1910s

GOLDMAN, SACHS & CO.
60 Wall Street
New York City

Goldman, Sachs & Co.
BANKERS AND BROKERS.

Goldman, Sachs & Co.

1920s

1950s   *1960s*   *1970s*

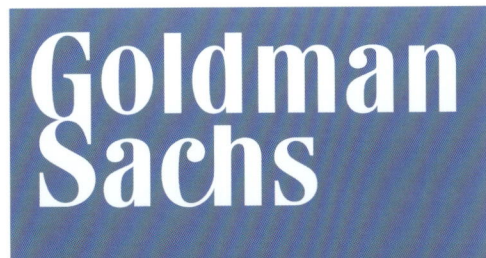

1999

A GLOBAL CITIZEN

In the decade after its initial public offering, Goldman Sachs grew fourfold in size and continued to expand globally, providing innovative solutions for clients and pioneering market-leading research and ideas. It coined the term Womenomics® in a groundbreaking research report that foretold the untapped potential of greater female engagement and inclusion to revive Japan's flagging economic growth. In addition, it was Goldman Sachs that introduced "BRICs" (Brazil, Russia, India and China) into the investing lexicon.

Senior leadership of the firm would turn over for the third time in less than a decade, as once again a leader stepped down to pursue a career in public service (Jon Corzine in 1999, to run for a US Senate seat, and Hank Paulson in 2006, to become US treasury secretary under President George W. Bush). In 2006, Lloyd Blankfein, who had helped to build and lead the firm's foreign exchange business from the earliest years of its global expansion, was named the firm's chairman and chief executive officer. Lloyd had joined Goldman Sachs in 1982 through J. Aron & Company, which had been acquired by the firm one year earlier.

The 2001 terrorist attacks on the World Trade Center would roil global markets, crippling New York's Financial District. Amid the sorrow of so many lost lives, the people of Goldman Sachs rallied to support recovery efforts and help stabilize financial markets, leading to much-needed economic momentum.

Looking forward, Goldman Sachs would break ground on an advanced, eco-friendly global headquarters in Lower Manhattan, bringing new vitality to a neighborhood just blocks from the September 11 attacks. Through its Environmental Policy Framework, established in 2005, the firm committed to leverage its people, capital and ideas to create effective market-based solutions that help address critical environmental issues. This leadership position in environmental stewardship would extend to South America and a landmark conservation effort that would preserve nearly three-quarters of a million acres of unique wilderness on the Chilean island of Tierra del Fuego. In 2008, the Goldman Sachs Foundation launched the *10,000 Women* initiative to help grow local economies and bring about greater shared prosperity and social change by providing thousands of underserved women entrepreneurs around the world with a business and management education. Being global for Goldman Sachs has always been about much more than having offices from Dallas to Dubai; rather, it is about undertaking work around the world to further the interests of its clients, and putting the firm's ideas, people and resources to work toward making a positive difference.

Top: Tierra del Fuego, Chile, 2004.

Bottom: Site visit to the business of 10,000 Women *scholar Anagha Kulkarni, Hyderabad, India, 2010. From left: Geetha Krishnan, director, The Center For Education at the Indian School of Business, Bunty Bohra, Anagha Kulkarni, David Solomon and Brooks Entwistle.*

Opposite: 10,000 Women *scholar Ayodeji Megbope at a* 10,000 Women *graduation, Lagos, Nigeria, 2008.*

Womenomics® reveals the power of the purse in Japan

The decade of the 1990s was one of economic stagnation in Japan, with GDP growing at a scant 0.5% per year. Often referred to as the "lost decade," it came on the heels of a boom period in the 1980s in which low interest rates stoked speculation in real estate and the stock market. When the government ultimately raised interest rates, the bubble burst and an equity market collapse and debt crisis ensued. By mid-1992, equity prices had fallen by roughly 60%. In 1998 alone, 181 small banks and credit cooperatives in Japan failed.

In August of 1999, Goldman Sachs' Global Investment Research Division (GIR) published a Japan Portfolio Strategy report titled "Women-omics: Buy the Female Economy." In it, Tokyo-based strategists Kathy Matsui, Hiromi Suzuki and Yoko Ushio highlighted female consumption in the country as an important pocket of strength in the flagging Japanese economy. In addition to providing a list of 16 Japanese companies that either were poised to benefit from female consumption or were proactive in fostering female employment, the Goldman Sachs strategists argued that an increase in Japan's female labor participation rate from the prevailing rate of 50% to 59% (the level in the United States) could boost the country's real GDP growth in 2000–2010 to 2.5% per annum from 2.2%.

Matsui and her colleagues would continue their research for the next two decades. Eventually the term *Womenomics* — and the concept itself — gained the attention of the Japanese government and would be adopted as a key pillar of reforms meant to revitalize the nation's economy.

Since the publication of the 1999 report, Japan's female labor participation ratio has risen to a record 71% — surpassing the United States and Europe. The Japanese government also introduced policies improving parental leave benefits and mandating equal pay for equal work.

In 2019, twenty years on, Kathy Matsui, Hiromi Suzuki and Kazunori Tatebe wrote "Womenomics 5.0." In the latest report, they estimate that closing Japan's gender employment gap could boost the country's GDP by 10%, and in a "blue-sky scenario" where the ratio of female vs. male working hours rises to the Organisation for Economic Co-operation and Development (OECD) countries' average, the GDP boost could expand further to 15%.

Above: "Women-omics" report authors Kathy Matsui and Hiromi Suzuki, New York City, 2019.

Above: Cover of "Women-omics: Buy the Female Economy" research report, 1999.

Right: Cover of "Womenomics 5.0" research report, 2019.

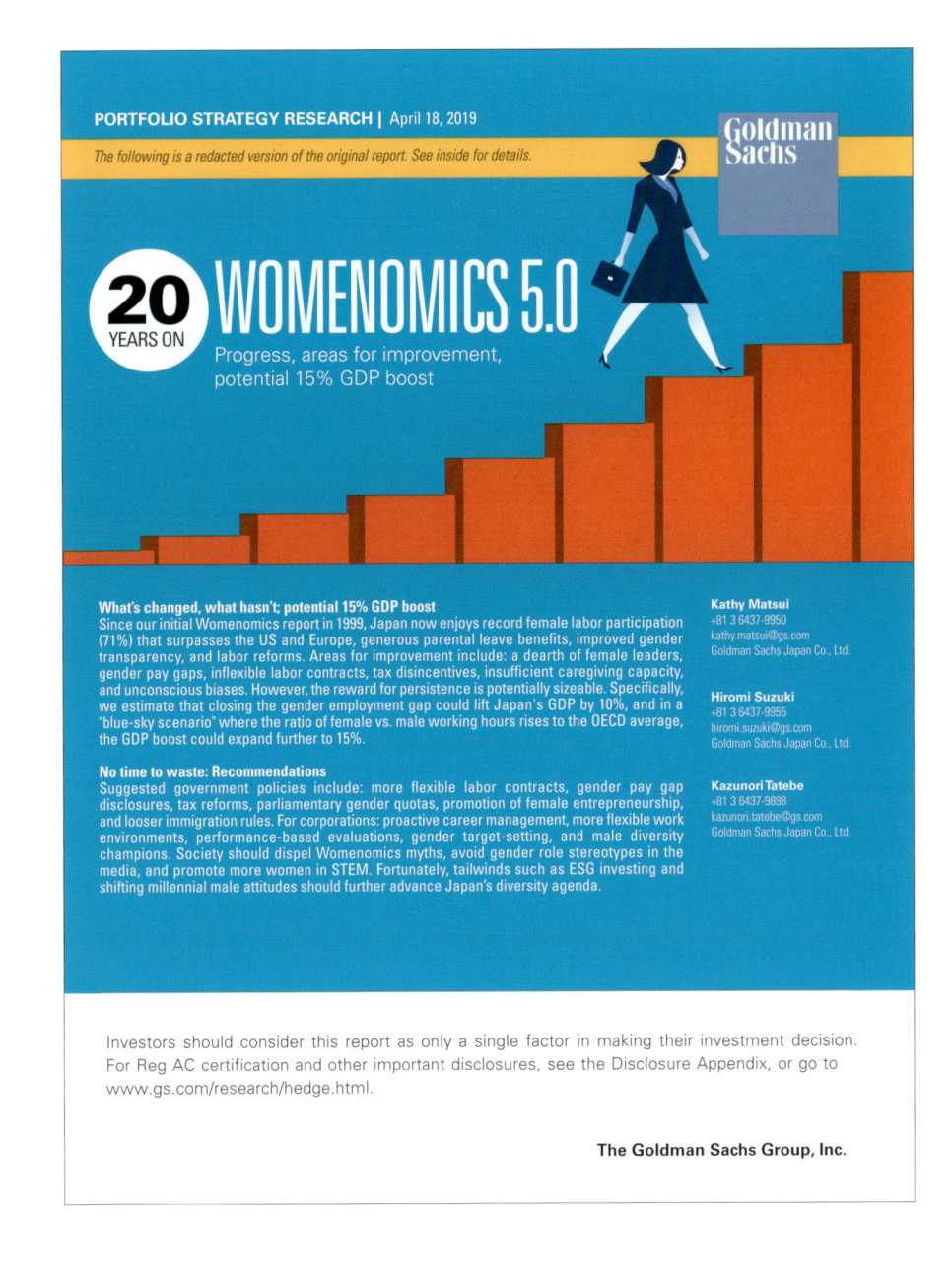

Left: Signing ceremony to form EADS, Strasbourg, France, 1999. From left: Jürgen Erich Schrempp, CEO, DaimlerChrysler; Jean-Luc Lagardère, CEO, Aérospatiale/Matra; Gerhard Schröder, chancellor, Germany; Lionel Jospin, prime minister, France; and Dominique Strauss-Kahn, minister of finance, France.

Firm helps with transactions behind historic European aerospace consortium

In October of 1999, Germany's DaimlerChrysler Aerospace AG (DASA) and French company Aérospatiale-Matra announced they would merge, creating the world's number three player in aerospace and defense, behind the United States' Boeing and Lockheed Martin. Earlier that year, DASA had merged with another European aerospace company, Spain's Construcciones Aeronáuticas S. A. (CASA). The company that combined all three firms, initially called European Aeronautic Defense and Space Company (EADS), became the largest aerospace concern in Europe when the DASA/Aérospatiale-Matra merger was completed in 2000. EADS was the controlling entity of a consortium called Airbus, which in addition to DASA/CASA and Aérospatiale, also included British Aerospace PLC (BAe, later known as BAE Systems).

For many years leading up to the creation of EADS, European policy makers had sought to strengthen the continent militarily and create more independence from foreign suppliers. The new entity, bringing German, French and Spanish companies together, represented a significant step in that direction. Goldman Sachs advised Daimler's DASA aerospace division in both mergers and was part of the underwriting consortium when EADS went public in 2000. Registered in the Netherlands, the company was listed on exchanges in Paris, Frankfurt and Madrid. Thirteen years later, working with Goldman Sachs as its advisor, Daimler would sell its 22.45% stake in EADS. A year later, in 2014, EADS was renamed Airbus Group. As of 2018, the company was ranked second globally in aerospace based on market share, behind Boeing.

Vodafone acquires Mannesmann in the largest acquisition in history

On February 4, 2000, Britain's Vodafone AirTouch PLC acquired Mannesmann AG in a deal that would reshape the mobile telecom marketplace. Goldman Sachs was a financial advisor to Vodafone on its acquisition of Mannesmann, which created the world's leading mobile telecom provider. The complex cross-border transaction, valued at more than $190 billion, was the largest merger in history and featured something largely unheard of at the time: the unsolicited acquisition of a German company. The historic transaction reflected the explosive growth in the European mergers and acquisitions (M&A) sector, which grew nearly three times faster than the global M&A market.

Of the 12 largest M&A transactions worldwide at the time, Goldman Sachs was involved in 11, illustrating the power of the firm's global franchise. Vodafone's successful — and complex — acquisition of Mannesmann strengthened the firm's already close relationship with the telecom giant. As a result, Goldman Sachs received mandates for a number of transactions related to the merger. This included serving as the joint arranger of a $30 billion Euro-bank loan, the largest ever; acting as a joint book runner on Vodafone's $5.25 billion global bond; and executing a $5.1 billion trade in Vodafone — the largest equity block trade in history. The firm also completed a number of related divestitures, including the $46 billion sale of Orange PLC to France Télécom S. A.

Top: Vodafone acquisition of Mannesmann deal toy, 2000.

Bottom: The Vodafone logo on the roof of the Mannesmann high-rise building, Düsseldorf, Germany, 2000.

With a prescient research report, "BRICs" are born

Between 2000 and 2009, the rapid growth of emerging economies outpaced that of developed countries for the first time. A 2001 Goldman Sachs Economic Research report focused on four fast-growing emerging market countries specifically as key drivers of future global economic growth: Brazil, Russia, India and China. With "Building Better Global Economic BRICs," a new term entered the investing vernacular.

The paper, authored by Jim O'Neill, then head of Global Economic Research, projected that over the coming 10 years, the weight of the "BRICs" — especially China — in world GDP would grow significantly, and thus so would the global economic impact of the spending power and demand growth of the four countries.

The BRIC moniker was adopted broadly in financial and economic circles as many of the original paper's insights proved timely: India's economy grew at an average pace of 6.9% per year from 2000 to 2009, and China's soared at a yearly average rate of 10.3%. Other BRICs-oriented research would follow from Goldman Sachs in the ensuing years, chronicling the divergent paths these economies would take.

By the middle of the decade, numerous BRICs-themed mutual funds, ETFs and indexes were created to track this distinct group of countries. By shining a research spotlight on a select group of emerging economies poised at the time to become the next global growth powerhouses, Goldman Sachs helped both investors and companies frame their thinking and decisions based on a shifting global economic power dynamic.

Top: Cover of "Building Better Global Economic BRICs" research report, 2001.

Bottom: Report author Jim O'Neill, 2011.

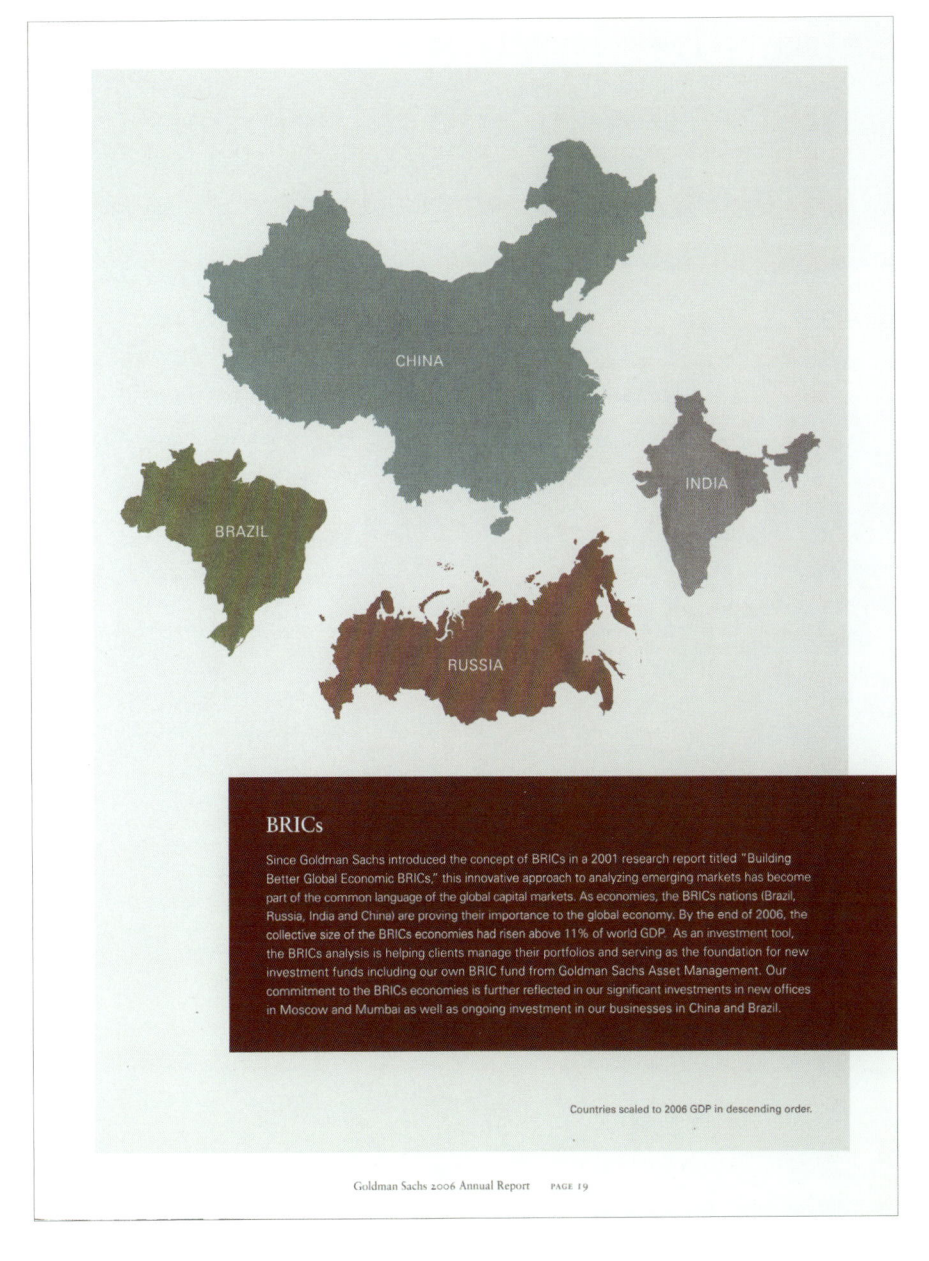

Above: Cover of "BRICs and Beyond" research report, 2007.

Right: Map of BRICs countries, Goldman Sachs Annual Report, *2006.*

September 11, 2001 terrorist attacks stun the world and jolt global financial markets

The deadliest terror attack in US history began when two hijacked commercial airliners crashed into New York's World Trade Center on September 11, 2001, collapsing its skyline-defining Twin Towers. Another hijacked airliner slammed into the Pentagon near Washington, DC, while a fourth hijacked plane crashed in a field near Shanksville, Pennsylvania. Nearly 3,000 people died in the coordinated assaults, and countless others sustained injuries and long-term illnesses. While no Goldman Sachs employees lost their lives in the 9/11 attacks, many family members and friends perished.

The attacks on the World Trade Center towers caused extensive damage to Lower Manhattan. Between 350,000 and 500,000 commuters isolated on the lower tip of the island were evacuated by an extraordinary ad hoc flotilla of boats that included US Coast Guard ships, police and fire boats, commuter ferries and a wide array of private vessels.

The destruction of the World Trade Center brought to a halt the world's leading financial center. In the wake of the Tuesday morning attacks, the New York Stock Exchange, the American Stock Exchange (now NYSE MKT) and Nasdaq remained closed for the remainder of the week, the longest NYSE shutdown since 1933.

The disruption to financial markets was met by an extraordinary global effort by team members at Goldman Sachs to continue to serve clients. Offices in Europe and Asia shouldered the workloads normally handled in New York. Members of the firm based in Manhattan relocated offices to nearby New Jersey and eventually went to great lengths — including chartering buses and ferryboats — to return to the firm's Manhattan offices once the immediate threat had subsided. Some slept on office floors given the difficulty of local travel.

A message from then-CEO Hank Paulson to the entire firm a month after the attacks summed up the tremendous effort put forth throughout the firm to transcend the challenges of the September 11 attacks: "Day by day, your resilience, your ingenuity and your teamwork are demonstrating that the success of any great enterprise always depends upon the character and qualities of its people. We have been facing the worst, and you have been giving us your very best."

Above: Page two of The New York Times, September 12, 2001.

Opposite: Front page of The New York Times, September 12, 2001.

Heroics amid the rubble

At the time of the September 11 attacks, Goldman Sachs' headquarters was located at 85 Broad Street, a few blocks from the World Trade Center's towers. The firm's employees became part of the mass exodus from Lower Manhattan, with no public transportation available. Colleagues banded together to assist each other navigating the debris and chaos that had descended on New York City. In the midst of this were many acts of kindness and heroics — some by helpers who remain anonymous to this day.

One such story involves an iconic photograph published in *The New York Times* the day after the attack featuring FDNY Chaplain Father Mychal F. Judge, the first official casualty of 9/11, being carried from the rubble. While the caption identifies the men in the photo as firefighters, the second man from the right is in fact John P. Maguire, an employee of Goldman Sachs. John was a 1995 graduate of the United States Military Academy at West Point and had been with the firm for less than one year.

In a letter to the firm's chairman and CEO Hank Paulson, John Maguire's parents shared the story behind the photo.

> When the attack occurred, John left his office and went to the Trade Center to help. Arriving shortly after the destruction of the first tower, he assisted in removing the dead and injured. He continued to help when the second tower collapsed almost burying him in the rubble. Fortunately, he survived with only minor injuries.
>
> We are very proud of John and we thought you should be aware of the caliber of people who work for Goldman Sachs.

The note closed with the postscript, "John does not know we have written this letter."

Urban Investment Group is formed to lead the firm's impact investing efforts

Believing that capital markets can and should play an important role in creating opportunities for underserved people and places, Goldman Sachs created the Urban Investment Group (UIG) in 2001 to develop innovative capital solutions that strengthen communities and promote long-term economic growth. Partnering with local public and private sector leaders, UIG makes investments to strengthen the fundamental building blocks of opportunity, including affordable housing, commercial and community facility space in underserved areas, quality education and healthcare, and growth capital for social enterprises and small businesses.

When Goldman Sachs became a bank holding company in 2008, the firm became subject to the Community Reinvestment Act (CRA), a federal law enacted in 1977 with the intent of encouraging depository institutions to help meet the credit needs of individuals and businesses in their communities, including in low- and moderate-income neighborhoods. UIG is responsible for ensuring Goldman Sachs Bank USA's (GS Bank USA) compliance with the federal and New York State CRA. GS Bank USA has received three consecutive "Outstanding" CRA ratings from the Federal Reserve Bank of New York and the New York State Department of Financial Services.

UIG has been a pioneer in creating innovative capital solutions to address complex community challenges. In 2012, the team created the United States' first social impact bond — a then-nascent financial instrument that leverages private investment to support high-impact social programs. In 2013, UIG launched the GS Social Impact Fund, one of the first domestic impact investing vehicles to be sponsored by a major financial institution. Two years later, UIG financed the largest public housing energy retrofit through a structure that linked investor repayment to energy savings achieved in low-income housing in Newark, New Jersey. UIG is now a leader in investing in federally designated opportunity zones, which are distressed areas around the United States. In 2018, UIG merged with the firm's Global Special Situations Group (GSSG), in order to further extend the breadth and depth of Goldman Sachs' principal investing businesses. By September 2019, UIG had committed nearly $8 billion to underserved American communities. That same year, UIG and GSSG — along with several other groups within the firm focused on principal investing — joined the firm's Merchant Banking Division (MBD), allowing Goldman Sachs to offer an integrated investing platform to its clients and position these critical businesses for sustainable long-term growth

Top: Margaret Anadu (third from left) during ribbon-cutting ceremony at 175 Delancey Street, a complex with special housing for low-income senior citizens, New York City, 2018.

Bottom: Faubourg Lafitte, an affordable housing complex rebuilt with funding from the Urban Investment Group (UIG) following Hurricane Katrina, New Orleans, 2012.

Goldman Sachs invests in a stronger Japanese banking system

In early 2003, Goldman Sachs and Sumitomo Mitsui Financial Group (SMFG) entered into a series of transactions that provided the latter with needed capital to shore up its balance sheet. A key part of the agreement was Goldman Sachs' investment of JPY150.3 billion (approximately $1.27 billion) in preferred stock of SMFG, convertible into a 7% stake in the Japanese bank.

The transactions occurred at a time when Japanese banks struggled to regain their footing in the long aftermath of the late 1980s and early 1990s real estate and stock market bubble. After the asset price bubble burst, the Japanese banking industry suffered from significant non-performing loans during the 1990s and early 2000s, resulting in some banks being nationalized. A major focus of the Goldman Sachs-SMFG agreement was the disposition of some of SMFG's non-performing assets.

In October 2003, Goldman Sachs agreed to buy an additional $9.1 billion in nonperforming Sumitomo loans while setting up a joint venture to repackage the debt and help troubled borrowers become more profitable. This infusion of both capital and expertise helped SMFG begin to rehabilitate its balance sheet and return to profitability.

The investment deepened a long-standing relationship between the two firms that dated back to Sumitomo Bank's $500 million investment in the Goldman Sachs partnership at a critical juncture for the firm in the mid-1980s. It also underscored Goldman Sachs' commitment to the Japanese financial markets at a time when capital and restructuring expertise were critically needed to strengthen the country's banking sector.

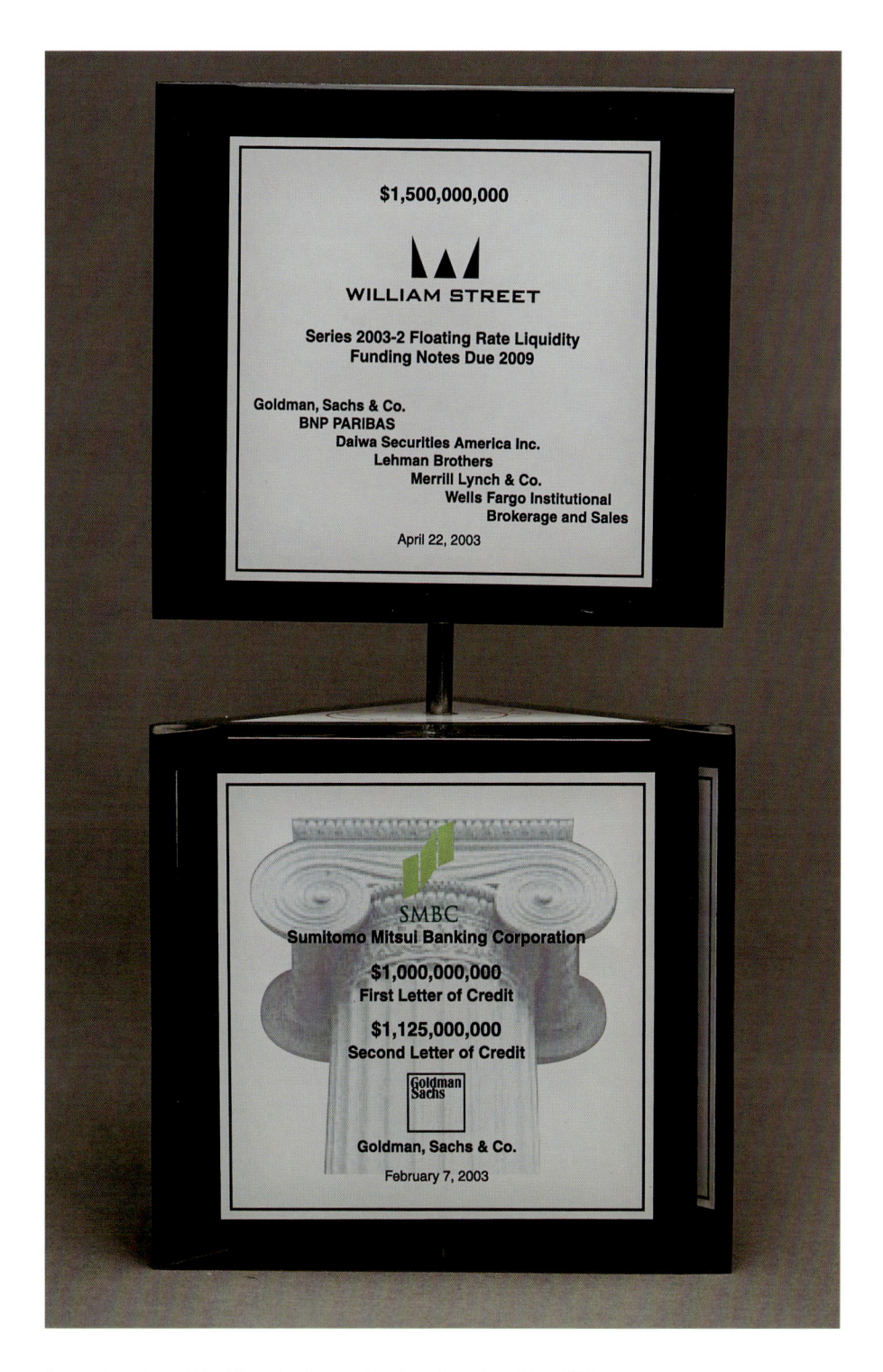

Above: Sumitomo Mitsui Banking Corporation investment deal toy, 2003.

An innovative partnership preserves the pristine wilderness in Tierra del Fuego

In 2004, the firm entered into a public-private partnership with the Wildlife Conservation Society (WCS) to establish the Karukinka Natural Park on the island of Tierra del Fuego, Chile.

Goldman Sachs and the Wildlife Conservation Society announced a first-of-its-kind partnership to protect in perpetuity a vast tract of wilderness at the southernmost edge of South America, on the Chilean side of the island of Tierra del Fuego. This unique public-private alliance created a 736,634-acre nature preserve for the Chilean people.

The naturalist Charles Darwin described Tierra del Fuego's uniqueness in the 1830s while on his historic scientific expedition aboard the HMS *Beagle*, writing, "A single glance at the landscape was sufficient to show me how widely different it was from anything I had ever beheld." Home to alpine meadows, old-growth forests, peat bogs, snow-capped mountains and extraordinary wildlife, the land was donated to ensure the conservation of this uncommon landscape and its wildlife for future generations.

Together, Goldman Sachs and WCS worked with Chilean conservationists and other partners to establish the park, develop a sustainable use plan and preserve the region's distinct ecological characteristics. Named Karukinka, meaning "our land" in the language of the Selk'nam people who once lived there, the park became a model for protecting endangered terrestrial and marine landscapes, combating invasive species and delivering successful public-private partnerships for conservation.

Nameless peaks stand guard over La Paciencia.

The Principal Finance Group saw an opportunity to preserve 680,000 acres of rare wilderness in Tierra del Fuego, Chile.

To learn more about this initiative, visit GSWeb.

Goldman Sachs — WILDLIFE CONSERVATION SOCIETY

Partners in Conservation

Above: Tierra del Fuego, Chile, 2004.

Right: Guanacos at Karukinka Natural Park, Tierra del Fuego, Chile, 2004.

Opposite: Announcement highlighting the Goldman Sachs and Wildlife Conservation Society partnership, 2004.

Embracing past and future, Goldman Sachs breaks ground on a new global headquarters in Manhattan

On November 29, 2005, Goldman Sachs broke ground for its new, state-of-the-art headquarters at 200 West Street, consolidating all of the firm's Lower Manhattan offices into one building, while once again demonstrating its commitment to the area. Since its founding on Pine Street, Goldman Sachs had enjoyed a continual presence in buildings along the city's historic cobblestone alleys within walking distance of the New York Stock Exchange.

When exploring locations to build a new, eco-friendly headquarters, Goldman Sachs selected a site just blocks from the site of the 9/11 attacks and what is today the location of the National September 11 Memorial and Museum. Ground breaking for the new building designed by Pei Cobb Freed & Partners took place on November 29, 2005, with the new headquarters officially opening for business on November 16, 2009.

Goldman Sachs' connection to 200 West Street dates back to its role in financing New York infrastructure projects more than three decades earlier. In 1972, under the leadership of then-senior partner Gus Levy, the firm co-managed the underwriting of a $200 million bond issued by the Battery Park City Authority to finance the construction of a massive landfill on the Hudson River. The space was envisioned as a vibrant community with office buildings, schools and shops — a destination that would help draw people together. For decades, however, the project languished, and the space stood undeveloped, until Goldman Sachs helped to bring to life the city's original vision of Battery Park City by establishing its global headquarters there — catalyzing what is today an attractive and thriving neighborhood and commercial center.

Above: Groundbreaking of the headquarters at the 200 West Street construction site, 2005. From left: Sheldon Silver, state senator, New York; Michael R. Bloomberg, mayor, New York City; Hank Paulson; George E. Pataki, governor, New York; Charles E. Schumer, senator, New York; James F. Gill, chairman, Battery Park City Authority and Hillary Rodham Clinton, senator, New York.

Below: 200 West Street, New York City, 2014.

Environmental Policy Framework establishes the firm's commitment to sustainable economic growth

In November 2005, Goldman Sachs established its Environmental Policy Framework, articulating the firm's conviction that a healthy environment is a prerequisite for a strong economy and sustainable future and its belief that markets can and should play an important role in addressing environmental challenges. At that time, Goldman Sachs was one of the first financial institutions to acknowledge the impact of climate change on issues including economic development, poverty alleviation, access to clean water, food security and adequate energy supplies.

Goldman Sachs also established a carbon emissions trading desk — the first and largest greenhouse gas emissions trading platform in the world — following the 2005 launch of the European Union Emissions Trading Scheme.

In 2006, the firm launched the Goldman Sachs Center for Environmental Markets to undertake strategic partnerships with like-minded sustainably focused corporations, academic institutions and nongovernmental organizations. The firm would go on to establish numerous joint programs and initiatives to facilitate independent research and the development of new environmental tools and metrics to inform climate policy and resource efficiency.

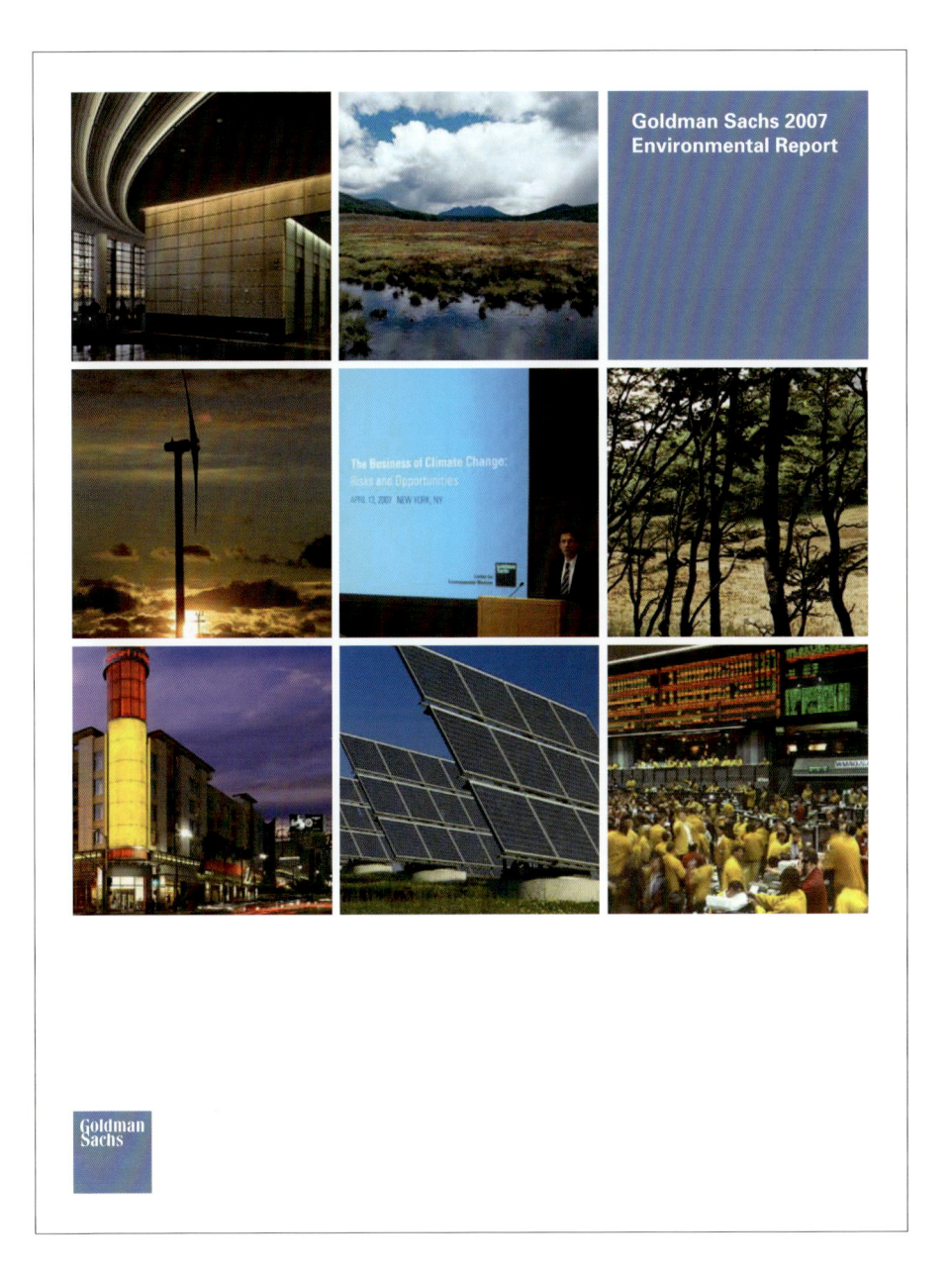

Above: Cover of Goldman Sachs 2007 Environmental Report.

Alumni network provides valuable connection to the firm and former colleagues

With its strong, unique culture, Goldman Sachs remains a powerful source of connection for its alumni around the world, long after their days working at the firm. No matter where their post–Goldman Sachs career may lead them — entrepreneur, client, public servant — many of the firm's alumni stay actively engaged with the firm and their former colleagues. The Goldman Sachs Alumni Network, established in 2005, fosters this tradition of connection through newsletters and special events for more than 93,000 alumni. It is not uncommon to generate a strong turnout for training program reunions as much as 25 years later — powerful testimony to the impact Goldman Sachs has on its people and their professional development, wherever it may lead them.

Top: 1989 Investment Banking Division (IBD) analyst class reunion, New York City, 2015.

Bottom: 1989 Securities Sales associates class reunion, New York City, 2019.
Front row, from left: Akiko Tabor, Robert Castrignano, Rhian-Anwen Hamill, Marta Cotton, Roy Zuckerberg, Matthias Eppenberger, Rod MacKay, James Herring and Maria Chrin. Back row, from left: Vincent Barnouin, Rory Tobin, Jeff Bernstein, Tracy Nixon, Andy Stenovec, Emmanuel Gavaudan, Marla Stewart, Randall Burkert, Olivier Rouget and Olivier Dupraz.

Top: Alumni networking event, Bengaluru, 2017.

Bottom: Group portrait at dinner celebrating George Ross and Richard Menschel's combined 100th anniversary with Goldman Sachs, New York City, 2009. Seated from left: Eric Schwartz, Eric Dobkin, Lewis Eisenberg, Stephen Kay and Richard Atlas. Standing from left: Roy Zuckerberg, Geoffrey Boisi, William Stutt, Joe Camarda, George Ross, Richard Menschel, Robert Menschel, Robert Freeman, Eugene Mercy and Robert Steel.

Diversity initiatives underscore the firm's commitment to an inclusive workforce

In an effort to promote a work environment that would attract and retain the best people, Goldman Sachs formed the firmwide Diversity Committee in 1989. The committee's first mandate was to identify and evaluate existing programs related to diversity-focused initiatives, "to ensure that Goldman Sachs continues to be a true meritocracy with an atmosphere of professionalism, cooperation and tolerance."

In 2001, the firm launched a Global Diversity Task Force to comprehensively examine and evaluate those diversity efforts. Over a period of six months, 25 professionals across all levels, regions and divisions reviewed the firm's diversity programs, benchmarked best-in-class companies, organized focus groups and conducted a firmwide survey about diversity and the work environment. As a result of these findings, the Goldman Sachs Office of Global Leadership and Diversity was created.

Another tangible result of the task force was the amendment of the Goldman Sachs Business Principles to underscore publicly the importance of diversity to the firm's success. In a message signed by Chairman and CEO Hank Paulson and co-COOs John Thain and John Thornton on October 16, 2001, Goldman Sachs announced that the seventh Business Principle had been expanded to emphasize the importance of building, supporting and leveraging a diverse and inclusive workforce at Goldman Sachs. The revised version (new language in italics), published in the firm's 2001 *Annual Report*, reads:

> We offer our people the opportunity to move ahead more rapidly than is possible at most other places. Advancement depends on merit and we have yet to find the limits to the responsibility our best people are able to assume. *For us to be successful, our men and women must reflect the diversity of the communities and cultures in which we operate. That means we must attract, retain and motivate people from many backgrounds and perspectives. Being diverse is not optional; it is what we must be.*

In 2006, a new Diversity Task Force was convened to re-examine the successes of Goldman Sachs' diversity efforts to date. The task force presented recommendations focusing on accountability, training, communication and governance. The Office of Global Leadership and Diversity would assume responsibility for the implementation and oversight of those recommendations, as well as provide ongoing efforts to continuously monitor and improve the firm's diversity and inclusion practices.

To advance specific areas critical to making progress on a more diverse and inclusive workforce, Chairman and CEO Lloyd Blankfein and President David Solomon announced that the firm would reconstitute a Global Diversity Committee in July 2018. The Committee focuses on recommending initiatives to promote an inclusive work environment and diverse leadership, as well as to develop metrics, accountability and new strategies for recruiting and integrating both entry-level and experienced diverse hires.

Left: Mahzarin Banaji, professor of social ethics in the Department of Psychology at Harvard University, leads "Blindspot: Hidden Biases of Good People," a leadership training program for employees, New York City, 2016.

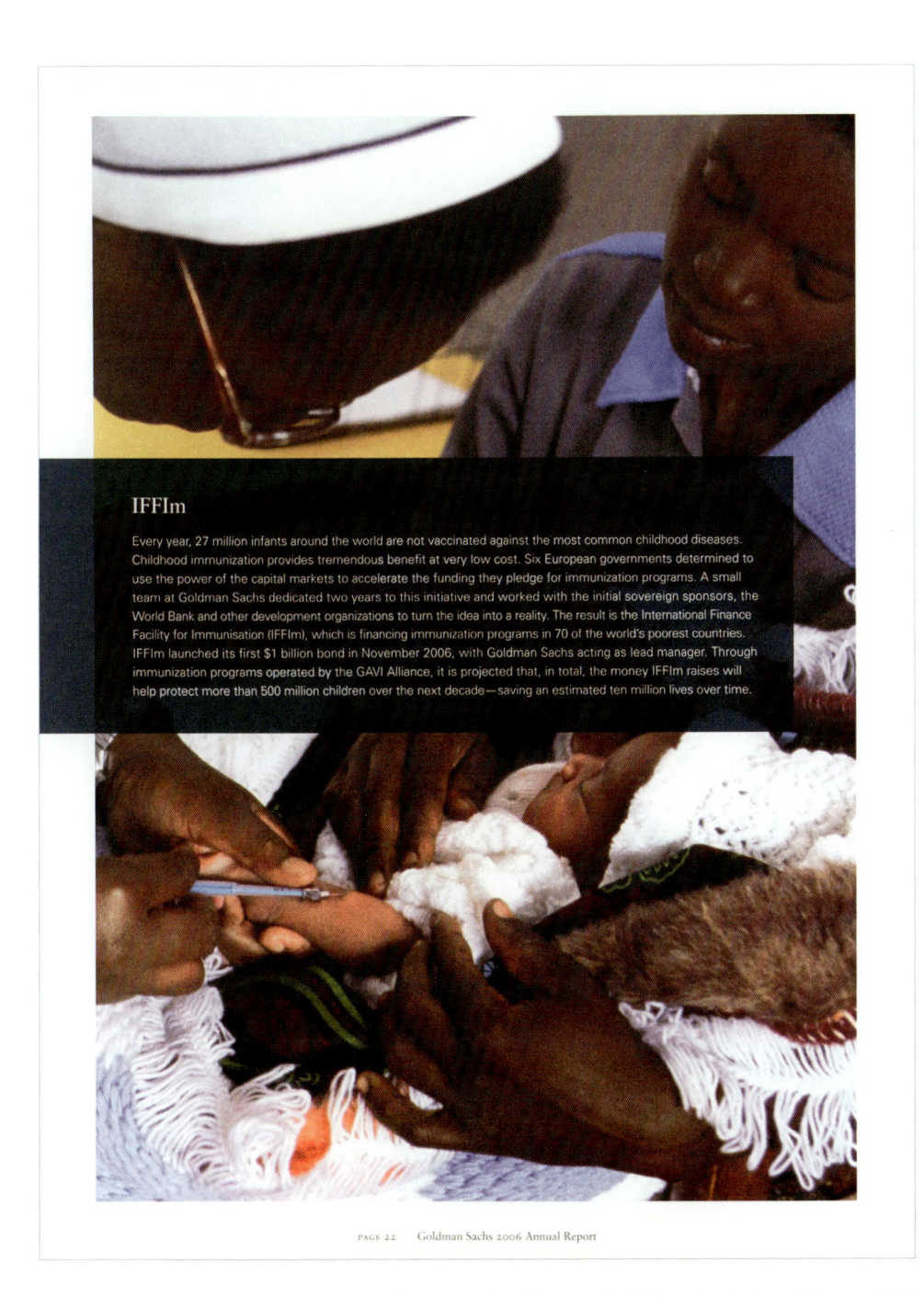

Above: IFFIm bond featured in Goldman Sachs Annual Report, 2006.

Financial innovation funds immunization in more than 60 countries

In the mid-2000s, more than 20 million infants annually around the world were not vaccinated against the most common childhood diseases, despite evidence that childhood immunization could provide tremendous benefit at very low cost. In light of this, the United Kingdom, France, Italy, Spain, Sweden and Norway determined to use the power of capital markets to accelerate the funding each nation pledged for immunization programs. For two years, a small team at Goldman Sachs worked with the initial sovereign sponsors, the World Bank and other development organizations, to transform this notion into a reality, resulting in the International Finance Facility for Immunisation (IFFIm).

The facility was designed to provide a steady stream of immunization funds for programs in more than 60 developing countries by issuing debt in capital markets, backed by multiyear grants from sovereign donor governments. Goldman Sachs acted as lead manager jointly with Deutsche Bank in launching the first IFFIm $1 billion bond in November 2006. The capital raised for this and other issues was projected to help protect the health of more than 500 million children over the following decade — saving an estimated 10 million lives over time.

Lloyd Blankfein is named chairman and CEO, beginning a tenure marked by historic challenge and innovation

Lloyd Blankfein was born in the Bronx, New York in 1954 and raised in Brooklyn. After graduating from Harvard University, which he attended on an academic scholarship, Lloyd earned a law degree at Harvard Law School. Initially he worked as a corporate tax lawyer for a New York firm, but a few years later, in 1982, he joined the commodities trading firm J. Aron & Co. as a precious metals salesperson. J. Aron had been acquired by Goldman Sachs the prior year, in 1981. Named partner in 1988, Lloyd pioneered Goldman Sachs' foreign exchange business, which would help to reinforce the firm's position as a leading provider of integrated financial and risk management solutions to its clients around the globe.

Lloyd was named head of sales and trading in 2002 and president and chief operating officer of Goldman Sachs two years later. In 2006, he became chairman and CEO after Hank Paulson was named secretary of the US Department of the Treasury under President George W. Bush. Despite his outwardly buoyant demeanor, Lloyd's years of experience as a trader had trained him to be intensely risk aware and deeply skeptical of the ability of even the most sophisticated quantitative models to properly project market outcomes.

Lloyd would steer the firm through the financial crisis of 2008, working ceaselessly to guide Goldman Sachs as it transitioned into a bank holding company. In addition to building on the firm's global momentum during his tenure, initiatives such as *10,000 Women* and *10,000 Small Businesses* would be launched, as well as Marcus®, the firm's digital consumer financial services business.

In 2018, Lloyd retired as chairman and CEO of the board and was succeeded by David Solomon.

Above: Lloyd Blankfein (right) and Russell Horwitz leave the New York Stock Exchange following a forum with leaders of New York's international business and finance community, October 10, 2008.

Above: Lloyd Blankfein moderates a Talks at GS *session with Cardinal Timothy Dolan, New York City, 2014.*

Left: Lloyd Blankfein, New York City, 1986.

New program harnesses the power of education and capital for women entrepreneurs around the world

In 2008, the Goldman Sachs Foundation launched *10,000 Women*, a global initiative to help grow local economies and bring about greater shared prosperity and social change by providing thousands of underserved women entrepreneurs with a world-class business and management education, as well as access to networks and capital.

10,000 Women was inspired by a growing body of research, including the firm's *Womenomics* reports, showing that female labor force participation is a key source of long-term economic growth and that investing in women's education can have a significant multiplier effect — leading to job creation; healthier, better-educated families; and more prosperous communities and nations.

In 2014, the program reached its 10,000th participant and published a report detailing its global impact. More than 60% of graduates had created new jobs, and over 70% had increased their revenues. Graduates also passed on their learnings within their communities, with over 90% mentoring eight other women on average.

Lack of access to funding historically has been an impediment to the growth of women-owned businesses. In a 2014 report, Goldman Sachs' Global Markets Institute estimated that closing this funding gap could increase per capita income in the BRIC and "Next 11" countries by up to 12% by 2030. The year the report was published, the *10,000 Women* initiative partnered with the International Finance Corporation to create *The Women Entrepreneurs Opportunity Facility* (WEOF) initiative, the first-ever global finance facility for women-owned small- and medium-sized businesses. As of June 2019, WEOF had invested $1.45 billion — far exceeding its original goal of $600 million — and had provided capital to more than 53,000 women entrepreneurs across 33 countries in the developing world.

Top: 10,000 Women *scholars and delegation, Lagos, Nigeria, 2008.*

Bottom, left: Su Xiaoyan, 10,000 Women *scholar, Changshu, China, 2012.*

Bottom, right: 10,000 Women *panel, New York City, 2016. From left, Jessica Johnson,* 10,000 Women *scholar; Ciiru Waweru,* 10,000 Women *scholar and Dina Powell.*

Opposite: 10,000 Women *brochure, 2009.*

Recruiting Talent

As noted in the firm's Business Principles, the people of Goldman Sachs are among its most valuable assets. The ability to attract and retain that talent is an essential pillar of the firm's success. While the tools and technology for engaging with prospective recruits have changed dramatically over the years, the mission remains essentially the same: to identify and connect with talented, driven, team-oriented individuals who can add to the firm's collective efforts on behalf of the clients and communities it serves.

"Minds. Wide. Open.," 2002

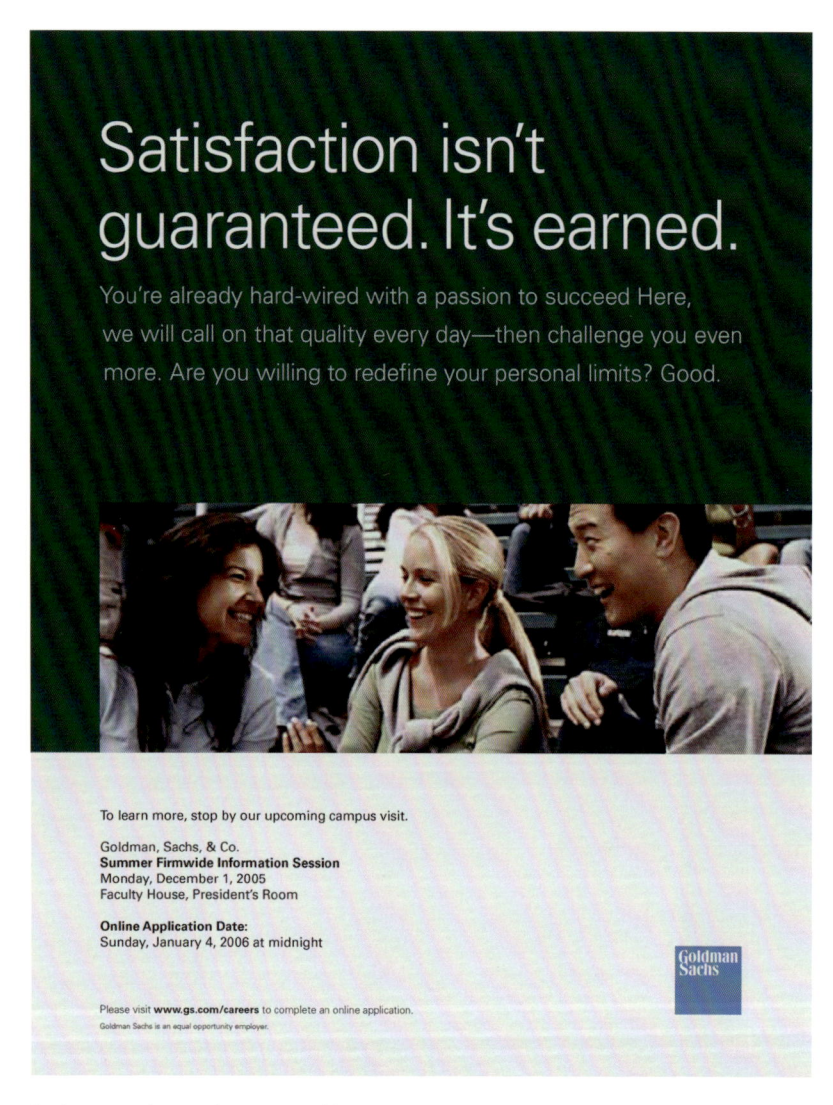

"Take Your Talent to the Next Level," 2005

"Matrix," 2008

"Matrix," 2008

"Make things possible," 2018

"Make an Impact," 2012

"Make an Impact," 2013

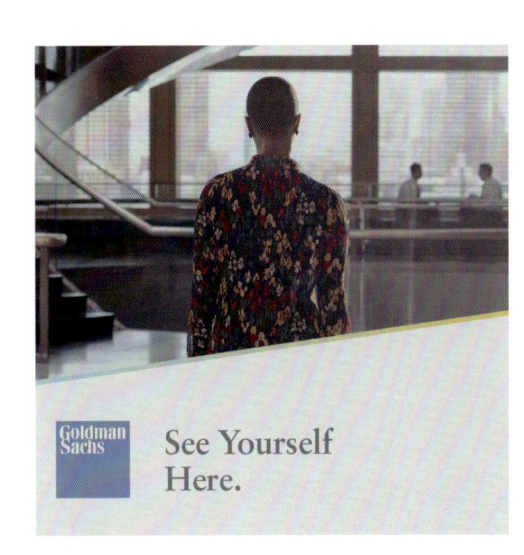

"Day in the Life," 2019

"Day in the Life" digital advertising, 2019

159

EVOLUTION

The year 2008 ushered in the worst economic disaster since the Great Depression. The global financial crisis made the risks of interconnected markets astonishingly clear when what started out in the United States as shock triggered by falling housing prices and loose credit standards quickly reverberated through capital markets around the globe. Financial institutions faced such profound losses from holdings in mortgage-backed securities that the US government was forced to step in and provide significant capital to the banks through the Troubled Asset Relief Program (TARP). In the court of public opinion, the banks became the objects of derision, perceived as having contributed to the crisis — or worse, having profited from it. While Goldman Sachs' reputation suffered during this period, the firm's leadership, with Lloyd Blankfein at the helm, helped to steer it through the most turbulent days of the global financial crisis and one of the most trying chapters in its history. Even amid a near-term crisis of epic proportions, the firm made some important, long-term strategic decisions. On September 21, 2008, 75 years after the US Congress separated investment banks from deposit-taking lenders, Goldman Sachs became a traditional bank holding company, ending the business model of an independent securities firm on Wall Street, but changing the opportunity set for the firm and its future course.

For Goldman Sachs, the global financial crisis triggered a period of intense introspection. For one, it contributed to a greater sense of accountability to the broader financial system that would culminate, two years later, in the creation of the Business Standards Committee (BSC). The BSC critically evaluated each of the firm's business standards and practices to ensure that they were of the highest quality; that they met or exceeded the expectations of clients, regulators and other stakeholders; and that they contributed to overall financial stability in the capital markets. As a public company with a significant and visible role in global markets, Goldman Sachs also recognized the need to engage with a broader set of external constituencies in order to foster a better understanding of the firm's business activities on behalf of clients and subsequent contribution to economic growth. The global financial crisis transformed the world of finance, with ripple effects that continued to be felt a decade later. As it did in crises past, Goldman Sachs used the difficult period as an opportunity to do the work necessary not only to survive but to emerge stronger on the other side.

Top: Front page of Financial Times *with Lloyd Blankfein's op-ed piece "Do not destroy the essential catalyst of risk," February 9, 2009.*

Bottom: Protestors rally outside the Goldman Sachs representative office to call on the US Congress to take on financial reform, Washington, DC, 2009.

Opposite: Traders on the New York Stock Exchange floor watch as stocks fall, 2008.

Goldman Sachs announces it will become a bank holding company

On September 21, 2008, Goldman Sachs announced it would become the fourth-largest bank holding company in the United States, regulated by the Federal Reserve (the Fed). The move was in response to the dramatically changing landscape in the investment banking industry caused by the collapse of Lehman Brothers merely six days before and the ensuing global financial crisis.

"We believe that Goldman Sachs, under Federal Reserve supervision, will be regarded as an even more secure institution with an exceptionally clean balance sheet and a greater diversity of funding sources," stated Chairman and CEO Lloyd Blankfein. He noted that the move addressed market perceptions that placed a premium on the value of oversight by the Fed and the ability to source Federal Deposit Insurance Corporation (FDIC)–insured bank deposits to increase funding capacity, while also providing access to a broader set of liquidity and financing alternatives.

The firm already had two active deposit-taking institutions — Goldman Sachs Bank USA, an industrial loan company established in Utah in 2004, and Goldman Sachs Bank Europe PLC, incorporated in Ireland in 2007 — which, together, held more than $20 billion in customer deposits. By merging a number of existing strategic businesses into GS Bank USA, it quickly became one of the ten largest banks in the United States, with more than $150 billion in assets at the end of 2008. GS Bank USA established a branch in London in March 2013 to service its non-US clients, and in April 2016, it acquired GE Capital Bank's US deposit platform — which would be relaunched as Marcus by Goldman Sachs® — to aid the firm's participation in the consumer finance sector.

By becoming a bank holding company, now regulated primarily by the Federal Reserve and subject to new capital and leverage tests, the firm had further strengthened its capital, liquidity and competitive position.

Above: Front page of The Wall Street Journal, *September 22, 2008.*

Berkshire Hathaway invests $5 billion in the firm

While many US firms looked overseas for capital infusions during the 2008 global financial crisis, Goldman Sachs found willing investors closer to home. These investments in the fourth quarter of 2008 strengthened the firm's capitalization while securing the endorsement — $5 billion dollars' worth — of one of the world's most admired investors.

Warren Buffett had worked with Goldman Sachs for more than 50 years and had first met senior partner Sidney Weinberg in 1940. This long-term relationship with the firm formed the basis for approaching the famed investor about making a potential investment in Goldman Sachs.

Berkshire Hathaway would purchase $5 billion in special preferred shares that would pay a 10% annual dividend. The firm had the option of buying back the shares for $5 billion plus a one-time dividend of $500 million. Berkshire Hathaway would also acquire warrants to buy an additional $5 billion of common stock at $115 per share.

Two days after Goldman Sachs became a bank holding company, the firm announced the private offering to Berkshire Hathaway. The next day, the firm also completed a public offering of 46.7 million shares of common stock at $123 per share, for proceeds of $5.75 billion in an offering that was oversubscribed.

Just a few weeks later, on October 27, the firm received an injection of an additional $10 billion under the Capital Purchase Program (CPP) funded by the US Treasury's Troubled Asset Relief Program (TARP). Lloyd Blankfein, the firm's chairman and CEO, noted that, while Goldman Sachs had not sought such an infusion of capital, it appreciated its value in light of market conditions. "We view the TARP as important to the overall stability of the financial system and, therefore, important to Goldman Sachs," said Blankfein in testimony to the US Congress.

Top: Warren Buffett addressing the people of Goldman Sachs, New York City, 2008.

Bottom: Isabelle Ealet, Gary Cohn, Lloyd Blankfein and Warren Buffett visiting a trading floor, New York City, 2008.

The firm repaid the US government's $10 billion TARP investment just eight months later, with $1.41 billion of profit for the lender. The repayment, when combined with preferred dividends paid, represented an annualized 23% return for US taxpayers.

In March 2011, Goldman Sachs announced it would exercise its option to buy back the Berkshire Hathaway shares two years early.

10,000 Small Businesses® helps to fuel the engines of job creation and spark innovation

In November 2009, Goldman Sachs announced it would spend $500 million to fund a program to help small businesses in the United States through a combination of education, mentoring and access to capital. Founded on the strong results achieved through the firm's *10,000 Women* initiative, *10,000 Small Businesses* would be guided by an advisory council co-chaired by Lloyd Blankfein; legendary investor Warren Buffett; Michael Bloomberg, founder of Bloomberg LP and Bloomberg Philanthropies and Dr. Michael Porter of the Initiative for a Competitive Inner City and Harvard Business School.

10,000 Small Businesses looks beyond the heavily-supported startup market to serve established small business owners poised for growth. The firm committed $200 million to fund business education and support services for these entrepreneurs. The curriculum was designed to target skills that participants could immediately apply, including accounting, marketing, negotiating and human resource management. In addition, the firm committed $300 million in lending and philanthropic support to community development financial institutions and other mission-driven small business lenders to spur greater access to capital.

Given the program's primary objective of unlocking the growth and job creation potential of small business owners, a core component of *10,000 Small Businesses* is measuring its impact. Revenue and job growth are key metrics used to assess the effectiveness of the program. As of 2019, eighteen months after completing the program, almost three-quarters (72%) of alumni had grown their revenues. This compares with just over half (53%) of US small businesses increasing their revenues as surveyed by the National Small Business Association for its "2017 Year-End Economic Report." *10,000 Small Businesses* maintains a 98% graduation rate and has created a vibrant network for entrepreneurs, with 86% of graduates reporting doing business together.

Above: Cover of 10,000 Small Businesses *Progress Report, 2018.*

In the United Kingdom, *10,000 Small Businesses* launched in 2010 with the same aim — to spur economic growth and prosperity by providing education to ambitious entrepreneurs. Its graduates are doubling revenues and creating 50% more jobs within two years of graduating, following the changes they implement because of the program.

In 2018, nearly ten years after the US launch of the *10,000 Small Businesses* program, more than 2,000 graduates of the program convened in Washington, DC for the *10,000 Small Businesses* Summit: The Big Power of Small Business — the largest-ever gathering of small business owners in the United States. During the two-day convening, business owners heard from the likes of Warren Buffett, Richard Branson, and Sara Blakely, and, in a landmark "Day on the Hill," participants met with representatives from their respective districts to advocate for policies that support the continued ability of small businesses to grow, thrive and compete.

Above: 10,000 Small Businesses *LaGuardia Community College graduation, New York City, 2010.*

Left: Angelica Rivera, *10,000 Small Businesses scholar, New Orleans, 2011.*

The Business Standards Committee is formed

The aftermath of the global financial crisis was a time of reflection for many market participants, and in some cases, a time for the strengthening or reinforcement of certain core values. In 2010, Goldman Sachs announced the creation of the Business Standards Committee (BSC), whose mandate was to conduct an extensive review to ensure that the firm maintained business standards and practices of the highest quality; that these standards and practices met or exceeded the expectations of the firm's clients, other stakeholders, and regulators; and that they contributed to overall financial stability and economic opportunity.

The committee was led by E. Gerald Corrigan, former president of the New York Federal Reserve from 1985 to 1993 and a Goldman Sachs partner since 1996; J. Michael Evans, a vice chairman of Goldman Sachs; 14 partner members; and Arthur Levitt, the longest-serving chairman of the US Securities and Exchange Commission (1993 to 2001) and advisor to the firm since 2009. The BSC operated with oversight by the firm's Board of Directors.

The areas of focus for the committee included client relationships and responsibilities; conflict management; disclosure and transparency of firmwide activities; structured products and suitability; education, training and business ethics.

The scope and intensity of the committee's eight-month review was significant, encompassing every major business, region and activity of the firm. The work of the committee included the active involvement of 130 of the firm's most senior leaders from across every division and region, hundreds of meetings, the engagement of two independent consulting firms and regular postings to the firm's regulators globally. The committee drew on an external survey of more than 200 clients worldwide and an internal culture survey of approximately 3,000 of the firm's employees.

Ultimately the BSC made 39 recommendations for change, spanning client service, conflicts and business selection, structured products, transparency and disclosure, committee governance, training and professional development and employee evaluation and incentives. It called for the creation of the Client and Business Standards Committee, a permanent body whose mandate is to focus on the interrelationships among clients, business standards and practices, and reputational risk management in an ever-more-complex operating and market environment.

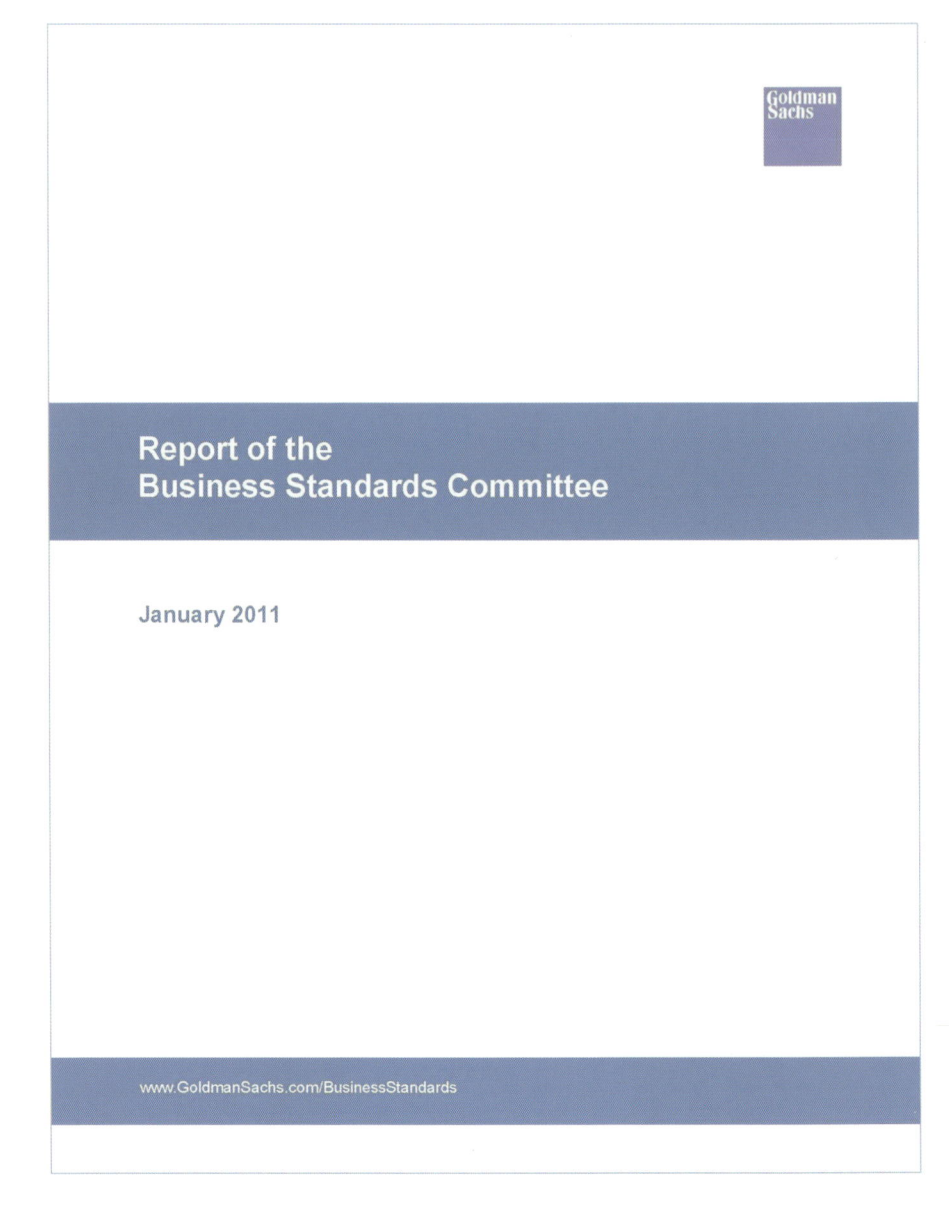

Above: Cover of Business Standards Committee report, 2011.

Above: Business Standards Committee meeting, New York City, 2010.

Left: Business Standards Committee co-chairs Mike Evans and Jerry Corrigan, New York City, 2010.

Influential entrepreneurs are celebrated at inaugural Builders + Innovators Summit

In October 2012, Goldman Sachs hosted its first annual Builders + Innovators Summit (B+I®) in Newport Beach, California. The summit brought together an elite group of entrepreneurs with seasoned innovators for a three-day forum at the Resort at Pelican Hill, where participants exchanged ideas, insights and strategies for growing and enhancing their businesses and for driving economic growth through innovation. Each year since, the summits have featured a newly selected list of the 100 Most Intriguing Entrepreneurs — hailing from industries as diverse as healthcare, IT, consumer products, energy and entertainment — sharing their vision for future innovation. In 2019, the first Builders + Innovators Summit in Asia was held, continuing the dynamic exchange of ideas among global business leaders.

Right: Builders & Innovators signage outside conference venue in Marana, Arizona, 2013.

Top, right: David Solomon and media executive Peter Chernin, Talks at GS session at Builders + Innovators Summit, Santa Barbara, California, 2018.

Bottom, right: Builders & Innovators breakout session with entrepreneurs, Santa Barbara, California, 2018.

Dodd-Frank Act ushers in a new era of post-crisis banking regulation

The global financial crisis of 2008 led policy makers around the world to coordinate their initial responses, rethinking key aspects of financial regulation. The results would have a profound impact on Goldman Sachs and on the financial industry as a whole.

In January 2009, the Group of 30 — a research group chaired by Paul A. Volcker (former chairman of the Board of Governors of the Federal Reserve System) — recommended prohibiting banks from sponsoring and managing "commingled private pools of capital" and limiting "large proprietary trading." This proposal would become part of the largest financial regulatory reform in the United States since the 1933 Glass-Steagall Act separating commercial and investment banking.

On January 21, 2010, President Barack Obama voiced his support for the ban on proprietary trading by banking entities, calling it the "Volcker Rule," and making it a key part of the Wall Street Reform and Consumer Protection Act (commonly known as the Dodd-Frank Act). Signed into law by President Obama on July 21, 2010, Dodd-Frank established new capital requirements for banks and mandated periodic "stress tests" to evaluate their performance during potential economic downturns. The Act created the Financial Stability Oversight Council, and it set up an Orderly Liquidation Authority to place failing non-bank financial firms in government receivership. Systemically important financial institutions were required to provide resolution plans in the event of material financial distress or failure.

Section 619 of Dodd-Frank contained the Volcker Rule, affecting banks with Federal Deposit Insurance Corporation (FDIC) deposit insurance and access to the Federal Reserve's discount window lending facility. These banking entities were prohibited from engaging in short-term proprietary trading of securities, derivatives, commodity futures and options on these instruments. Banks were also

Above: Signing of the Dodd-Frank Act by President Barack Obama, Washington, DC, 2010. From left: Vice President Joe Biden, House Speaker Nancy Pelosi, Senate Majority Leader Harry Reid, Representative Mel Watt, Representative Maxine Waters, Senator Chris Dodd, and Representative Barney Frank.

limited from having equity, partnership or ownership interest in hedge funds or private equity funds.

International efforts to reform financial regulation yielded the Basel III framework in 2010, increasing the required capital for banks, constraining bank leverage and improving their liquidity coverage.

In its final 2014 version, the Volcker Rule allowed banks to trade loans, government bonds, physical commodities and foreign exchange. A banking entity could trade for market making only on behalf of its clients, in the distribution of securities underwriting and for risk-hedging in their asset-liability management.

Implementation of the Volcker Rule across the financial industry required an extensive and ongoing effort of control and compliance. Goldman Sachs liquidated substantially all of its principal strategies and global macro proprietary trading positions in 2010 and 2011. The firm began redeeming interests in hedge funds in March 2012 and established a firmwide Volcker Oversight Committee. Goldman Sachs has been and remains supportive of reforms that improve the oversight, transparency and overall health and stability of the financial system.

Firm helps to rebuild US communities following Hurricane Sandy

When Hurricane Sandy slammed ashore in late October of 2012, storm surges inundated Lower Manhattan, Brooklyn, Queens and Staten Island. With floodwaters in the city's streets and subway tunnels paralyzing Lower Manhattan, Nasdaq and the New York Stock Exchange (NYSE) were forced to close for two days, the first such multiday closing for the NYSE due to weather in more than 120 years. By the storm's end, Sandy would cause roughly $19 billion in damage to homes and businesses in the New York City area.

While much of Lower Manhattan lost power, pockets of functioning utilities dotted the map. Goldman Sachs' headquarters building at 200 West Street, which had opened in 2009, sustained only slight damage.

As the storm receded, Goldman Sachs took on a greater role in rebuilding efforts. The firm committed $5 million in small business loans through its Urban Investment Group and an additional $5 million in grants from *Goldman Sachs Gives*, the firm's donor-advised fund, to aid with long-term housing and small business reconstruction and recovery. Through Goldman Sachs' Community TeamWorks initiative, nearly 1,200 employees — including CEO Lloyd Blankfein — along with their friends and relatives, participated in widespread on-the-ground cleanup efforts.

Top: South entrance of 200 West Street headquarters surrounded by sandbags during Hurricane Sandy, New York City, 2012.

Center: Hurricane Sandy Relief and Recovery Community TeamWorks project, New York City, 2012.

Bottom: Hurricane Sandy Relief and Recovery Community TeamWorks team members with Team Rubicon, New York City, 2012.

Opposite: Lower Manhattan skyline with lights on at 200 West Street office building during Hurricane Sandy, 2012.

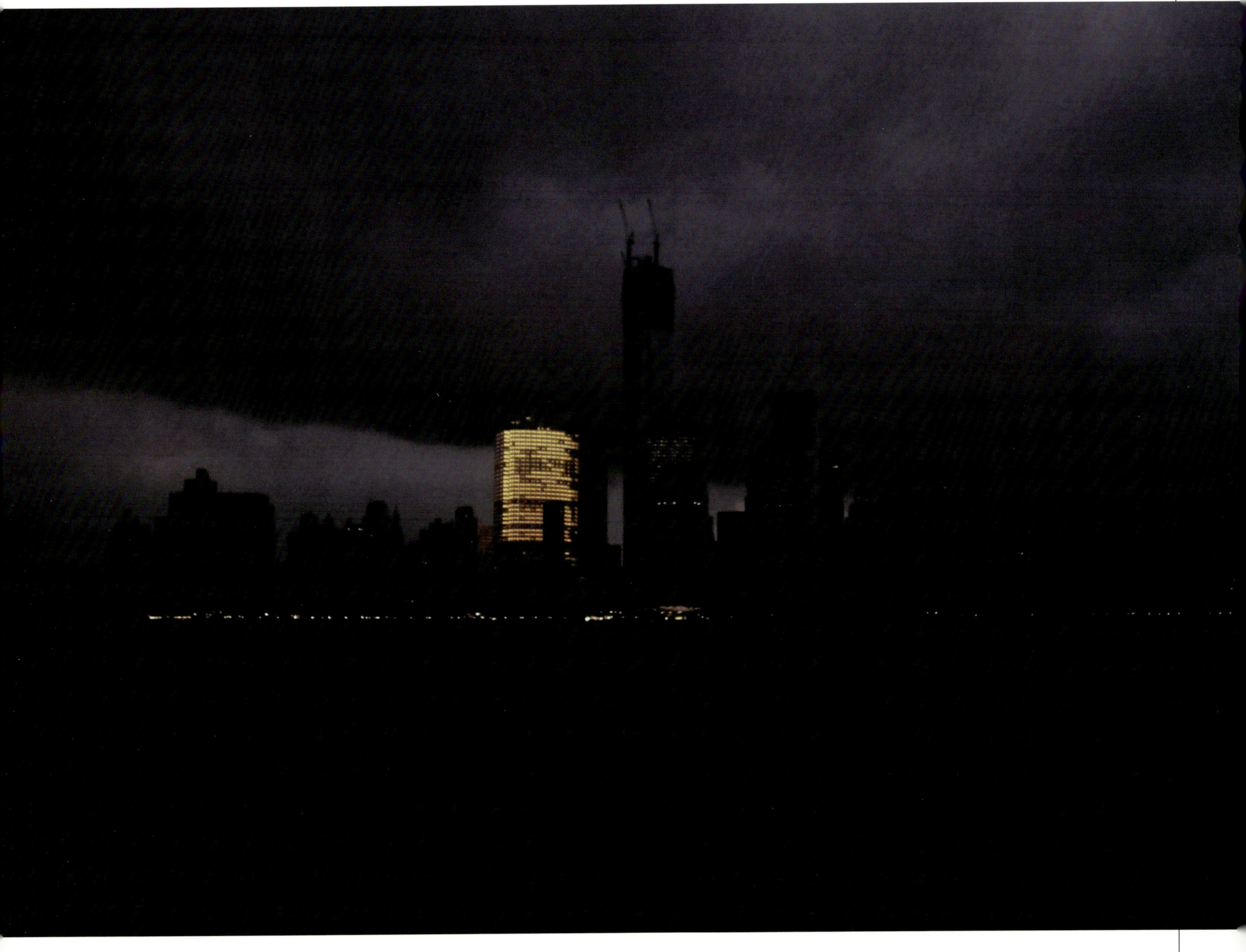

Firm signs amicus brief supporting marriage equality

On February 28, 2013, Goldman Sachs joined other Wall Street firms and corporations, as well as representatives from government, advocacy groups and religious organizations, to show support for marriage equality in Washington, DC. The firm signed an amicus brief that was filed with the US Supreme Court, as the court weighed in on *United States v. Windsor* to determine whether the Defense of Marriage Act (DOMA) was constitutional.

DOMA was a federal law, enacted in 1996, which defined marriage as being exclusively between a man and a woman. The amicus brief was a "friend of the court" legal document that provided information about the benefits for the economy as a result of advancing marriage equality.

The specific case before the US Supreme Court involved Edith Windsor (1929–2017), who was challenging a decision by the Internal Revenue Service forcing her to pay estate taxes following the death of Thea Spyer (1931–2009), her female spouse to whom she was legally married in New York. Under federal law, heterosexual couples would not incur the same tax.

The firm's support of marriage equality aligned with its Business Principles, specifically the importance of building, supporting and leveraging a diverse and inclusive workforce. As the firm's seventh business principle had stated since 2001, "For us to be successful, our men and women must reflect the diversity of the communities and cultures in which we operate. That means we must attract, retain and motivate people from many backgrounds and perspectives. Being diverse is not optional; it is what we must be."

On June 26, 2013, the US Supreme Court ruled Section 3 of DOMA to be unconstitutional in a five-to-four decision, declaring it "a deprivation of the equal liberty of persons that is protected by the Fifth Amendment."

Above: Pride flag at 200 West Street, New York City, 2018.

Exactly two years later, on June 26, 2015, the US Supreme Court ruled in *Obergefell v. Hodges* that all US states recognize same-sex marriages. Goldman Sachs noted the significance of the ruling, stating, "We applaud today's US Supreme Court ruling on marriage equality, which will help families across the country, make it easier for businesses to hire and keep talented people, and promote both economic growth and individual freedom."

In a message to its members and allies that same day, the firm's LGBT Network echoed this sentiment: "Today's decision comes two years to the day after the US Supreme Court struck down the 1996 Defense of Marriage Act. Goldman Sachs has been an outspoken supporter of marriage equality. In 2013, Lloyd Blankfein became the first Fortune 500 CEO to support same-sex marriage publicly. We are pleased to fly the Pride flag outside of 200 West Street today in response to the decision and to highlight our continued focus on supporting the LGBT community."

Dow to Add Goldman, Nike, Visa

Continued from page C1

York aluminum maker Alcoa closed Monday at $8.06, down from $40 as recently as 2007. H-P, the Palo Alto, Calif., computer maker, ended at $22.27, down from $50 in 2010. Bank of America of Charlotte, N.C., finished at $14.61, down from $50 in 2007.

Goldman Sachs shares rose 3.5%, while Visa shares gained 3.4% and Nike added 2.2%. Alcoa's shares slipped 0.3%, while H-P dropped 0.4%. Bank of America rose 0.9%.

"We are pleased to join this historic and significant market benchmark, and remain dedicated to delivering value for our shareholders as a member of the Dow 30," a Goldman Sachs spokesman said.

In a statement, Alcoa said: "The composition of the Dow Jones Industrial Average has no impact on Alcoa's ability to successfully execute our strategy, and we remain focused on delivering shareholder value.

"This decision has no impact on our business or our strategy for providing solid returns to shareholders," Bank of America said in a statement.

A Visa spokesman didn't have an immediate comment. Representatives for H-P and Nike couldn't be reached for comment.

S&P Dow Jones said the moves won't have any effect on the level of the index, which at Tuesday's finish of 1683.99 was up 18% for the year and just 1.5% below its Aug. 2 all-time high.

The Dow is a price-weighted measure, meaning the bigger the stock price, the larger the sway for a component, and vice versa. That is different from stock-market indexes such as the Standard & Poor's 500, which are weighted by components' market capitalizations.

David Blitzer, chairman of the index committee at S&P Dow Jones Indices, said the methodology for calculating the Dow allows for the companies to exit and enter without affecting the measure's level. The value following the moves will be "100% dependent on what the market does and not on these changes," Mr. Blitzer said on a conference call.

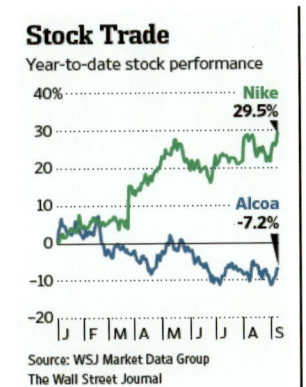

While a big change for the Dow industrials, observers say the impact on the individual stocks should be limited. That is because unlike other well-known indexes, such as the S&P 500 or the Russell 2000, relatively few index-tracking investment products follow the Dow and will need to buy or sell shares based on the changes.

"Despite the popularity of the Dow Jones Industrial Average in the press, it's a lot less significant than an add to the Russell 2000 or an add to the S&P 500, because it's just not an index that institutions benchmark to," said Phil Mackintosh, global head of trading strategy at Credit Suisse Group AG.

The change in the Dow industrials is the biggest since April 2004, when **American International Group** Inc., **Pfizer** Inc. and **Verizon Communications** Inc. replaced **AT&T** Inc., Eastman Kodak Co. and **International Paper** Co. Numerous changes have taken place since. A year ago, insurer **UnitedHealth Group** Inc. replaced **Kraft Foods** Inc., as the global snacks company moved toward a spinoff of its North American grocery business. The committee that determines the blue-chip average's makeup said Kraft's reduced size made it unfit.

—*Andrew R. Johnson contributed to this article.*

Stock Trade
Year-to-date stock performance

Nike 29.5%
Alcoa -7.2%

Source: WSJ Market Data Group
The Wall Street Journal

Online »
Review 25 years of changes in the Dow industrials in an interactive at **WSJ.com/Markets.**

Above: News clipping from The Wall Street Journal, *September 11, 2013.*

Goldman Sachs is added to Dow Jones Industrial Average

In September 2013, Goldman Sachs was added to the Dow Jones Industrial Average (DJIA or "the Dow"), along with Visa and Nike. The DJIA is designed to be a collection of blue-chip companies that represent the core of the US economy. The 2013 move represented part of the Dow's long-term effort to diversify the index in order to better represent the broader economy. According to the Index Committee, "While stock selection is not governed by quantitative rules, a stock typically is added to the Dow only if the company has an excellent reputation, demonstrates sustained growth and is of interest to a large number of investors." Changes in DJIA constituents are relatively infrequent, with the previous three-member exchange occurring in 2004. At the time of the announcement, Goldman Sachs entered as the third-largest company in the index, behind leader IBM and the newly added Visa. The Dow Jones Industrial Average dates to 1896 (the same year Goldman Sachs joined the New York Stock Exchange) and originally comprised 12 stocks.

With Marquee®, clients access data and cutting-edge ideas from Goldman Sachs

In 2014, a new platform called *Marquee* launched. Built leveraging the leading technology of the firm's proprietary SecDB system, the *Marquee* platform used application program interfaces (APIs) to tie in with end users' own systems, enabling clients to access the same pricing data, risk models and proprietary datasets used by Goldman Sachs traders and risk managers. The *Marquee* platform was both broad and deep, with more than 20 years of historical data for select asset classes. In addition to current and historical market data, *Marquee* users could now access research reports from the firm's Global Investment Research Division (GIR), specific trade ideas from traders in the Securities Division, powerful analytics and charting tools, and execution services.

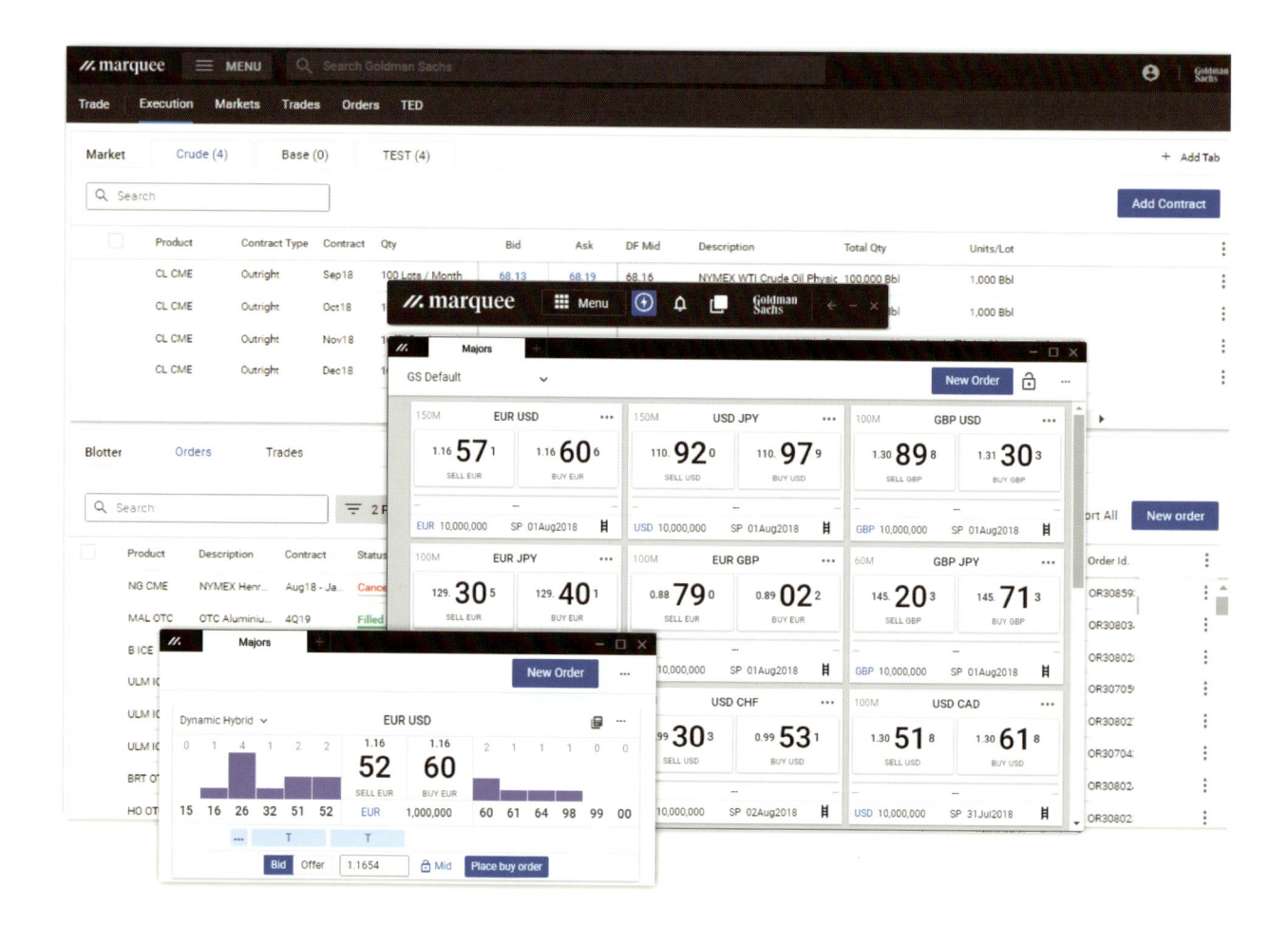

Top: Marquee *logo, 2019.*

Bottom: Image of Marquee *desktop, 2019.*

174

Goldman Sachs manages the concurrent IPOs of Japan Post Holdings, Japan Post Bank and Japan Post Insurance

Japan established its first postal system in 1871. Four years later, it added postal banking services modeled on Great Britain's system, which allowed savers to deposit funds at local post offices. By 2013, Japan Post Holdings' banking subsidiary was the largest retail bank in the country measured by savings and deposits and had diversified into insurance and other financial services, becoming a crucial arm of the Japanese state.

The year 2015 marked the culmination of a plan nearly a decade in the making to privatize the massive, multipronged public institution, with a key aim of stimulating investment by Japanese households, whose high savings rates were constraining the country's economic growth. Japan's Ministry of Finance (MOF), the government institution in charge of budget and public finance matters, engaged Goldman Sachs as a joint global coordinator and joint book runner for the IPO, of which 80% of the shares were reserved for domestic investors. The offering was met with strong demand from the Japanese public, raising nearly $12 billion, and was the largest IPO of 2015.

For Goldman Sachs, the offering was another important milestone in a history of strong partnership with Japan's MOF, particularly in the privatization of state-owned enterprises. The firm had assisted with the MOF's first global equity offering (Japan Tobacco) in 1996 and had served jointly as global co-lead for NTT DoCoMo's IPO in 1998, the largest-scale global IPO in history at the time.

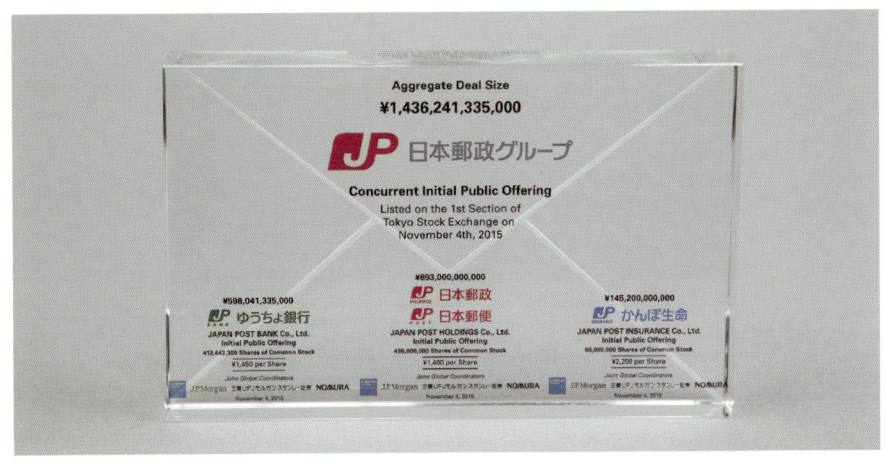

Top: Taizo Nishimuro, president of Japan Post Holdings, at the launching of Japan Post concurrent IPOs, Tokyo, 2015.

Bottom: Japan Post concurrent IPOs deal toy, 2015.

Junior talent's competitive spirit drives grants for nonprofits

Goldman Sachs established the Analyst Impact Fund in 2016. This annual contest provides an opportunity for more-junior employees to compete with their peers to win grants from *Goldman Sachs Gives*, the firm's donor-advised fund, to benefit the nonprofit organization of their choice. The contest is judged by members of the firm's Partnership Committee, part of whose mission is to steward the firm's culture and cultivate its current and future leaders. Since its launch, nearly 2,000 analysts from all divisions and 55 offices globally have participated, benefiting nonprofit organizations in Germany, India, the United States and more. The initiative has grown dramatically and become a featured part of the firm's long-established philanthropic culture. For its 2019 edition, 975 analysts representing all Goldman Sachs divisions submitted 369 applications, nearly three times the number of submissions in the inaugural year of the program.

Top: Analyst Impact Fund winners, New York City, 2018. From left: Hamza Farrukh, Pascale Barget, Gloria Setordjie and Jude Fernando.

Bottom: Partnership Committee co-chairs Pablo Salame (far left) and Edith Cooper (second from right), and Lloyd Blankfein with Analyst Impact Fund finalists, New York City, 2016. From left, front row: Ashley Macaulay Wolff, Kevin Chang, Anthony Alvarez, Allison Kandel, Caitlin Murphy, Rachel Serwetz and Chelsea Shupe. Second row: Peter Heye, Sam Obletz, Olivia Benjamin, Paul Antonios, Mainak Ghosh, Andre Dixon and Brent Jackson.

Firm advises and helps fund Amazon's $13.7 billion acquisition of Whole Foods

On June 16, 2017, Amazon.com, Inc. stunned the world with a proposed $13.7 billion acquisition of Whole Foods Market, Inc. Goldman Sachs advised Amazon on the transaction, and while the deal came together quickly, the groundwork to secure the assignment was long in the making.

Goldman Sachs had been expanding its presence in major North American cities, deploying more-senior coverage bankers in Seattle, Atlanta, Dallas, Toronto and others, as each became a hub of greater corporate activity. In Seattle, Goldman Sachs worked to deepen its connection with not only large corporations, such as Amazon, Microsoft and Starbucks, but also with the region's flourishing startup ecosystem and to leverage the firm's network across multiple business lines, including investment banking and private wealth management. The strategy paid dividends when Amazon selected the firm as sole advisor and lead financier for its acquisition of Whole Foods in what would be Amazon's first such deal, valued at more than $1.2 billion.

Amazon's initial offer to buy Whole Foods for $41 per share represented a premium over its then-current price of $35 and valued the company at $13.1 billion. A counteroffer of $45 per share from Whole Foods was rejected, as Amazon appeared to cool to the prospects of acquiring the retailer. Goldman Sachs, representing Amazon, presented a firm and final $42 per share offer, which ultimately was approved, valuing Whole Foods at $13.7 billion. In addition to serving as advisor on the acquisition, Goldman Sachs provided bridge financing for the acquisition and acted as book runner for Amazon's $16 billion bond offering to finance the acquisition.

Top: Store sign announcing Amazon acquisition of Whole Foods, San Ramon, California, 2017.

Bottom: Amazon acquisition of Whole Foods deal toy, 2017.

The Power of Convening

The first step in making progress on any issue is bringing key stakeholders to the table. By combining the power of the firm's deep relationships with policymakers, business leaders and innovators around the globe with cutting-edge thought leadership, Goldman Sachs has endeavored to be a catalyst for productive dialogue on important economic and social issues shaping the world.

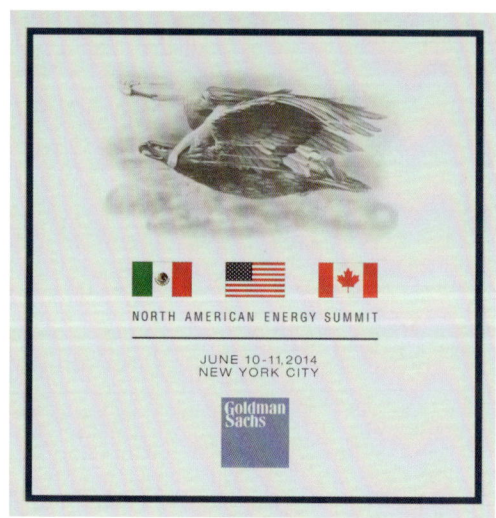

CHINA-U.S. CEO BILATERAL INVESTMENT DIALOGUE
中美CEO双边投资对话
July 2, 2014 | 2014年7月2日
Goldman Sachs 高盛
THE PAULSON INSTITUTE
CDRF 中国发展研究基金会
USCBC THE US-CHINA BUSI

Fireside Chat with Gunjan Samtani
WOMEN EMERGING IN FINANCE

VOWS
Veterans on Wall Street

PERSPEKTYWY
WOMEN IN TECH SUMMIT

NEW YORK
MELBOURNE
TOKYO
HONG KONG
LONDON
GSAM SYMPOSIUM

IBD • FINANCING GROUP
Shared Vision
Global Reach
2004 GLOBAL CONFERENCE
Leadership Roundtable

HBCU
Leadership
Summit

150
THE LONG VIEW

The world in which Goldman Sachs operates today could not look more different than when Marcus Goldman started his modest commercial paper trade a century and a half ago. Over that time, globalization and technological change have transformed the capital markets to an extent that would have been unimaginable in the firm's early days. Yet, while on the surface today's Goldman Sachs looks nothing like the small family-run business it was in the latter half of the nineteenth century, the culture of that small business remains intact: a commitment to excellence in all endeavors; a focus on service to clients and communities; innovation in approaching problems; and values such as teamwork and integrity.

Being grounded in these core principles has allowed Goldman Sachs to confidently and boldly look to the future throughout its 150-year history. The firm has learned that navigating constant change requires focus, creativity, nimbleness and a willingness to take risk. By continuously seeking new and better ways to solve problems, the firm has repeatedly pioneered change in the financial services industry. From social impact and green bonds to the Apple Card, Goldman Sachs' ability to identify and seize new opportunities on behalf of clients around the globe has taken many forms and will continue to evolve with the markets within which it operates.

Following Lloyd Blankfein's retirement from the firm in late 2018, David Solomon was appointed chairman and CEO of Goldman Sachs, marking the early years of his tenure with a focus on expanding the firm's product offering, harnessing the power of technology in all its businesses and ensuring a diverse and inclusive workforce. Underpinning these distinct goals is the central commitment to clients that has endured since 1869 and will help guide Goldman Sachs into its next 150 years — and beyond.

Opposite: Summer interns, Salt Lake City, 2019.

Firm launches Marcus by Goldman Sachs®, a startup with 150 years of experience

In 2016, Goldman Sachs introduced its consumer business, *Marcus by Goldman Sachs* to offer products and services designed to address consumer pain points regarding finance. Named after the firm's founder, the *Marcus* platform combines the freshness of a digital offering with the strength and heritage of the firm, leveraging core competencies in risk management and technology.

As one of the few large banks without a legacy consumer business or infrastructure, Goldman Sachs was uniquely positioned to redefine how financial services are distributed and consumed.

The *Marcus* platform, user experience and products were based on extensive research and direct feedback from consumers regarding their frustrations with consumer finance — confusing jargon, inflexible products and hidden fees. Over time, the *Marcus* teams heard from more than 100,000 consumers, incorporating their insights into building *Marcus* products that are simple and transparent.

The firm made the decision to enter the consumer finance sector in 2015. In April 2016, Goldman Sachs Bank USA (GS Bank USA) acquired GE Capital Bank's US online deposit platform — a transaction that doubled the firm's client count. This enabled the firm to provide an online bank for retail customers, offering savings products. Later that year, the firm launched the *Marcus* platform, initially offering no-fee unsecured personal loans.

By the end of 2017, *Marcus*' online lending platform originated $2 billion in loans, and the firm integrated GS Bank USA's online deposit platform under the *Marcus* brand.

In April 2018, GS Bank USA acquired Clarity Money, Inc., a personal finance management app offering actionable insights, and welcomed the more than one million Clarity Money® customers to the *Marcus* family. Later that year, Goldman Sachs launched a *Marcus* online savings platform in the United Kingdom, expanding its consumer footprint internationally.

Most recently, in August 2019, Apple Card launched in the United States, the result of an innovative collaboration between the *Marcus* team and Apple, offering the first credit card product issued by Goldman Sachs in its 150-year history.

Since launch, *Marcus* has grown into a multiproduct platform, with $50 billion in deposits, $5 billion in consumer loan balances and four million customers in the United States and the United Kingdom — all without the traditional brick-and-mortar branch model.

With the *Marcus* platform, the firm is focused on developing an enduring consumer franchise and helping millions of consumers take control of their financial lives. As Goldman Sachs Chairman and CEO David Solomon explained, "We have the ambition to build a large, differentiated, highly profitable digital consumer platform."

Above: Marcus by Goldman Sachs logo, 2016.

Above: Marcus by Goldman Sachs *team, London, 2019.*

David Solomon is appointed chairman and CEO

In mid-2018, Goldman Sachs announced that as of September 30 that year, Lloyd Blankfein would step down as chairman and CEO of Goldman Sachs after 12 years of service in those roles. David Solomon, then president and chief operating officer, would succeed Lloyd, becoming CEO in October 2018 and chairman in January 2019.

Born in 1962 in Hartsdale, New York, David grew up in the northern suburbs of New York City and then attended Hamilton College, where he earned a BA in political science. After college, David embarked on a career in financial services that would include senior roles at Irving Trust Company, Drexel Burnham and Bear Stearns. He joined Goldman Sachs from Bear Stearns in 1999 as a partner and co-head of Goldman Sachs' High Yield and Leveraged Loan Business within the Investment Banking Division.

Over the years, David also served as global head of the firm's Financing Group, which handles all capital markets and derivative products for the firm's corporate clients. He was appointed to the Management Committee in 2004 and, in 2006, was named co-head of the Investment Banking Division (IBD), a role he held for ten years. David became Goldman Sachs' president and co-chief operating officer in January of 2017 and sole COO in March 2018, before ultimately stepping into the CEO position in October of 2018 and that of chairman in January 2019.

A dynamic leader who embodies the firm's culture, David brought extensive experience managing client relationships to his new leadership role, plus a distinct combination of strategic insight, deep business knowledge and an ability to engage effectively with both internal and external stakeholders. He has encouraged the people of Goldman Sachs to embrace a new way of thinking and working that reflects both the firm's changing workforce and promising new technologies Goldman Sachs can harness to better serve its clients.

Above: David Solomon during Global Partners Meeting, New York City, 2019.

Opposite, top: David Solomon and Lloyd Blankfein at the Quarterly Managing Directors meeting where Solomon was announced as the firm's next CEO and chairman, New York City, July 2018.

Opposite, bottom: David Solomon moderates a Talks at GS *session with Tyra Banks during a* 10,000 Small Businesses *event at the Iowa State Fair, Des Moines, 2019.*

Talented teams make up the heart of a global enterprise

Behind the headlines of marquee transactions on behalf of its clients, Goldman Sachs relies on an extraordinary array of resources and expertise in a wide variety of essential roles.

With state-of-the-art offices in 34 countries and 73 cities, Goldman Sachs operations require a sophisticated, integrated network of services led by skilled professionals from a range of disciplines.

The complexity of the highly regulated financial services industry demands broad and deep expertise in areas such as operations, risk, compliance, legal, internal audit and various fields within finance. These provide the fiscal and risk management essential to ensuring safety and soundness and optimal performance on behalf of the firm's shareholders.

As a leader in the industry, the firm relies on technology innovators who bring advanced engineering capabilities more commonly associated with a fast-moving startup. These engineers have significantly improved the way Goldman Sachs does business and the way it interfaces with clients.

Deeply committed to the care of its people, the firm has built an enterprise-wide network of world-class services — from wellness to learning opportunities to comprehensive benefits — that make it an employer of choice around the globe.

Behind everything that is accomplished at Goldman Sachs are the executive assistants, a team of professionals who, over the years, have "made things happen," without fanfare and with unfailing dedication.

Over time, the depth of talent of the people in these roles has grown exponentially. The range of skill sets that are an enduring strength of the firm vary widely — professionals at every level whose abilities and perspectives are as distinct as the nearly 40,000 individuals themselves. Yet, they are united by a deeply rooted culture of teamwork, integrity and commitment to client service. Their efforts remain indispensable to the reputation and success of Goldman Sachs.

One Goldman Sachs seeks to coordinate holistic client solutions

In the first days of his tenure as CEO, David Solomon, along with Goldman Sachs President and Chief Operating Officer John Waldron and Chief Financial Officer Stephen Scherr, set to work on an initiative called *One Goldman Sachs*. Recognizing that the firm and its clients continue to evolve into many-layered, often globally diversified businesses, this leadership team launched an effort to take a more comprehensive view of the client relationship. With participation and input from business leaders across the firm, *One Goldman Sachs* was created to bring the full resources of the firm to bear on clients' multifaceted needs and, importantly, to make it seamless and easy for clients to access the breadth of services the firm can provide.

As corporations have become more complex, so too have their risks, challenges and opportunities. Technology is breaking down barriers but also posing new challenges to be managed. Macroeconomic and geopolitical forces are impacting businesses small and large, often in unpredictable ways. The thinking behind *One Goldman Sachs* is to coordinate the comprehensive resources of the firm to address all of the components of a client's "big picture" needs, cutting across divisional and geographic lines to present integrated advice, thinking and solutions.

Louisa, the digital ecosystem connecting the firm's people to deliver *One Goldman Sachs*, leverages several firm-developed systems to communicate with clients, connect them with expertise across the firm and help them execute on commercial opportunities. The ecosystem was named after Louisa Goldman Sachs, the daughter of Marcus Goldman and wife of Samuel Sachs.

One Goldman Sachs, which is being piloted in 2019 with approximately 30 clients, ranging from insurance companies to large-scale family offices and institutional investors, is a testament to Goldman Sachs' unwavering commitment to evolving the way it does business to best meet the changing needs of its diverse, dynamic global client base.

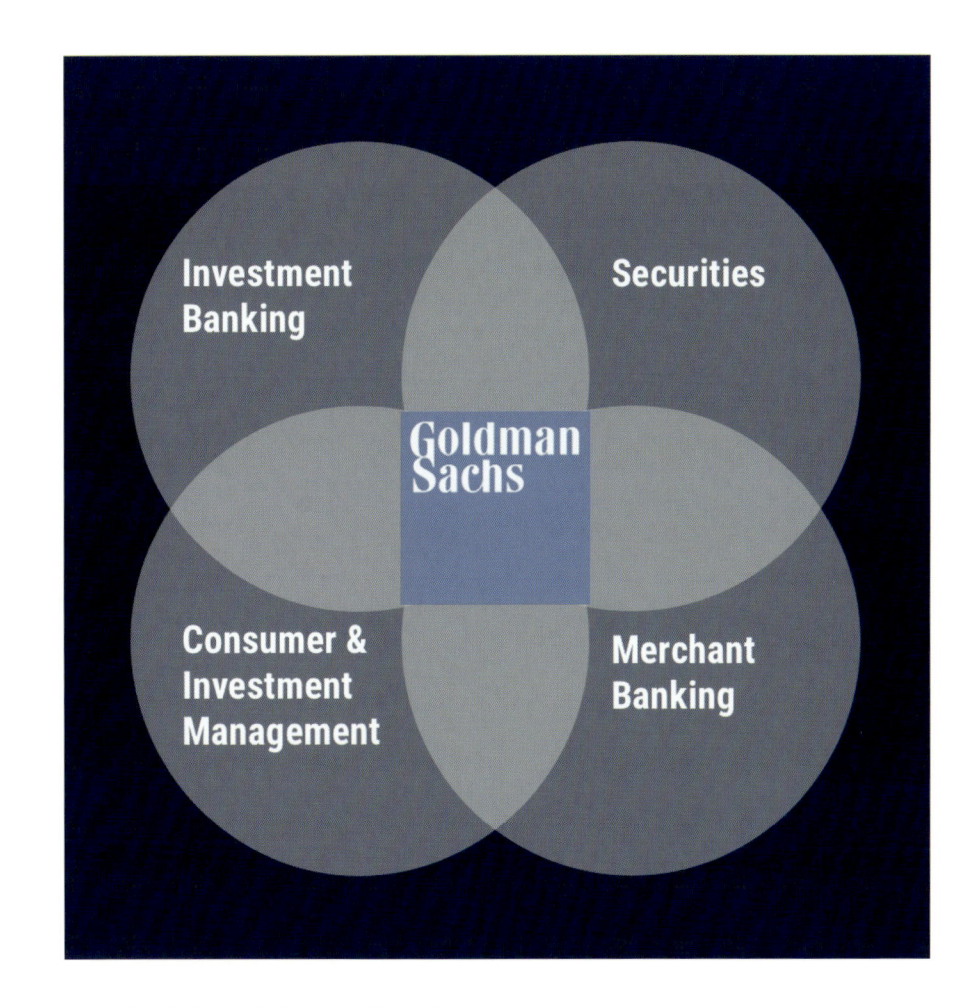

Above: One Goldman Sachs *schematic, 2019.*

GS Accelerate taps the firm's entrepreneurial spirit to drive innovation from within

According to Goldman Sachs' first Business Principle, its people are one of the firm's greatest assets. Throughout its history, many of the firm's most impactful business innovations have come from within — born of the ideas of the people of Goldman Sachs. To tap the full creative potential of its global talent base, in 2018 Goldman Sachs announced the launch of *GS Accelerate*, an initiative to foster innovation and provide investment in ideas that can help the firm grow and deliver best-in-class solutions for its clients.

In its first year, *GS Accelerate* received nearly 1,000 submissions from the firm's people globally. Of these, it selected eight for continued investment. Chosen teams participate in an "entrepreneurial bootcamp" to learn skills including how to build and articulate a detailed business case and budget, seek support and sponsorship from firm leaders and ultimately, execute on their ideas.

In 2019, the program is focused on driving innovation across three key areas: client experience and engagement, strategic business growth and investment in efficiency. Each year, *GS Accelerate* will open up its submission process anew, kindling the spirit of entrepreneurship that dates back to the days of Marcus Goldman and harnessing it in the service of continued growth, innovation and client-centered solutions.

Right: GS Accelerate *entrepreneurs collaborating in their incubator space, New York City, 2019.*

Below: Dane Holmes, Stephanie Cohen and Tanya Baker host GS Accelerate *kick-off, New York City, 2019.*

Launch With GS™ commits $500 million to narrow investing gaps

In 2018, Goldman Sachs announced Launch With GS™, a $500 million commitment to invest in women-led companies and women investment managers. Within the first year, the firm deployed more than $100 million toward this goal, and expanded *Launch With GS* to include businesses founded and led by Black, Latinx and other entrepreneurs who have been historically underserved by the funding ecosystem.

Launch With GS is an investment strategy grounded in the view that diverse management teams make better decisions, outperform peers and drive strong returns. Through *Launch With GS*, Goldman Sachs aims to narrow investing gaps via three mutually enforcing activities: investing the firm's balance sheet capital in companies with diverse and gender-balanced leadership; partnering with clients to invest in emerging investment managers; and creating an ecosystem to support and expand the pipeline of entrepreneurs and investors.

Goldman Sachs has long believed that the global economy is propelled by innovation, creativity and the sharing of diverse perspectives. This belief fueled the creation of *10,000 Women* in 2008 and *10,000 Small Businesses* in 2009, both of which have experienced enormous success. *Launch With GS* builds on Goldman Sachs' thesis that fostering inclusivity makes sound economic sense and extends it to the firm's core investing businesses.

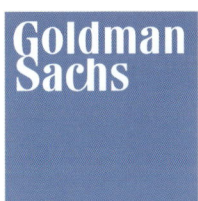

Top: Launch With GS *forum, London, 2019.*

Bottom: Launch With GS *visual identity, 2018.*

Goldman Sachs partners with Apple on a game-changing credit card

In August 2019, Apple and Goldman Sachs launched a groundbreaking new credit card. Designed to help consumers lead a healthier financial life, Apple Card aims to revolutionize the credit card experience.

With features including no fees, daily cash back and seamless integration into Apple's mobile devices, Apple Card introduces a new level of privacy, security and transparency to credit cards, allowing consumers to quickly and easily analyze their spending patterns and calculate how much they could save in interest charges by paying off different portions of their balances.

Goldman Sachs is the issuer of the card and is responsible for underwriting, customer service, the underlying platform and all matters related to regulatory compliance through Goldman Sachs Bank USA.

"Simplicity, transparency and privacy are at the core of our consumer product development philosophy," said Chairman and CEO David Solomon. "We're thrilled to partner with Apple on Apple Card, which helps customers take control of their financial lives."

This partnership marks another significant step in growing the firm's consumer franchise and realizing the broader vision of *Marcus by Goldman Sachs* to create a leading digital consumer platform, with partnerships as a core pillar of its strategy.

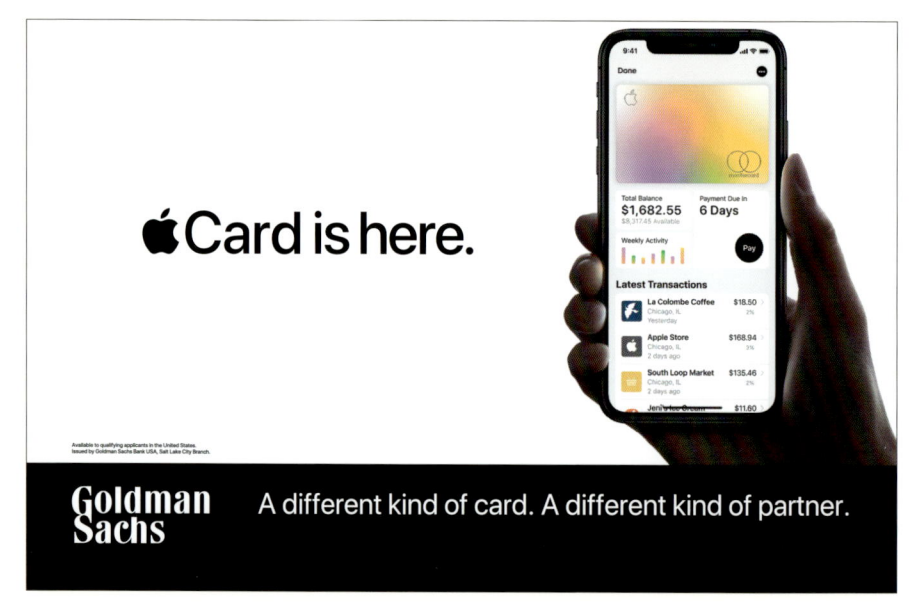

Top: Eric Lane and Harit Talwar announcing the launch of Apple Card at a daily meeting, New York City, 2019.

Bottom: Apple Card promotional material, 2019.

Above: Ronald Lee with Ann Colgin, founder of Colgin Cellars, and Andrew Wu, president of Greater China, LVMH Group, Builders & Innovators, Ningbo, China, 2019.

Below: Todd Leland at Builders & Innovators, Ningbo, China, 2019.

Builders & Innovators expands to Asia

Goldman Sachs demonstrated its commitment to supporting entrepreneurs and helping them expand and grow their businesses when it held its inaugural Builders + Innovators (*B+I*) Summit in Newport Beach, California, in 2012. In 2019, the firm brought *B+I* to Ningbo, China, for the first Builders + Innovators Asia Summit, convening emerging and seasoned entrepreneurs from a diverse set of industries for a two-day exchange of ideas in a former trade hub on China's Silk Road.

ESG and impact investing leverage capital with purpose

Goldman Sachs has a long history of deploying its expertise and position in the capital markets to help address issues that impact society and the environment. The firm released its Environmental Policy Framework in 2005, becoming one of the first global financial institutions to underscore the urgency to address climate change. Since then, Goldman Sachs has harnessed its core capabilities to drive progress, as reflected in its broad-based environmental, social and governance (ESG) and impact investing initiatives.

The firm has mobilized over $100 billion in clean energy financing and investments, with a target to deploy $150 billion by 2025, and invests in entrepreneurs through its *10,000 Women*, *Launch With GS* and *10,000 Small Businesses* programs. Through its Urban Investment Group (UIG), Goldman Sachs commits capital to underserved American communities. The firm has underwritten over $45 billion in green, social and sustainability bonds, including leading some of the most innovative transactions. Goldman Sachs' sustainability efforts extend to the management of the firm itself, driving efficiency efforts in its operations around the world, including being carbon neutral since 2015.

In recent years, sustainable growth — notably inclusive growth and climate transition — has emerged as a growing focus for investors, shareholders and the world at large. For Goldman Sachs, fostering more-inclusive economic growth and addressing climate change represent both commercial opportunities and competitive necessities. In response, in 2019 the firm formed the Sustainable Finance Group (SFG), which partners with the firm's businesses to drive innovation and capture sustainability opportunities using a holistic, integrated approach. The group is embedded in all areas of the firm, providing clients with the most comprehensive sustainability expertise across financing, advisory, risk management and asset management.

Goldman Sachs has been recognized repeatedly for its long-standing commitment to sustainable finance. In 2019, the firm was named Best Bank for Sustainable Finance in North America by *Euromoney*, for bringing innovation to social and environmental finance.

Goldman Sachs Asset Management also received an A+ score on its overall ESG strategy for the fourth consecutive year in 2019 from the United Nations-supported Principles for Responsible Investment (PRI) annual assessment, earning an A or A+ score across all categories.

Above: "What Is a Social Impact Bond?" infographic, 2012.

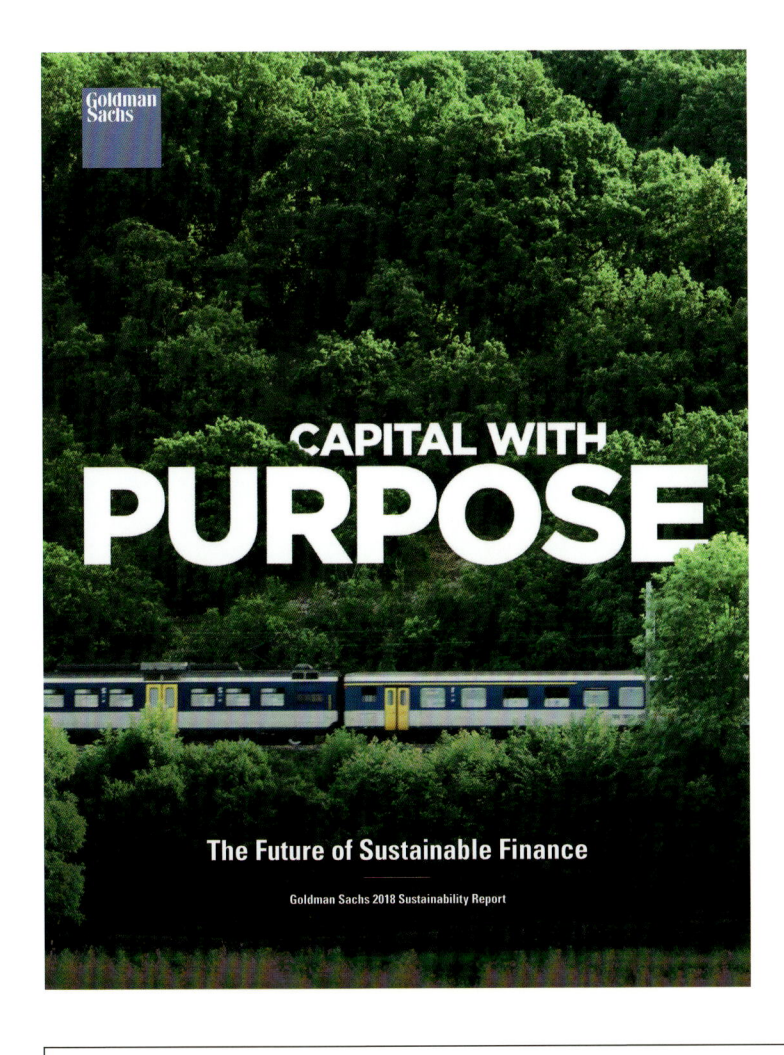

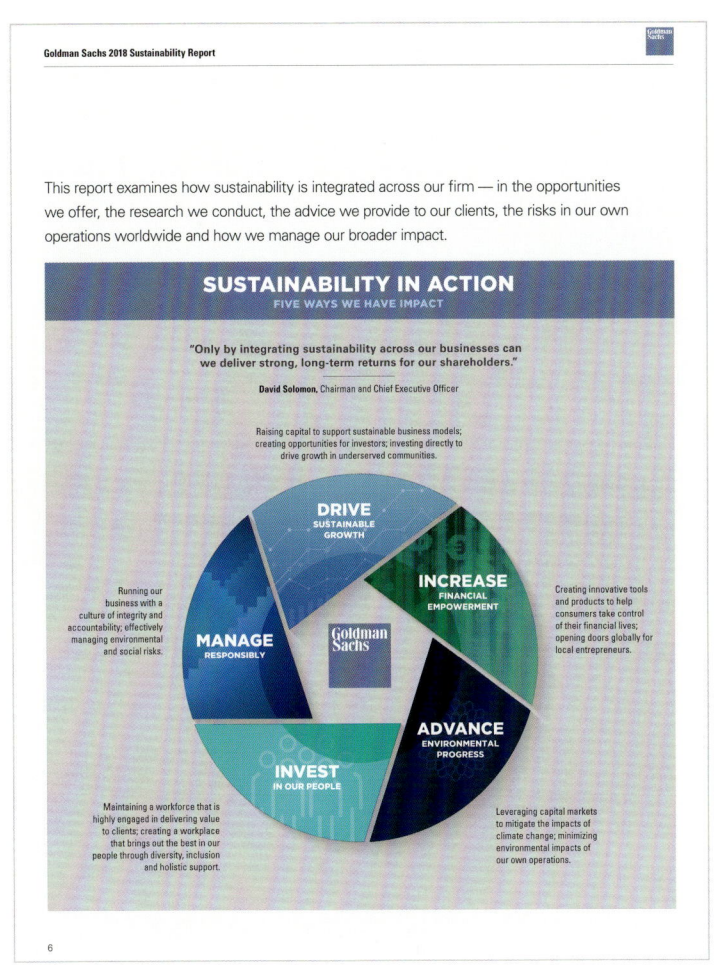

Left: Page from Goldman Sachs Sustainability Report, *2018*.

Far left: Cover of Goldman Sachs Sustainability Report, *2018*.

Firm accelerates progress toward sustainability goals

Sustainability is a growing driver of how Goldman Sachs engages with clients and the industry more broadly and how the firm conducts its business. From raising capital to support sustainable business models to creating tools to help individuals take control of their financial lives to effectively managing the environmental and social risks of its own operations, Goldman Sachs' commitment to sustainability is closely integrated across the firm's activities. Reflective of this continued focus has been the sustained growth in environmental, social and governance (ESG) and impact assets under supervision — from $550 million in 2015 to $35 billion in 2019 — in the firm's Consumer and Investment Management Division (CIMD).

In 2018, Goldman Sachs reached several milestones toward some of its near-term sustainability targets. Since 2005, when the firm adopted and launched its Environmental Policy Framework, Goldman Sachs has made more than $4.5 billion in green investments to reduce its own impact on the environment. The firm achieved carbon neutrality (zero net carbon emissions) across its global operations and business travel in 2015 and intends to use 100% renewable power for its global electricity needs by 2020.

Goldman Sachs deepens and expands initiatives to foster greater diversity and inclusion

Goldman Sachs is committed to building and supporting a diverse and inclusive workforce that is reflective of the countries and cultures in which the firm operates. As the seventh Business Principle states, "Being diverse is not optional; it is what we must be."

To strengthen its global team, reinforce its core values and best serve its clients, the firm continues to seek innovative ways to implement recruitment and retention practices that help close gaps in its workforce across race, gender, sexual orientation, socioeconomic status, disability status, military service and other dimensions. Among the targets the firm has set is to have 50% of its global talent represented by women, as announced in an email to all employees from Lloyd Blankfein and David Solomon in March 2018. In 2019, these hiring goals were expanded to include all analysts and entry-level associates, a combined group that represents more than 70% of the firm's annual hiring. Within this group, the firm also aspires to increase the representation of black professionals to 11% and Hispanic/Latinx professionals to 14% in the Americas and that of black professionals in the United Kingdom to 9%.

Specific initiatives geared to attracting and retaining the broadest possible range of qualified candidates include leveraging technology, engaging new media to identify talent and creating pipeline programs designed to attract people who might never otherwise look to pursue a career in financial services. Goldman Sachs is also working to establish a common language, skill set and system of accountability around inclusiveness, including classroom curricula aimed at increasing awareness and addressing inclusion with a focus on race and ethnicity. In addition, the firm has developed more than 80 diversity-based affinity networks and interest forums globally to provide opportunities for its people to share their distinct experiences, offer feedback to the firm and deepen professional relationships across business units and divisions. As of 2018, more than half of the firm's employees had opted in to one or more of these affinity networks globally, and more than 300 of its senior managers held network leadership roles.

Goldman Sachs recognizes that, for its teams to excel, all members must feel that they are operating in an inclusive environment that welcomes and supports differences and encourages input from all perspectives. Appreciating that it can best serve its clients and shareholders by tapping the rich insights, talents and judgments of a diverse workforce, the firm continues to approach diversity and inclusion as a business imperative.

Top: Senior leaders address the Firmwide Black Network Townhall, New York City, 2019. From left: Asahi Pompey, Lisa Opoku, Laurence Stein, Erika Irish Brown, Brian Fortson, Dane Holmes and Earl Hunt.

Bottom: Goldman Sachs Global Affinity Networks fair, Bengaluru, 2018.

Firm broadens engagement through social media

One of the keys to the enduring success of Goldman Sachs is its ability to adapt to an evolving marketplace while remaining true to its principles. This is particularly evident in the firm's breadth of engagement on social media and innovative use of emerging digital platforms. Leveraging the power of multiple social channels, Goldman Sachs shares timely, thought-provoking content with its ever-growing audience of stakeholders.

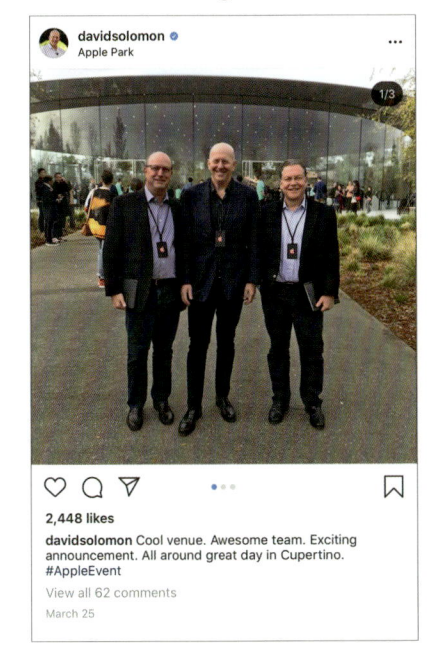

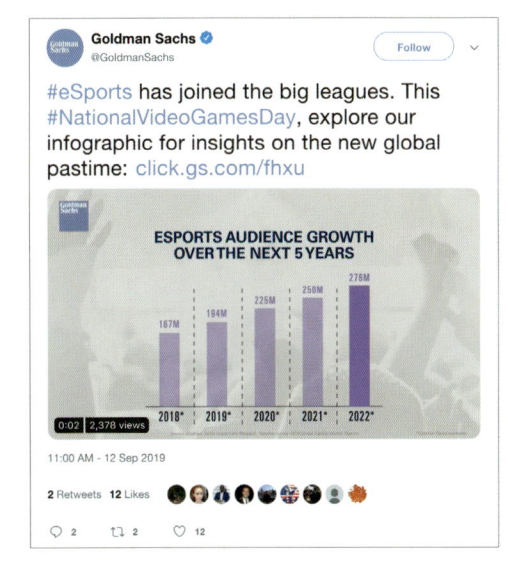

New Bengaluru campus becomes firm's third-largest office

On May 30, 2019, Goldman Sachs inaugurated its newest campus at 150 Outer Ring Road in Bengaluru, India. The address commemorates both the firm's 150th anniversary as well as the Bengaluru office's 15 years of operation.

Reflecting Goldman Sachs' commitment to sustainability, the campus of three interconnected ten-story wings uses energy from clean sources, such as solar and wind; harvests and stores rainwater; and reuses 100% of wastewater for landscaping, cooling and plumbing. Designed by Pei Cobb Freed & Partners, the architects who designed the firm's global headquarters at 200 West Street in Lower Manhattan, the new office can house more than 8,600 individuals and features two and a half acres of landscaped outdoor parks.

Bengaluru is often referred to as the "Silicon Valley of India." Its proximity to leading universities means it offers access to a large pool of entrepreneurial talent. Goldman Sachs' presence in the city dates to 2004, and since then, the office has grown significantly, making it the third-largest by head count.

Above: Laurence Stein and N. R. Narayana Murthy, co-founder of Infosys, at the ribbon-cutting ceremony for the opening of 150 Outer Ring Road, Bengaluru, 2019.

Right: 150 Outer Ring Road, Bengaluru, 2019.

Plumtree Court combines design, functionality and sustainability in new European headquarters

In 2019, Goldman Sachs completed construction of Plumtree Court, its new European headquarters, bringing its people from three London buildings together under one roof. Located just a few minutes' walk from the firm's existing London campus and designed by the firm Kohn Pederson Fox, Plumtree Court is a 1.1-million-gross-square-foot building designed to foster productivity, connectivity and employee well-being. The building includes a 350-seat auditorium for conferences and special events and an expansive client center on the top floor, featuring 29 conference rooms.

Plumtree Court is designed to meet the BREEAM Excellent rating for its environmental performance. In its construction, Goldman Sachs prioritized the hiring of local small businesses in the supply chain and encouraged the involvement of apprentices. Plumtree Court's green roof contributes to its sustainable operation while also offering stunning panoramic views of the city. The building also features a dedicated facility for those who cycle to work, with 455 bicycle parking spaces. The building was completed and opened for occupancy in July 2019.

Above: Coffee bar at Plumtree Court, London, 2019.

Left: Plumtree Court, London, 2019.

Thought Leadership

For generations, Goldman Sachs has served as a trusted advisor to clients on a broad range of business challenges and opportunities. For most of the firm's history, that counsel was provided to clients and related audiences. Today, Goldman Sachs is a leading public voice, commenting on the key issues and emerging opportunities in markets worldwide. The formats have changed dramatically, with a broad spectrum of media now utilized to share the insights of its people. But whether shared through podcasts, video interviews or white papers, their value is the same as it has ever been — providing unique, valuable perspectives on markets, business and the global economy.

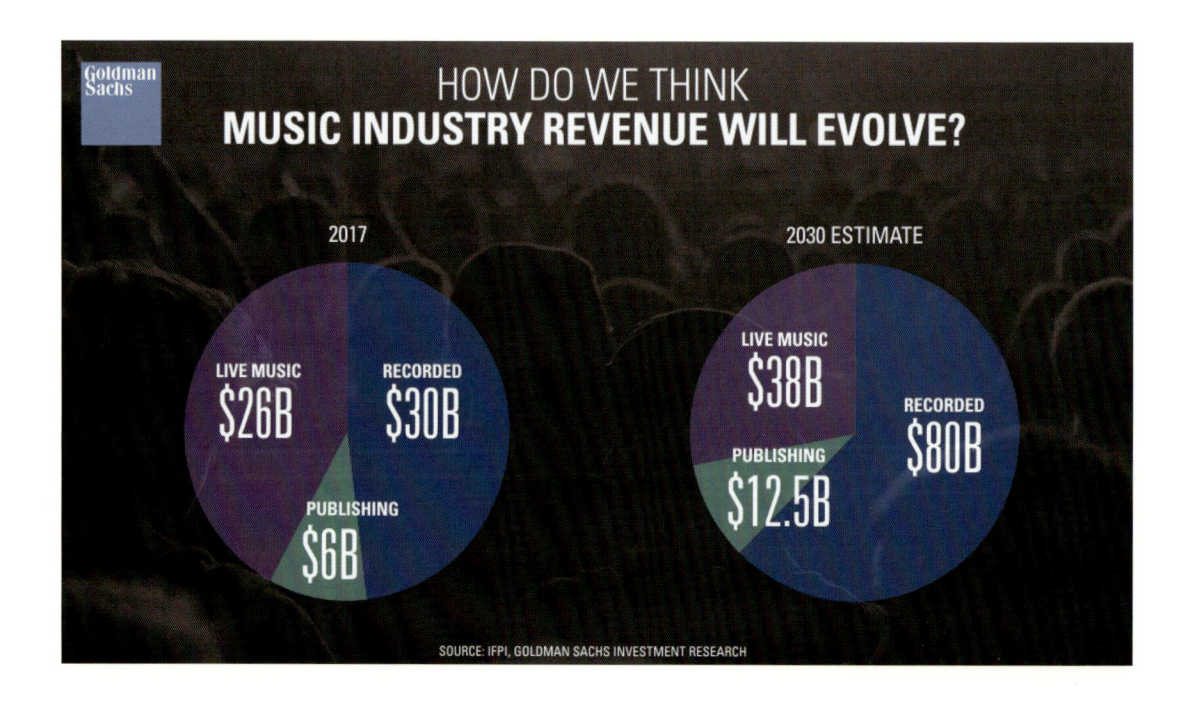

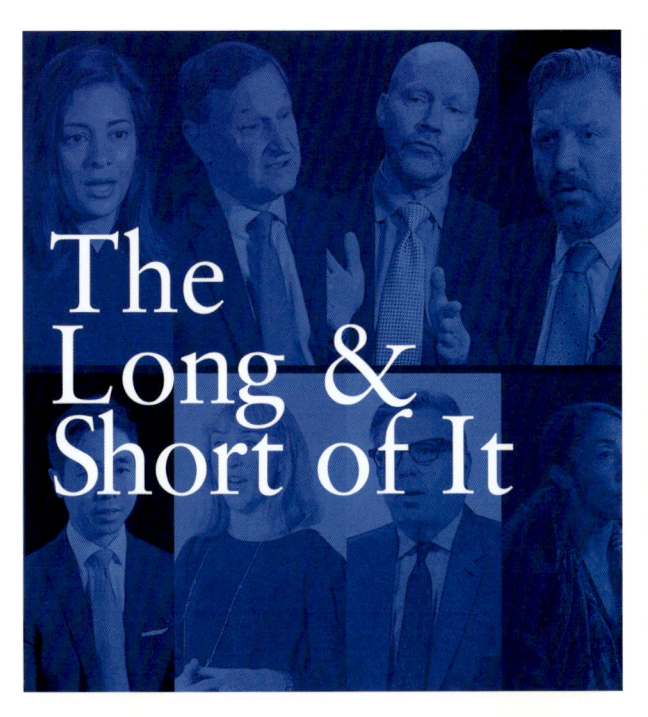

The Long & Short of It

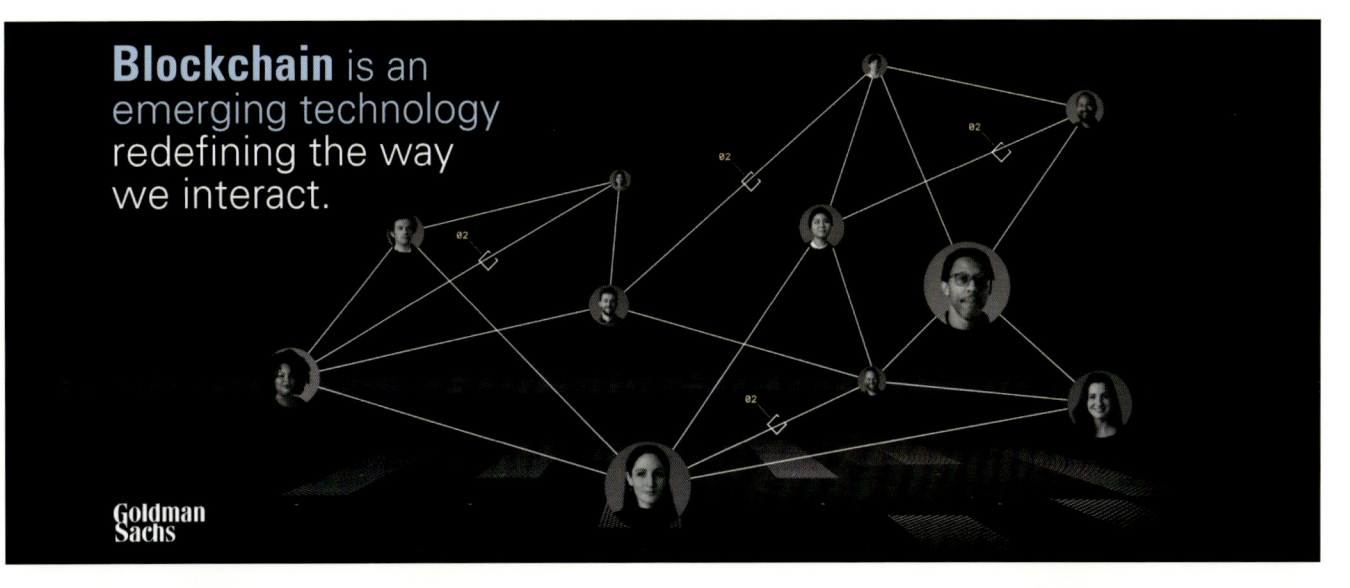

Blockchain is an emerging technology redefining the way we interact.

Goldman Sachs

CATCH-UP *WITH DAVID*

TOP *of* MIND

A Shared Lexicon

The unique culture of Goldman Sachs is manifested, in part, in words and phrases familiar to its people globally. These maxims inform how the firm's people interact with clients and with one another; they emanate from a collective sense of mission and a shared set of values that guide both the day-to-day judgments and efforts of its people and the long-term vision of the firm.

The client always comes first. Experience has shown us that if we serve our clients well, our own success will follow.

Clients are simply in your custody. Someone before you established the relationship and someone after you will carry it on.

Hubris, ego, arrogance, a sense of self-importance: if you allow them to develop, that's when you fall off the track.

Money can be made back easily, but losses of confidence, trust and valued staff are infinitely more difficult to recoup.

Client trust must be earned over many years.

The firm demands you be a contributor. No one can survive as just an employee.

Relationships stand on confidence and trust.

It's we. Not I.

Our assets are our people, capital and reputation. If any of these is ever diminished, the last is the most difficult to restore.

We work with those who lead and those who have the ingredients to lead.

The firm is not bigger than the markets.

As long as there are risks, there will be losses. If the day ever comes when there are no risks, there will also be no profits.

Focus on the future.

Look at the horizon, not just at this moment in time.

Have an uncompromising determination to achieve excellence in everything you do.

We would, if it came to a choice, rather be best than biggest.

Never before have so many people had a share in their future.

The people of Goldman Sachs are Goldman Sachs.

Trees do not grow to the sky.

In addition to brains, we seek humor, motivation, a sort of restrained audacity, confidence and maturity.

Underpromise and overdeliver.

Realize that the world of finance will not stand still and that complacency can lead to extinction.

A Brief History by the Numbers

ANNIVERSARY	25th	50th	75th	100th
Year	**1894**	**1919**	**1944**	**1969**
Partners	5	7	11	38
Headquarters Address	9 Pine Street	60 Wall Street	30 Pine Street	55 Broad Street
Capital	$640 thousand	$8.17 million	$8.9 million	$45 million
Capital (2019 dollars)	$19.3 million	$119 million	$127 million	$308 million
Employees	10	100	250	1,300
Countries	1	1	1	1
Cities	1	4	5	10

Over time, Goldman Sachs has evolved its footprint and impact through the composition of its leadership team, assets and global presence. More deliberate growth in the first half of the firm's existence yielded to a decidedly accelerated expansion in the past 50 years. In the twenty-first century, Goldman Sachs continues to grow its presence and capabilities to meet client needs and opportunities — wherever they may be found.

	125th	*150th*
	1994	**2019**
	150	474[1]
	85 Broad Street	200 West Street
	$4.77 billion	$90 billion [2]
	$8.08 billion	$90 billion
	9,000	37,700 [2]
	17	34 [2]
	31	73 [2]

[1] As of January 2019   [2] As of June 2019

The Partners of Goldman Sachs – 1869 to 2019

1869 to 1909
Marcus Goldman
Samuel Sachs
Henry Goldman
Ludwig Dreyfuss
Harry Sachs
Arthur Sachs
Paul J. Sachs
Walter E. Sachs

1910 to 1930
Henry S. Bowers
Howard J. Sachs
Waddill Catchings
Sidney J. Weinberg

1931
Samuel W. Anderson
Grant Keehn
Ernest Loveman

1942
Miles J. Cruickshank
Alfred E. Hamill
James C. Hemphill
Robert V. Horton

1943
Walter F. Blaine

1944
T. Spencer Shore

1946
Walter J. Creely
Gustave L. Levy

1949
Edward A. Schrader

1950
Robert E. Anderson Jr.
Stanley R. Miller

1952
Durwin D. Algyer

1954
Charles E. Saltzman

1956
L. La Verne Horton
John L. Weinberg
John C. Whitehead

1958
Howard R. Young

1959
Arthur G. Altschul
John W. Callaghan
Charles L. Grannon
James D. Robertson
L. Jay Tenenbaum
Harold S. Wass

1963
Robert S. Danforth
Richard J. Fay
H. Frederick Krimendahl II
William H. Montgomery
John H. Rhoades III

1965
George E. Doty
Donald R. Gant
James P. Gorter
Peter A. Hager
Lewis J. Kaufman
James S. Marcus
Alan L. Stein
J. Fred Weintz Jr.

1967
Robert B. Menschel
Robert E. Mnuchin
Richard P. Oakley
Sidney J. Weinberg Jr.
Lewis M. Weston
Robert G. Wilson

1968
Peter A. Levy
L. Thomas Melly
Thomas B. Walker Jr.

1969
George T. Boyer
Michael H. Coles
Henry H. Fowler
John C. Jamison
Richard L. Menschel
Ross E. Traphagen Jr.

1971
H. Corbin Day
James J. Kelly
Bruce J. McCowan
Eugene Mercy Jr.
George M. Ross
Robert E. Rubin
Eric P. Sheinberg
David B. Stocker
George M. Van Cleave

1973
Daniel G. Dubrovich
Stephen Friedman
John D. Gilliam
Peter M. Sacerdote
Lloyd Stockel
William C. Stutt
Hyman Weinberg

1975
Pieter A. Fisher
Charles M. Harmon Jr.
Stephen B. Kay
Sheldon Seevak

1976
Francis X. Coleman Jr.

1977
Dan W. Cook III
Leon G. Cooperman
Robert N. Downey
Lewis M. Eisenberg
Anthony E. Fahnestock
Stephen R. Goldenberg
Frank P. Smeal
Roy C. Smith
Burton E. Sorensen
James D. Timmons
Roy J. Zuckerberg

1978
Daniel G. Amstutz
Geoffrey T. Boisi
Kenneth D. Brody
David C. Clapp
Peter R. Coneway
Robert M. Conway
Robert M. Freeman
James C. Kautz
David M. Silfen
Gary M. Wenglowski
Barrie A. Wigmore

1980
Jon S. Corzine
Eugene V. Fife
Robert A. Friedman
Richard M. Hayden
Robert J. Hurst
William J. Kealy
Terence J. Mulvihill
Peter G. Sachs
Howard A. Silverstein

1981
Jack R. Aron
Robert Aron
Claude M. Ballard Jr.
Herbert J. Coyne
Martin L. Coyne
Charles P. Griffis
Howard C. Katz
Edward R. Roberts
Marvin H. Schur
Dennis A. Suskind
Ronald S. Tauber

1982
J. Nelson Abanto
Michael R. Armellino
Peter K. Barker
Eric S. Dobkin
Peter M. Fahey
David A. George
Roger M. Lynch
Willard J. Overlock Jr.
Henry M. Paulson Jr.
Philip C. Scott
Joseph H. Wender
Marius O. Winkelman

1984
Eugene D. Atkinson
Richard S. Atlas
Nicola L. Caporale
Jonathan L. Cohen
Alfred C. Eckert III
John R. Farmer
Robert G. Frahm II
Fredric B. Garonzik
J. Markham Green
Kevin W. Kennedy
Joel Kirschbaum
William C. Landreth
T. Gordon McMahon
Daniel M. Neidich
Gary D. Rose
Edward Spiegel
Victor R. Wright

1986
Thomas W. Berry
Fischer Black
Robert A. Cenci
Robert F. Cummings Jr.
Charles A. Davis
Angelo De Caro
Michael C. Delaney
David F. DeLucia
Steven G. Einhorn
Joseph H. Ellis
Wade Fetzer III
David B. Ford
Robert M. Giordano
John A. Golden
Richard W. Herbst
Paul F. Jacobson
P. Henry James
James N. Lane
David M. Leuschen
Jeanette W. Loeb
Michael R. Lynch
Michael D. McCarthy
Thomas G. Mendell
Todd M. Morgan
Robert E. O'Hara III
Donald C. Opatrny Jr.
John J. Oros
R. Ralph Parks Jr.
Edward A. Poppiti Jr.
Thomas R. Pura
Thomas L. Rhodes
Jacob Z. Schuster
Gary L. Seevers
Alan A. Shuch
Thomas E. Tuft
Artur Walther
Garland E. Wood

1987
George F. Adam Jr.
Michael P. Mortara

1988
Henry C. Barkhorn III
Lloyd C. Blankfein
Frank P. Brosens
John P. Curtin Jr.
Marcus J. Dash
Gavyn Davies
Dexter D. Earle
John Ehara
J. Christopher Flowers
Gary Gensler
John F. Gilmore Jr.
William R. Gruver
Charles T. Harris III
Thomas J. Healey
Stephen Hendel
Robert E. Higgins
Robert J. Katz
Ernest S. Liu
Robert I. Lund
Eff W. Martin
Charles B. Mayer Jr.
David Morrison
Michael J. O'Brien
Mikael Salovaara
Stuart J. Schlesinger
Mark Schwartz
Stephen M. Semlitz
Robert K. Steel
Daniel J. Sullivan Jr.
John A. Thain
John L. Thornton
Moses K. Tsang
Bracebridge H. Young Jr.
Joseph R. Zimmel
Barry L. Zubrow
Gary L. Zwerling

1990
Vinod Ahooja
Jonathan R. Aisbitt
Andrew M. Alper
William J. Buckley
Frank L. Coulson Jr.
Connie K. Duckworth
Richard A. Friedman
Alan R. Gillespie
Joseph H. Gleberman
Jacob D. Goldfield
Steven M. Heller
Ann F. Kaplan
Robert S. Kaplan
Peter D. Kiernan III
John P. McNulty
T. Willem Mesdag
Gaetano J. Muzio
Robin Neustein
Timothy J. O'Neill
Scott M. Pinkus
John J. Powers

1992
Lance A. Bakrow
Carlos A. Cordeiro
John O. Downing
W. Mark Evans
Michael D. Fascitelli
Sylvain M. Hefes
Reuben Jeffery III
Suzanne Nora Johnson
Lawrence H. Linden
Jun Makihara
Masanori Mochida
Robert B. Morris III
Philip D. Murphy
Terence M. O'Toole
Gregory K. Palm
Carl G. E. Palmstierna
Michael G. Rantz
J. David Rogers
Joseph Sassoon
Peter Savitz
Charles B. Seelig Jr.
Ralph F. Severson
Michael L. Smirlock
Gene T. Sykes
Gary A. Syman
Leslie C. Tortora
John L. Townsend III
Lee G. Vance
David A. Viniar
John S. Weinberg
Peter A. Weinberg
Laurence M. Weiss
Stephen D. Quinn
Arthur J. Reimers III
James P. Riley Jr.
Richard A. Sapp
Bernard M. Sussman
Donald F. Textor
Thomas B. Walker III
Patrick J. Ward
Jeffrey M. Weingarten
Jon Winkelried
Richard E. Witten

George W. Wellde Jr.
Jaime E. Yordan

1993
Sharmin Mossavar-Rahmani

1994
Paul M. Achleitner
Armen A. Avanessians
Joel S. Beckman
David W. Blood
Zachariah Cobrinik
Gary D. Cohn
Christopher A. Cole
Henry Cornell
Robert V. Delaney
Joseph Della Rosa
J. Michael Evans
Lawton W. Fitt
Joseph D. Gatto
Peter C. Gerhard
Nomi P. Ghez
David T. Hamamoto
Walter H. Haydock
David L. Henle
Francis J. Ingrassia
Hideo Ishihara
Scott B. Kapnick
Kevin M. Kelly
John C. Kleinert
Jonathan L. Kolatch
Peter S. Kraus
Robert B. Litterman
Jonathan M. Lopatin
Thomas J. Macirowski
Peter G. C. Mallinson
Oki Matsumoto
E. Scott Mead
Eric M. Mindich
Steven T. Mnuchin
Thomas K. Montag
Edward A. Mulé
Kipp M. Nelson
Christopher K. Norton
Robert J. O'Shea

Wiet H. M. Pot
Jack L. Salzman
Eric S. Schwartz
Michael F. Schwerin
Richard S. Sharp
Richard G. Sherlund
Michael S. Sherwood
Cody J. Smith
Daniel W. Stanton
Esta E. Stecher
Fredric E. Steck
Byron D. Trott
Barry S. Volpert
Peter S. Wheeler
Anthony G. Williams
Gary W. Williams
Tracy R. Wolstencroft
Danny O. Yee
Michael J. Zamkow
Mark A. Zurack

1995
Terence J. O'Neill
Peter D. Sutherland

1996
Ron E. Beller
Milton R. Berlinski
Peter L. Briger Jr.
Lawrence R. Buchalter
E. Gerald Corrigan
Randolph L. Cowen
Timothy D. Dattels
Paul C. Deighton
C. Steven Duncker
Glenn P. Earle
Geoffrey T. Grant
Eric P. Grubman
Joseph D. Gutman
Robert S. Harrison
David B. Heller
Mary C. Henry
Jacquelyn M. Hoffman-Zehner
Barry A. Kaplan
Erland S. Karlsson

Douglas W. Kimmelman
Bradford C. Koenig
David G. Lambert
Ronald G. Marks
Karsten N. Moller
Alok Oberoi
Timothy C. Plaut
Girish V. Reddy
Stuart M. Rothenberg
John C. Ryan
Muneer A. Satter
Howard B. Schiller
Steven M. Shafran
James M. Sheridan
Marc A. Spilker
Mark R. Tercek
John R. Tormondsen
Steven J. Wisch
Gregory H. Zehner
Jide J. Zeitlin

1997
Simon M. Robertson

1998
Bradley I. Abelow
David M. Baum
Richard J. Bronks
Michael J. Carr
Christopher J. Carrera
Mary Ann Casati
Andrew A. Chisholm
Abby Joseph Cohen
Claudio Costamagna
Philip M. Darivoff
David A. Dechman
Alexander C. Dibelius
Gordon E. Dyal
Paul S. Efron
Pieter Maarten Feenstra
Edward C. Forst
Christopher G. French
Richard J. Gnodde
Jeffrey B. Goldenberg
Amy O. Goodfriend
Andrew Gordon

M. Roch Hillenbrand
Timothy J. Ingrassia
Stefan J. Jentzsch
Chansoo Joung
Thomas D. Lasersohn
Anthony D. Lauto
Matthew G. L'Heureux
Robert H. Litzenberger
David J. Mastrocola
Sanjeev K. Mehra
Wayne L. Moore
Thomas S. Murphy Jr.
Avi M. Nash
Michael E. Novogratz
Greg M. Ostroff
Robert J. Pace
Michael A. Price
Scott S. Prince
Emmanuel Roman
Ralph F. Rosenberg
Michael S. Rubinoff
Richard M. Ruzika
Michael D. Ryan
Tsutomu Sato
Jonathan S. Savitz
Antoine Schwartz
Dinakar Singh
Christian J. Siva-Jothy
Jonathan S. Sobel
Hsueh J. Sung
Robert B. Tudor III
Malcolm B. Turnbull
John E. Urban
George H. Walker IV
Kendrick R. Wilson III
Yasuyo Yamazaki
Yoel Zaoui

1999
David M. Solomon

2000
Raanan A. Agus
Zarthustra J. Amrolia
Stuart N. Bernstein
Jean-Luc Biamonti

Randall A. Blumenthal
Antonio Borges
Charles W. A. Bott
Craig W. Broderick
John J. Bu
Timothy B. Bunting
Andrew Cader
Lawrence V. Calcano
Richard M. Campbell-Breeden
Carmine C. Capossela
Chris Casciato
Robert J. Christie
Todd J. Christie
Peter T. Cirenza
Laura C. Conigliaro
Frank T. Connor
Karen R. Cook
Edith W. Cooper
Philip A. Cooper
Eduardo A. Cruz
John Stephen Daly
Simon Dingemans
Suzanne O. Donohoe
James H. Donovan
Michael B. Dubno
Jay S. Dweck
Isabelle Ealet
Herbert E. Ehlers
John E. Eisenberg
Edward K. Eisler
Michael P. Esposito
Charles P. Eve
Thomas M. Fitzgerald
Randy W. Frankel
Shirley Fung
Emmanuel Gavaudan
Robert R. Gheewalla
H. John Gilbertson Jr.
Gary F. Goldring
James S. Golob
Frank J. Governali
David J. Greenwald
Christopher M. Grigg
Douglas C. Grip
Nobumichi Hattori

Terry P. Hughes
William L. Jacob III
Dan H. Jester
David A. Kaplan
Robert C. King Jr.
Ewan M. Kirk
Mark J. Kogan
Kathy Mitsuko Koll
Peter J. Layton
Kenneth H. M. Leet
Hughes B. Lepic
Jack Levy
Thomas B. Lewis Jr.
Gwen R. Libstag
Mitchell J. Lieberman
Syaru Shirley Lin
Antigone Loudiadis
John A. Mahoney
Sean O. Mahoney
Charles G. R. Manby
Barry A. Mannis
Arthur S. Margulis
Robert J. Markwick
Theresa E. McCabe
Mark E. McGoldrick
Stephen J. McGuinness
John C. McIntire
Audrey A. McNiff
Roberto Mendoza
Amos Meron
Edward S. Misrahi
Jeffrey M. Moslow
Ian Mukherjee
Timothy R. Mullen
Duncan L. Niederauer
Richard T. Ong
Mukesh K. Parekh
David B. Philip
Stephen R. Pierce
John J. Rafter
Paul M. Roberts
John F.W. Rogers
Paul M. Russo
Katsunori Sago
Pablo J. Salame
J. Michael Sanders

Gary B. Schermerhorn
Jeffrey W. Schroeder
Steve M. Scopellite
Robert J. Shea Jr.
Ravi M. Singh
Ravi Sinha
Edward M. Siskind
Michael M. Smith
Randolph C. Snook
Steven R. Starker
Stuart L. Sternberg
Ronald K. Tanemura
Mark J. Tracey
Hank Uberoi
Hugo H. van Vredenburch
Corrado P. Varoli
John J. Vaske
Hsueh Ming Wang
David M. Weil
William M. Wicker
Todd A. Williams
Michael S. Wishart
Zi Wang Xu
W. Thomas York Jr.
Paolo Zannoni
James P. Ziperski

2001
Philippe K. Khuong-Huu
Alison J. Mass
Donald R. Mullen

2002
Peter C. Aberg
Syed H. Ahmad
Akio Asuke
Dean C. Backer
Frances R. Bermanzohn
Gary D. Black
John D. Campbell
Geoffrey G. Clark
Lawrence A. Cohen
Brahm S. Cramer
Neil D. Crowder
Michael David Daffey
Michael G. De Lathauwer

Mark F. Dehnert
Juan A. Del Rivero
Martin R. Devenish
Armando A. Diaz
Mario Draghi
William C. Dudley
Stephen Fitzgerald
Robert K. Frumkes
Enrico S. Gaglioti
Rajiv A. Ghatalia
Scott A. Gieselman
William M. Grathwohl
Stefan Green
Celeste A. Guth
Melina E. Higgins
Kenneth W. Hitchner
Maykin Ho
Peter Hollmann
Phillip S. Hylander
Robert C. Jones
Carsten Kengeter
Shigeki Kiritani
Eric S. Lane
Gregg R. Lemkau
Ryan D. Limaye
Josephine Linden
Anthony W. Ling
Victor M. Lopez-Balboa
Mark G. Machin
John J. Masterson
George N. Mattson
Joseph M. McConnell
John W. McMahon
Robert A. McTamaney
Christian A. Meissner
Andrew J. Melnick
Andrew L. Metcalfe
Therese L. Miller
William C. Montgomery
Gregory T. Mount
Lawrence P. O'Hagan
Andrea Ponti
Richard H. Powers
Charlotte P. Ransom
Joseph Ravitch
Ivan Ross

Masanori Sato
Marcus Schenck
Stephen M. Scherr
Harvey M. Schwartz
Lisa M. Shalett
Sarah E. Smith
Daniel L. Sparks
Steven H. Strongin
Andrew J. Stuart
Greg W. Tebbe
Stephen S. Trevor
Michael A. Troy
Eiji Ueda
Kaysie Uniacke
Ashok Varadhan
John E. Waldron
Gregg S. Weinstein
Matthew C. Westerman
C. Howard Wietschner
Susan A. Willetts
John S. Willian
Paul M. Young
William J. Young

2004
Yusuf A. Alireza
John A. Ashdown
Neil Z. Auerbach
Steven M. Barry
Christopher M. Barter
Stacy Bash-Polley
Jonathan A. Beinner
Driss Ben Brahim
Paul D. Bernard
Gerald J. Cardinale
Mark M. Carhart
Anthony H. Carpet
Amy L. Chasen
Jane P. Chwick
Alan M. Cohen
Thomas G. Connolly
Thomas W. Cornacchia
Matthew H. Cyzer
Stephen D. Daniel
Diego De Giorgi
Francois-Xavier de Mallmann

Daniel L. Dees
Joseph P. DiSabato
Jana Hale Doty
Michael L. Dweck
Kenneth M. Eberts III
Kathleen G. Elsesser
Elizabeth C. Fascitelli
Steven M. Feldman
Pierre-Henri Flamand
James R. Garvey
Gary T. Giglio
Justin G. Gmelich
Gregg A. Gonsalves
Peter Gross
Vishal Gupta
Rumiko Hasegawa
A. John Hass
Keith L. Hayes
Robert D. Henderson
Bruce A. Heyman
Stephen P. Hickey
Margaret J. Holen
Philip Holzer
Robert Howard
Fred Z. Hu
Edith A. Hunt
Raymond J. Iwanowski
Adrian M. Jones
Ravindra J. Joseph
Fumiko Kanenobu
Toshinobu Kasai
James C. Katzman
Richard L. Kauffman
Thomas J. Kenny
Timothy M. Kingston
Remy Klammers
Joseph A. LaNasa III
John J. Lauto
George C. Lee II
Johan Leven
Peter B. MacDonald
Jason E. Maynard
Ian R. McCormick
Michael R. Miele
Philip Moffitt
J. Ronald Morgan III

continued on following page

The Partners of Goldman Sachs – 1869 to 2019

Simon P. Morris
Marc O. Nachmann
Jeffrey P. Nedelman
Anthony Noto
Taneki Ono
James R. Paradise
Geoffrey M. Parker
Arthur J. Peponis
Ellen R. Porges
Kevin A. Quinn
Jean Raby
Jeffrey A. Resnick
Linnea K. Roberts
William M. Roberts
Eileen P. Rominger
David C. Ryan
Karen D. Seitz
David G. Shell
Jeffrey S. Sloan
Shahriar Tadjbakhsh
Roland W. Tegeder
David H. Tenney
Massimo Tononi
Donald J. Truesdale
Irene Y. Tse
David H. Voon
Theodor Weimer
Lance N. West
Elisha Wiesel
Jon A. Woodruff
Wassim G. Younan
Kevin Yi Zhang

2005
Dorothee Blessing
Salvatore Di Stasi
Fenglei Fang
Sanjay Patel

2006
Mark E. Agne
Gregory A. Agran
David M. Atkinson
Mark Beveridge
Leslie A. Biddle
Johannes M. Boomaars
Jason M. Brown
Melissa R. Brown
Steven M. Bunson
Nicholas F. Burgin
Mary D. Byron
Jin Yong Cai
Valentino D. Carlotti
Lik Shuen David Chan
R. Martin Chavez
James B. Clark
Peter H. Comisar
William J. Conley Jr.
Colin J. Corgan
Jean A. De Pourtales
Giorgio De Santis
Katinka I. Domotorffy
Donald J. Duet
Jason H. Ekaireb
Peter C. Enns
James P. Esposito
Carl Faker
Douglas L. Feagin
Luca D. Ferrari
Mark B. Florian
Timothy B. Flynn
Elisabeth Fontenelli
Silverio Foresi
Colleen A. Foster
Orit Freedman Weissman
Matthew T. Fremont-Smith
James R. Garman
Kevin S. Gasvoda
Lorenzo Grabau
Michael J. Graziano
Kenneth L. Hirsch
Simon N. Holden
Alastair J. Hunt
Zubin P. Irani
Andrew J. Jonas
Andrew J. Kaiser
Richard Ayer Kimball
Koji Kotaka
John D. Kramer
Jonathan A. Langer
Gregory D. Lee
Ronald Lee
Tim Leissner
Todd W. Leland
Allan S. Levine
Brian T. Levine
George C. Liberopoulos
Peter J. Lyon
Paula B. Madoff
Puneet Malhi
Simon I. Mansfield
Allan S. Marson
James A. McNamara
Bernard A. Mensah
Julian R. Metherell
Michael J. Millette
Timothy H. Moe
Thomas C. Morrow
Ken N. Murphy
Arjun N. Murti
Kenichi Nagasu
Gavin G. O'Connor
Peter C. Oppenheimer
Robert W. Pack
Kostas N. Pantazopoulos
Sheila H. Patel
Kenneth A. Pontarelli
Dioscoro-Roy I. Ramos
Krishna S. Rao
Buckley T. Ratchford
Sara E. Recktenwald
Gene Reilly
Elizabeth E. Robinson
David M. Ryan
Ankur A. Sahu
Guy E. Saidenberg
Susan J. Scher
Clare R. Scherrer
John A. Sebastian
Peter D. Selman
David A. Shiffman
Kunihiko Shiohara
Theodore T. Sotir
Christoph W. Stanger
Laurence Stein
Chase O. Stevenson
Morgan C. Sze
Thomas D. Teles
Daisuke Toki
Peter K. Tomozawa
Andrew Lucas van Praag
Robin A. Vince
Alejandro Vollbrechthausen
Casper W. Von Koskull
Theodore T. Wang
Alan S. Waxman
Nicholas H. Weber
Martin M. Werner
Andrew F. Wilson
Samuel J. Wisnia
Andrew E. Wolff
Neil J. Wright
Shinichi Yokote
Sanaz Zaimi

2007
Gregg Jon Felton
Serge Marquie
Peter K. Scaturro
Jonathan R. Symonds
Andrea Vella

2008
Paul Aaron
Sanggyun Ahn
Philip S. Armstrong
Charles Baillie
Philip R. Berlinski
Robert A. Berry
Oliver R. Bolitho
Atanas Bostandjiev
Patrick T. Boyle
Stephen Branton-Speak
Anne F. Brennan
Samuel S. Britton
Jason G. Cahilly
Martin Cher
Denis P. Coleman III
Kevin P. Connors
James V. Covello
Jeffrey R. Currie
Albert F. Dombrowski
Thomas M. Dowling
L. Brooks Entwistle
Stephan J. Feldgoise
Benjamin W. Ferguson
Wolfgang Fink
Timur F. Galen
Sean J. Gallagher
Gonzalo R. Garcia
Paul E. Germain
Paul Graves
Edward G. Hadden
Jonathan J. Hall
Jan Hatzius
Martin Hintze
Todd Hohman
James P. Houghton
Paul J. Huchro
Hidehiro Imatsu
Alan S. Kava
Dimitrios Kavvathas
Larry M. Kellerman
Hideki Kinuhata
Michael E. Koester
J. Christopher A. Kojima
Michiel P. Lap
Brian J. Lee
David A. Lehman
Deborah R. Leone
Wai Man Kaven Leung
John S. Lindfors
Hao-Cheng Liu
David M. Marcinek
Blake W. Mather
John J. McCabe
John J. McGuire Jr.
James McMurdo
Milton R. Millman III
Christopher Milner
Christina P. Minnis
Takashi Murata
Todd G. Owens
Craig W. Packer
Gilberto Pozzi
Lorin P. Radtke
Richard N. Ramsden
Michael J. Richman
Michael Rimland
Luigi G. Rizzo
Lora J. Robertson
Scott A. Romanoff
Julian Salisbury
Paul D. Scialla
Peter E. Scialla
Peter A. Seccia
Rebecca M. Shaghalian
Devesh P. Shah
Heather K. Shemilt
Magid N. Shenouda
Suhail A. Sikhtian
Gavin Simms
Marshall Smith
John D. Storey
Patrick M. Street
Ram K. Sundaram
Robert J. Sweeney
Michael J. Swenson
Jeffrey M. Tomasi
David G. Torrible
Frederick Towfigh
Greg A. Tusar
Jeffrey L. Verschleiser
Andrea A. Vittorelli
Paul Walker
Alasdair J. Warren
Dominic A. Wilson
Steve Windsor
Martin Wiwen-Nilsson
Denise A. Wyllie
Han Song Zhu

2009
Dalinc Ariburnu

2010
Charles F. Adams
Nick S. Advani
Philippe J. Altuzarra
William D. Anderson Jr.
Steven K. Barg
Scott B. Barringer
Gareth W. Bater
Tracey E. Benford
Avanish R. Bhavsar
V. Bunty Bohra
Stefan R. Bollinger
Robert Boroujerdi
Alison L. Bott
Sally A. Boyle
Christoph-Matthias Brand
Torrey J. Browder
Philippe L. Camu
Donald J. Casturo
Chia-Lin Chang
Sonjoy Chatterjee
Steven N. Cho
David T. Y. Chou
Efthalia Chryssikou
Colin Coleman
Kenneth W. Coquillette
Cyril M. M. Cottu
Massimo Della Ragione
Michele I. Docharty
David P. Eisman
Charalampos Eliades
Christopher H. Eoyang
Samuel W. Finkelstein
Ramani Ganesh
Matthew R. Gibson
Michelle Gill
Michael J. Grimaldi
Dylan S. Halterlein
Elizabeth M. Hammack
Dane E. Holmes
Ning Hong
Shin Horie
Ming Yunn Stephanie Hui
Eric S. Jordan
Pierre-Emmanuel Y. Juillard
Vijay M. Karnani
Christopher Keogh
Peter Kimpel
Lee Guan Kelvin Koh
Adam M. Korn
David J. Kostin
Jorg H. Kukies
Andre Laport Ribeiro
Geoffery Lee
Laurent Lellouche
Eugene H. Leouzon
Wayne M. Leslie
John R. Levene
Leland Lim
Lindsay P. LoBue
David B. Ludwig
Raghav Maliah
Matthew F. Mallgrave
Alain Marcus
Robert A. Mass
Alastair Maxwell
Matthew B. McClure
Patrick S. McClymont
Dermot W. McDonogh
Richard P. McNeil
Avinash Mehrotra
Jonathan M. Meltzer
Bruce H. Mendelsohn
Peeyush Misra
Bryan P. Mix
Atosa Moini
Ricardo Mora
Ezra Vitali Nahum
Brett Alan Olsher
Nigel M. O'Sullivan
Nirbhan Pathmanabhan
Jonathan M. Penkin
Michelle H. Pinggera
Dhruv Piplani
Dina H. Powell
Sumit Rajpal
James H. Reynolds
Stuart Riley
Karl J. Robijns
Peter Craig Russell
Luke A. Sarsfield III
Stephen B. Scobie
John Shaffer
Konstantin A. Shakhnovich
Daniel M. Shefter
Michael L. Simpson
Mark R. Sorrell
J. Richard Suth
Jasper Tans
Patrick Tassin de Nonneville
Megan M. Taylor
Teresa Teague
Pawan Tewari
Klaus B. Toft
Kenro Tsutsumi
Richard J. Tufft
Toshihiko Umetani
Jonathan R. Vanica
Philip J. Venables
Simone Verri
Daniel Wainstein
Kevin A. Walker
Robert P. Wall
David D. Wildermuth
Michael Wise
Chang-Po Yang
Xing Zhang
Xudong Zhang

2011
Ronald Hua
Christian Johnston
Anthony Miller
Daniel Petrozzo
Andrew Rennie
Simon Rothery
Carl Stern
Kent Wosepka

2012
Vivek J. Bantwal
Heather Bellini
Brian W. Bolster
Jill A. Borst
Michael J. Brandmeyer
Jason H. Brauth
Stuart A. Cash
Alex S. Chi
Kent A. Clark
Richard N. Cormack
John F. Daly
Anne Marie B. Darling
David H. Dase
James Del Favero
Olaf Diaz-Pintado

Robert Drake-Brockman
Alessandro Dusi
Edward A. Emerson
Antonio F. Esteves
Patrick J. Fels
Peter E. Finn
David A. Fishman
Sheara J. Fredman
Jacques Gabillon
Francesco U. Garzarelli
Nick V. Giovanni
Bradley J. Gross
Anthony J. C. Gutman
Michael L. Hensch
Ericka T. Horan
Russell W. Horwitz
Roy R. Joseph
John J. Kim
Marie Louise Kirk
Hugh J. Lawson
Scott L. Lebovitz
Luca M. Lombardi
John V. Mallory
Joseph S. Mauro
Charles M. McGarraugh
Xavier C. Menguy
Amol S. Naik
Jyothsna Natauri
Una M. Neary
Gregory G. Olafson
Lisa Opoku
Gerald B. Ouderkirk III
Francesco Pascuzzi
Anthony W. Pasquariello
Richard Phillips
Hugh R. Pill
Dmitri Potishko
Sean D. Rice
Francois J. Rigou
Scott M. Rofey
Johannes Rombouts
Michael Ronen
Jami Rubin
Yann Samuelides
Joshua S. Schiffrin
David A. Schwimmer

Gaurav Seth
Michael H. Siegel
Michael T. Smith
Joseph J. Struzziery III
Damian E. Sutcliffe
Michael S. Swell
Ryan J. Thall
Christoph Vedral
Simon R. Watson
Toby C. Watson
Yoshihiko Yano

2013
Kate G. Richdale

2014
Fadi Abuali
Aaron M. Arth
Jennifer A. Barbetta
Thomas J. Barrett
Gerard M. Beatty
Shane M. Bolton
William C. Bousquette Jr.
Clarence K. Brenan
Tavis C. P. Cannell
Thomas J. Carella
Gary W. Chropuvka
Darren W. Cohen
Stephanie E. Cohen
Kathleen A. Connolly
Sara V. Devereux
Iain N. Drayton
Carlos Fernandez-Aller
Jonathan H. Fine
David A. Friedland
Johannes P. Fritze
Dino Fusco
Micheal H. Garriott
Jeffrey M. Gido
John L. Glover III
Cyril J. Goddeeris
Alexander S. Golten
Jason A. Gottlieb
Joanne Hannaford
Julie A. Harris
Edouard Hervey

Matthias Hieber
Charles P. Himmelberg
Sean C. Hoover
Pierre Hudry
Irfan S. Hussain
Etsuko Kanayama
Kevin G. Kelly
Tammy A. Kiely
Maxim B. Klimov
Edward C. Knight
Meena K. Lakdawala
Nyron Z. Latif
Gregory Paul Lee
Dirk L. Lievens
Kyriacos A. Loupis
John G. Madsen
Richard M. Manley
Michael Marsh
Ali S. Melli
David Miller
Kayhan Mirza
Joseph Montesano
Eric D. Muller
Alice Jane Murphy
Manikandan Natarajan
Fergal J. O'Driscoll
Jernej Omahen
Paul G. Parker
Nicholas W. Phillips
Robert M. Pulford
Colin J. Ryan
Carsten Schwarting
Kunal Kishore Shah
Jake Siewert
Jason E. Silvers
Kristin O. Smith
Kevin M. Sterling
Umesh Subramanian
Joseph D. Swift
Ben W. Thorpe
Oliver Thym
Joseph K. Todd
Hiroyuki Tomokiyo
Thomas A. Tormey
Mark A. Van Wyk
Rajesh Venkataramani

Matthew P. Verrochi
Owen O. West
Ronnie A. Wexler
Xiaoyin Zhang
Adam Zotkow

2015
James Ellery
Raja A. Mahajan
Harit Talwar

2016
Nicole V. Agnew
Andrew J. Bagley
Jonathan Barry
Jonathan A. B. Bayliss
Deborah R. Beckmann
Michael Bruun
Robert A. Camacho
David E. Casner
Kenneth G. Castelino
Christian Channell
Massimiliano Ciardi
David Coulson
Christopher A. Crampton
Canute H. Dalmasse
Michael J. Daum
Jennifer L. Davis
David A. Fox
Andrew J. Fry
Charles H. Gailliot
Gabriel E. Gelman
Joshua Glassman
Court Golumbic
Parameswaran Gopikrishnan
Sarah J. Gray
Carey Halio
Brian M. Haufrect
Peter U. Hermann
Amanda S. Hindlian
Harold P. Hope III
Erdit F. Hoxha
Kathleen Hughes
Russell E. Hutchinson
Omer Ismail
Geraldine Keefe

Andre H. Kelleners
Aasem G. Khalil
Simon J. Kingsbury
Kathryn A. Koch
Tuan Lam
David W. Lang
Bruce M. Larson
Gavin J. Leo-Rhynie
Tianqing Li
Paget MacColl
Clifton C. Marriott
Elizabeth G. Martin
Sarah Marie Martin
Jason L. Mathews
Alexander M. Mayer
Brendan M. McGovern
Sean T. McHugh
Celine-Marie G. Mechain
Jung Min
Sam A. Morgan
Edward G. Morse
Heather L. Mulahasani Majedabadi Kohne
Dimitrios Nikolakopoulos
Michael M. Paese
Kim-Thu Posnett
Alexander E. Potter
Macario Prieto
Xiao Qin
Marko J. Ratesic
Lawrence J. Restieri Jr.
Jason T. Rowe
David T. Rusoff
Maheshwar R. Saireddy
Thierry Sancier
Adam H. Savarese
Jason M. Savarese
John R. Sawtell
Stacy D. Selig
Tejas A. Shah
Nicholas Sims
Nishi Somaiya
Li Hui Suo
Aurora J. Swithenbank
Christopher W. Taendler
Jeremy R. Taylor

Richard J. Taylor
David S. Thomas
Andrew R. Tilton
Padideh N. Trojanow
Peter van der Goes Jr.
Damien R. Vanderwilt
Peter A. Weidman
Neil E. Wolitzer

2017
Michael L. Blum
Jeffrey W. Douthit
Jeffrey S. Wecker

2018
Philip J. Aldis
Margaret C. Anadu
Anthony M. Arnold
Jacqueline Arthur
Farshid M. Asl
Yibo Bao
David C. Bicarregui
Beat M. Cabiallavetta
Niharika Cabiallavetta
Wei Cai
Gregory D. Calnon
Katrien E. Carbonez
Michael J. Casey
Nikhil Choraria
Colin R. Convey
Adam R. Dell
Anthony Dewell
Arun Dhar
Xiang Fan
Jeffrey M. Fine
Brian C. Friedman
Daniel I. Friedman
Benjamin M. Frost
Christopher M. Gallea
Antonio Gatti
Jamie Goodman
John F. Greenwood
David Gribble
David H. Hammond
Magnus C. Hardeberg
Carl J. Hartman

Earl E. Hunt
Nell C. Hutton
Nitin Jindal
Tanweer Kabir
Zaid M. Khaldi
Tobias Koester
Thomas A. Leake
Ke Li
Zheng Li
Thomas Malafronte
Lisa S. Mantil
Shogo Matsuzawa
Heather Kennedy Miner
Igor Modlin
Steven R. Moffitt
Hari Moorthy
Eric Murciano
Craig Murray
Eric S. Neveux
Adam J. Nordin
Barry J. O'Brien
Daniel S. Oneglia
James Andrew Ozment
Andrew Philipp
Asahi Pompey
Stephanie L. Rader
Radovan Radman
Akila S. Raman
Thomas S. Riggs III
Philip J. Salem
Laurie E. Schmidt
Jameson C. Schriber
Anshul Sehgal
Karen P. Seymour
Ashish Shah
Kurt N. Simon
James Sinclair
Amit Sinha
Anna K. Skoglund
Stephanie P. Smith
Richard J. Spencer
David M. Stark
Sinead M. Strain
Michele Titi-Cappelli
Philippa A. Vizzone
Edward B. Waltemath

Miriam S. Wheeler
Rana Yared
Mikhail Zlotnik

2019
Marco Argenti
Joseph J. Duran
Atte Lahtiranta

Image Credits

The images in this book were sourced using published materials as well as original documents, publications, photographs and artifacts from the Goldman Sachs Archives, private collections and other repositories. Every attempt has been made to accurately credit photographers, authors and other rights holders and to gain permission for reproduction. We apologize for any errors or omissions.

Slipcase	30 Pine Street (Photographer unknown / Museum of the City of New York. X2010.11.3025).
Endsheets	Perspective map of Manhattan (Library of Congress Geography and Map Division, Washington, DC).
2	Page from client services brochure (Goldman Sachs Archives).
5	30 Pine Street (Photographer unknown / Museum of the City of New York. X2010.11.3025).
7	Marcus Goldman (Goldman Sachs Archives); Hurricane Katrina Relief, New Orleans, 2006 (Goldman Sachs Archives); Hackathon, Hong Kong, 2019 (Goldman Sachs Archives); Capital Markets team members, Tokyo, 1992 (Goldman Sachs Archives); Research Department library, New York, 1960 (Goldman Sachs Archives); Equities floor employees, New York, 1990 (Goldman Sachs Archives); Greenhouse Sports Challenge participants with Richard Gnodde and Michael Sherwood, London, 2013 (Goldman Sachs Archives); Mergers and Acquisitions Department summer picnic, New York, 1992 (Goldman Sachs Archives, courtesy of Margaret Langan); Securities Sales New Associates, New York, 1986 (Goldman Sachs Archives, courtesy of Terise Slotkin); 55 Broad Street office, New York, 1969 (Goldman Sachs Archives); Securities Division trading floor, New York, 2011 (Goldman Sachs Archives); J. Aron & Company coffee tasters, c. 1985 (Goldman Sachs Archives, courtesy of Terise Slotkin); São Paulo office employees, 2018 (Goldman Sachs Archives); and Stephen Scherr, David Solomon and John Waldron, New York, 2019 (Goldman Sachs Archives).
8	Marcus Goldman (Goldman Sachs Archives).
9	Perspective map of Manhattan (Library of Congress Geography and Map Division, Washington, DC).
10	City Hall in Trappstadt, Bavaria (Goldman Sachs Archives). Dun & Company Credit Report (New York, v. 417, p. 200 A134, R.G. Dun & Co. Credit Report Collection, Baker Library, Harvard Business School).
11	Group portrait at golden wedding anniversary of Marcus and Bertha Goldman (Goldman Sachs Archives). Ship manifest (Hamburg Archives via Ancestry.com).
12	The Goldman Family Tree (Goldman Sachs Archives).
13	The Sachs Family Tree (Goldman Sachs Archives). Portrait of Samuel Sachs (Goldman Sachs Archives). Announcement of Samuel Sachs joining the partnership (*Journal of Commerce*, courtesy of Federal Reserve Archival System for Economic Research – FRASER).
14	Henry Goldman (Goldman Sachs Archives). Announcement of the new name of Goldman, Sachs & Co. (*Journal of Commerce*, courtesy of FRASER).
15	Tower Bridge, London (Science & Society Picture Library via Getty Images). Envelope from Goldman, Sachs & Co. to Bloomingdale Brothers (Goldman Sachs Archives, courtesy of Rebecca J. Gordon).
16	New York Stock Exchange trading floor (Bettmann via Getty Images).
17	Page from Kleinwort, Sons & Co. ledger (Goldman Sachs Archives). Check from Kleinwort, Sons & Co. (Goldman Sachs Archives).
18	Boston office building on State Street (Boston Pictorial Archive Collection, Boston Public Library. "Boston, Massachusetts. State Street." Photograph. 1885. Digital Commonwealth, https://ark.digitalcommonwealth.org/ark:/50959/nv935g94r). Home Insurance office building (Chicago History Museum via Getty Images). Advertisement showing new Chicago address (Goldman Sachs Archives).
19	United Cigars store (History and Art Collection / Alamy Stock Photo). United Cigar Manufacturers Company announcement (Goldman Sachs Archives). United Cigar Manufacturers Company prospectus (Goldman Sachs Archives).
20	Sears, Roebuck & Co. profit sharing certificate (Goldman Sachs Archives). Sears, Roebuck & Co. catalogue (The LIFE Images Collection via Getty Images; Photo by George Karger / Pix Inc.). Sears, Roebuck & Co. prospectus (Goldman Sachs Archives). Facsimile of Sears, Roebuck & Co. balance sheet (Goldman Sachs Archives).
21	Facsimiles of authorized signatures (Goldman Sachs Archives). Portrait of Walter Sachs (Goldman Sachs Archives). Letter from W. E. B. Du Bois to Walter Sachs (Courtesy of UMass-Amherst, Special Collections and University Archives, reprinted with the permission of The Permissions Company, LLC on behalf of The David Graham Du Bois Trust).
22	F. W. Woolworth Co. company store (Bettmann via Getty Images).
23	F. W. Woolworth Co. prospectus (Goldman Sachs Archives). Woolworth Building (Library of Congress / Photo by Photo12 / Universal Images Group via Getty Images).
24	Aerial view of New York Stock Exchange (Corbis via Getty Images).
25	Front page of the *Brooklyn Daily Eagle*, October 24, 1929 (Icon Communications via Getty Images). Goldman Sachs Trading Corporation stock certificate (Courtesy of the Museum of American Finance, Collection ID 2010.01.539).
26	Letter from Henry Goldman to Kleinwort, Sons & Co. (Goldman Sachs Archives).
27	Waddill Catchings (Source: Albert Russel Erksine, *History of The Studebaker Corporation, 1852-1923*, South Bend, IN: The Studebaker Corporation, 1924, Goldman Sachs Archives). Letter announcing Henry Goldman's retirement and Waddill Catchings joining the firm (Goldman Sachs Archives).
28	Passage of Nineteenth Amendment (Photo12 / Universal Images Group via Getty Images). Treaty of Versailles signing (Universal History Archive, Universal Images Group via Getty Images).
29	Cote d'Azur Pullman Express vintage poster (Photograph by Found Image Holdings / Corbis via Getty Images). Paris-Lyons-Mediterranean Railroad Company prospectus (Goldman Sachs Archives).
30	Warner Bros. Studios (Photo by Hulton Archive via Getty Images). Warner Bros. Pictures, Inc. prospectus (Goldman Sachs Archives).
31	Goldman Sachs Trading Corporation prospectus (Goldman Sachs Archives). Front page of *The New York Times*, October 29, 1929 (From *The New York Times*. © 1929 The New York Times Company. All rights reserved. Used under license).
32	Arthur Sachs (Geni.com).
33	Harry Sachs (Engraved by Henry Glover & Co., Goldman Sachs Archives). Front page of *Security Dealers Daily Financial Reporter*, December 19, 1935 (Goldman Sachs Archives). Partners' Accounts ledger page (Goldman Sachs Archives). Paul Sachs (Courtesy of Dumbarton Oaks Library and Collection).
34	First annual employee outing (Goldman Sachs Archives).
35	Page from the Goldman Sachs Trading Corporation *Weekly Review* (Goldman Sachs Archives). National Dairy Product Corporation Board of Directors (Goldman Sachs Archives).
36	Construction in front of 30 Pine Street (Borough President Manhattan Collection: Courtesy NYC Municipal Archives).
37	Signing of the Glass-Steagall Act (Bettmann via Getty Images).
38	Sidney Weinberg in US Navy uniform (Goldman Sachs Archives).
39	Sidney Weinberg (Barton Silverman / *The New York Times* / Redux). Medal for Merit Certificate facsimile (Goldman Sachs Archives). "Mr. Wall Street" story, November 16, 1967 (From *The New York Times*. © 1967 The New York Times Company. All rights reserved. Used under license.).
40	75th anniversary dinner photo and program (Goldman Sachs Archives).
41	Signing of Ford Motor Company's IPO (Ford Motor Company / Ford Images). Correspondence from Henry Ford II to Sidney Weinberg (Goldman Sachs Archives).
42	Memorandum from Sidney Weinberg to John Whitehead (Goldman Sachs Archives). Chart from John Whitehead's report to Sidney Weinberg (Goldman Sachs Archives).
43	Walt Disney Productions stock certificate (Goldman Sachs Archives). Walt Disney Productions prospectus (Goldman Sachs Archives). Walt Disney at Disneyland (Allan Grant / The LIFE Picture Collection via Getty Images).
44	Management Committee (Goldman Sachs Archives).
45	Management Committee (Goldman Sachs Archives).
46	Quarter Century Club first annual meeting (Goldman Sachs Archives). 2019 Quarter Century Club inductees (Goldman Sachs Archives, courtesy of Marc Bryan-Brown).
47	20 Broad Street office (Goldman Sachs Archives).
48	Gus Levy on *Finance* magazine cover, May 1968 (Source: Steeplechase Films). Gus Levy and US Vice President Hubert Humphrey at the 175th anniversary of the New York Stock Exchange (Courtesy of NYSE Group).
49	Gus Levy in his office (Ernest Sisto / *The New York Times* / Redux).
50	Goldman Sachs employees in front of London International Financial Futures Exchange (Goldman Sachs Archives).
51	"Fraud Laid To PennC by the SEC" article, *New York Post*, May 2, 1974. (Copyrighted 1974. Associated Press. 2126584:1019PF). Seaboard World Airlines Boeing 747 (AFP via Getty Images).
52	Gus Levy at London office opening (Goldman Sachs Archives). Announcement of London office opening (Goldman Sachs Archives).
53	Penn Central train at Grand Central Station (Alfred Gescheidt / The Image Bank via Getty Images).
54	Robert Litterman and Fischer Black (Goldman Sachs Archives). Emanuel Derman, Brian Carrihill, Cemal Dosembet and Piotr Karasinski (Goldman Sachs Archives, courtesy of Terise Slotkin). Black-Scholes formula (Source: Fischer Black and Myron Scholes, "The Pricing of Options and Corporate Liabilities," *Journal of Political Economy*, vol. 81 (3), May-June 1973, p. 644).
55	Électricité de France power plant (Goldman Sachs Archives).
56	Aerial view of the Marunouchi district in Chiyoda City, Tokyo (The Asahi Shimbun via Getty Images). Announcement of Tokyo office opening (Goldman Sachs Archives).
57	Goldman Sachs employees in Zurich (Goldman Sachs Archives).
58	Goldman Sachs *Annual Reviews*, 1970-1990 (Goldman Sachs Archives).
59	Goldman Sachs *Annual Reviews*, 1991 and *Annual Reports*, 1999-2019 (Goldman Sachs Archives).
60	Top row, from left: Sidney Weinberg, Henry Ford II and Werner Gullander, White House, Washington, DC, 1967 (Photo by Yoichi Okamoto / The LIFE Picture Collection via Getty Images). Bottom row, from left: Don Truesdale, Rachel Winokur, Milton Berlinski, Anthony Terraciano and Wolfgang Schoellkopf, First National Bank, 1995 (Goldman Sachs Archives); and Sung-June Hwang, Janice Wallace and Jan Lee in front of Bank of China, Hong Kong, 1993 (Goldman Sachs Archives).
61	Top row, from left: Juan Del Rivero, Jose Ruiz Castroviejo, Alberto Piedra, Jr., Ignacio Ybarra and Richard Sapp at La Cruz del Campo S.A., Seville, 1991 (Goldman Sachs Archives); and Joseph Saunders, Marschall Carter, Byron Pollitt and John Partridge, Visa IPO, New York Stock Exchange, New York, 2008 (Goldman Sachs Archives). Bottom row, from left: Ernest Liu, David Jefferies and Anthony Moore, National Grid Company, London, 1990 (Goldman Sachs Archives); and Brooklyn Navy Yard site visit, New York, 2013 (Goldman Sachs Archives, photography by Craig Jelniker).
62	Top row, from left: Jack Sandner, chairman, Chicago Mercantile Exchange (CME); Bill Brodsky, president, CME; Merton Miller, Nobel laureate and professor of finance, University of Chicago; Stephen Friedman; and John Gilmore sounding the bell to begin trading in the GSCI Futures and Options on the CME, Chicago, 1992 (Goldman Sachs Archives); and Mike Evans and Chen Dongsheng, chairman and CEO, Taikang Life Insurance, New York, 2011 (Goldman Sachs Archives). Bottom row, from left: Employee and overseas client, Paris, 1979 (Goldman Sachs Archives); and Mark Schwartz, Robert Kaplan, Rita Reid and Rick Rowland, Macy's Herald Square, New York, 1986 (Goldman Sachs Archives).
63	Top row, from left: William Stutt and Mark Lawrence, Jr. in front of a Delta Air Lines airplane financed by Goldman Sachs, 1982 (Goldman Sachs Archives, courtesy of William Stutt); and Matthew McEvoy, Jeffrey Cheung, C. Roger Moss and Sandy Thompson, Hong Kong, 1986 (Goldman Sachs Archives). Bottom row, from left: Christina Minnis, Ashley Everett and Maurice Taylor, chairman and CEO, Titan International, Bryan, Ohio, 2012 (Goldman Sachs Archives, photography by Bradford Young); and Bradley Abelow; David Courtney; Mary Ann Casati; John Eisenberg; Randy Laney, vice president of Finance, Corporate Risk and Benefits, Wal-Mart; Tracy Wolstencroft; and Betty Dutton, store manager, Wal-Mart; 1991 (Goldman Sachs Archives).
64	*Institutional Investor* magazine cover, January 1984 (Reprinted with permission of *Institutional Investor* magazine).
65	International Stock Exchange, London (Goldman Sachs Archives). "Unrelenting Thinking" corporate advertisement (Goldman Sachs Archives).
66	John Whitehead and John Weinberg (Goldman Sachs Archives).
67	Goldman Sachs 2004 *Annual Report* page on the 25th anniversary of the Business Principles (Goldman Sachs Archives).
68	J. Aron coffee tasters (Goldman Sachs Archives).
69	International Advisory Board (Goldman Sachs Archives). Henry Kissinger visit to 55 Water Street office (Goldman Sachs Archives, courtesy of Steve Goldenberg).

70 Dedication at the 85 Broad Street construction site (Goldman Sachs Archives). 85 Broad Street (Goldman Sachs Archives).

71 Investment Research team in Central, Hong Kong (Goldman Sachs Archives). Hong Kong office (Goldman Sachs Archives).

72 Tokyo Stock Exchange (Goldman Sachs Archives).

73 Goldman Sachs corporate advertisement (Goldman Sachs Archives). London Stock Exchange (Georges De Keerle via Getty Images).

74 Microsoft IPO tombstone advertisement (Goldman Sachs Archives). Bill Gates (Photo by Keith Beaty / *Toronto Star* via Getty Images).

75 British Gas roadshow (Goldman Sachs Archives).

76 John Weinberg, Sidney Weinberg and Jim Weinberg (Goldman Sachs Archives).

77 Peter Weinberg, Jim Weinberg, John L. Weinberg and John S. Weinberg (Goldman Sachs Archives, courtesy of Terise Slotkin). John S. Weinberg at investment banking award ceremony (Goldman Sachs Archives, courtesy of Terise Slotkin).

78 Clockwise, from center: Creation of Mondelez International and Kraft Foods as two independent publicly traded companies, 2012 (Courtesy of Eric Dobkin); Teléfonos de Mexico, S.A. de C.V. $2.17 billion global offering, 1991 (Goldman Sachs Archives, courtesy of Robert B. Morris, III); British Steel PLC 18 million American Depositary Shares offering, 1988 (Courtesy of Eric Dobkin); Goldman Sachs and Development Bank of Japan ¥25 billion investment in Universal Studios Japan, 2005 (Courtesy of Masa Mochida); Energias de Portugal, S.A. (edp) acquisition of Horizon Wind Energy, 2007 (Courtesy of Michelle Breyer); P. T. Telekomunikasi Indonesia (Persero) $1.68 billion stock offering, 1995 (Goldman Sachs Archives, courtesy of Robert B. Morris, III); and NTT DoCoMo sale of stake in AT&T Wireless, 2004 (Courtesy of Masa Mochida).

79 Top row, from left: Toshiba ¥599.99 billion private placement of 2.28 billion shares, 2017 (Courtesy of Masa Mochida); China Telecom (Hong Kong) Ltd. global offering of 2.7 billion shares, 1997 (Courtesy of Eric Dobkin); Daimler Benz $795 million offering, 1996 (Goldman Sachs Archives, courtesy of Frank Oliver Lehmann); and Goldman Sachs, Allianz Versicherungs AG, Industrial and Commercial Bank of China, and American Express Company strategic $3.78 billion investment and cooperation agreements, 2006 (Goldman Sachs Archives, courtesy of Esta Stecher). Center row, from left: Imperial Chemical Industries PLC acquisition of Acheson, 1998 (Goldman Sachs Archives); Coca-Cola 1 million shares block trade, 1977 (Goldman Sachs Archives); NTT DoCoMo ¥2.1 trillion global IPO of 545 thousand shares, 1998 (Courtesy of Masa Mochida); Beijing Gao Hua Securities Co. Ltd. unit purchase of 8,800 shares of Emei Shan Tourism Co., 2005 (Courtesy of Eddie Naylor); and Mars, Inc. and Wm. Wrigley Jr. Co. merger, 2008 (Goldman Sachs Archives, courtesy of Kyung-Ah Park). Bottom row, from left: Apple $1.5 billion green bond, 2016 (Courtesy of Kevin Smith); Bertelsmann AG block trade of 3.6 million shares of America Online, Inc., 1996 (Goldman Sachs Archives, courtesy of Frank Oliver Lehmann); Hutchison Port Holdings acquisition of Korean marine terminal assets of Hyundai Merchant Marine Co., Ltd., 2002 (Courtesy of Kyung-Ah Park); and Goldman Sachs, Sumitomo Mitsui Banking Corporation and Daiwa Securities SMBC ¥300 billion investment in Sanyo Electric Co., Ltd., 2006 (Courtesy of Masa Mochida).

80 Clockwise, from top: Operations employees handling brokerage volume, 1971 (Goldman Sachs Archives); 200 West Street lobby, New York, 2011 (Goldman Sachs Archives); Operations employees processing securities transactions for clients, 1972 (Goldman Sachs Archives); and Cycle for Survival at 200 West Street, New York, 2017 (Goldman Sachs Archives).

81 Clockwise, from top left: 150 Outer Ring Road south dining, Bengaluru, 2019; Goldman Sachs TV control booth, New York, 2019 (Goldman Sachs Archives); 200 West Street fitness center, New York, 2015 (Goldman Sachs Archives); Lee Garden Three community hub, Hong Kong, 2019 (Goldman Sachs Archives); and Corporate Finance employee training, New York, 1971 (Goldman Sachs Archives).

82 Clockwise, from top: Artificial Intelligence infographic in "Artificial Intelligence: AI, Machine Learning and Data Fuel the Future of Productivity" report 2016; *Millennials: Coming of Age* infographic, 2015; "Virtual & Augmented Reality" report cover, 2016; "The World Cup and Economics" report cover, 2002; Graphic representation comparing the price fluctuations of 79 industrial preferred stocks with the price fluctuations of 21 Goldman, Sachs & Co. preferred stocks listed on the New York Stock Exchange, 1923; Page from Goldman Sachs Trading Corporation *Weekly Review*, September 21, 1931 (All in Goldman Sachs Archives).

83 Top row, from left: Rethinking Mobility in Numbers infographic in "Rethinking Mobility. The 'pay-as-you-go' car: Ride hailing just the start" report, 2017 (Goldman Sachs Archives); "Silicon Carbide: The next leg of growth in power semiconductors" report cover, 2018 (Goldman Sachs Archives); "A Survivor's Guide to Disruption" report cover, 2019 (Goldman Sachs Archives); and "Petrochina" / "The Dragon Awakens" report cover, Chinese version, 2001 (Goldman Sachs Archives, courtesy of Paul Bernard). Bottom row, from left: "The Store of the Future. Reimagining Retail in the E-Commerce Era" report cover, 2017 (Goldman Sachs Archives); "China's Rise in Artificial Intelligence: The New New China" report cover, 2017 (Goldman Sachs Archives); "India Consumer Close-up: Tapping the spending power of a young, connected Urban Mass" report cover, 2016 (Goldman Sachs Archives); and "CEEMEA Focus List: Diverse markets, diverse opportunities" report cover, 2019 (Goldman Sachs Archives).

84 Former Prime Minister Margaret Thatcher at Peterborough Court opening (Goldman Sachs Archives).

85 Fall of Berlin Wall (Carol Guzy / *The Washington Post* via Getty Images). Stephen Friedman and Robert Rubin (Goldman Sachs Archives).

86 Partner Class of 1986 (Goldman Sachs Archives). Municipal Bonds meeting (Goldman Sachs Archives).

87 Global Finance meeting (Goldman Sachs Archives). Jeanette Winter Loeb Room Dedication (Goldman Sachs Archives).

88 Sumitomo agreement signing (Goldman Sachs). John Weinberg and Ichiro Isoda (Goldman Sachs Archives).

89 Office at 6, rue Newton, Paris (Goldman Sachs Archives).

90 Michael Armellino, Marcia Beck, Alan Shuch and others in Goldman Sachs Asset Management meeting (Goldman Sachs Archives). Robert Jones, David Ford and Sharmin Mossavar-Rahmani (Goldman Sachs Archives).

91 Front page of *The New York Times*, October 20, 1987 (From *The New York Times*. © 1987 The New York Times Company. All rights reserved. Used under license.). British Petroleum logo (Martin Gerten / Picture Alliance via Getty Images).

92 President Ronald Reagan and Secretary of Transportation Elizabeth Dole at Conrail privatization announcement (Contact sheet C39946, White House Photo Office collection, Ronald Reagan Library). Conrail deal toy (Goldman Sachs Archives).

93 Telmex privatization team (Goldman Sachs Archives).

94 Robert Rubin and Stephen Friedman (Goldman Sachs Archives). Stephen Friedman and Robert Rubin (Goldman Sachs Archives).

95 Robert Rubin (Goldman Sachs Archives). Stephen Friedman (Goldman Sachs Archives).

96 Peterborough Court office opening (Goldman Sachs Archives).

97 *Moving Times* newsletter (Goldman Sachs Archives).

98 Diagram from the notebook of SecDB co-founder Michael Dubno (Goldman Sachs Archives). Group portrait at "SecDB – Celebrating 25 Years" event (Goldman Sachs Archives).

99 Stephen Friedman at The Children's Center opening (Goldman Sachs Archives). Children at The Children's Center (Goldman Sachs Archives, courtesy of Terise Slotkin).

100 Daimler-Benz stock trading at the New York Stock Exchange (Goldman Sachs Archives).

101 125th anniversary advertisement (Goldman Sachs Archives). Eurotunnel train (Philippe Huguen / AFP via Getty Images).

102 Shanghai office opening (Goldman Sachs Archives). Beijing office opening (Goldman Sachs Archives).

103 Ralph Lauren and Stephen Friedman (Goldman Sachs Archives, courtesy of Dave Turner Photography).

104 Jon Corzine (Goldman Sachs Archives).

105 Jon Corzine with Republic of South Africa meeting participants (Goldman Sachs Archives). Jon Corzine and Mark Winkelman (Goldman Sachs Archives).

106 GS Financial Workbench development team mousepad (Goldman Sachs Archives, courtesy of Gerry Beatty). Global Economics portal on GS Financial Workbench website (Goldman Sachs Archives).

107 Rockefeller Center deal team (Goldman Sachs Archives, courtesy of Jun Makihara).

108 Deutsche Telekom offering (Goldman Sachs Archives). Deutsche Telkom deal toy (Goldman Sachs Archives).

109 NTT DoCoMo visit (Goldman Sachs Archives).

110 Community TeamWorks photos (Goldman Sachs Archives).

111 Community TeamWorks photos (Goldman Sachs Archives).

112 Top: Team Goldman Sachs at the Wall Street Run & Heart 5K Walk benefitting the American Heart Association, New York, 2018 (Goldman Sachs Archives). Middle row, from left: Employee football team, London, 1993 (Goldman Sachs Archives); Event in honor of Diwali, the Hindu festival of light, hosted by firmwide and cross-divisional Asian professional networks, Jersey City, New Jersey, 2017 (Goldman Sachs Archives); and The GS Singing Choir at the *10,000 Small Businesses* UK Festive Market, London, 2017 (Goldman Sachs Archives). Bottom row, from left: Holiday photo with J. Aron team, including Lloyd Blankfein, New York, 1990 (Goldman Sachs Archives); and Securities Sales and Trading & Arbitrage New Associates, New York, 1984 (Goldman Sachs Archives, courtesy of Terise Slotkin).

113 Clockwise, from top left: Women's Career Strategies Initiative program participants, New York, 2019 (Goldman Sachs Archives); Private Wealth Management team-building hike for new colleagues, Swiss Alps, Zurich, 2018 (Goldman Sachs Archives); Hong Kong-based dragon boat team competing at the Stanley International Dragon Boat Championships, Hong Kong, 2018 (Goldman Sachs Archives); 75th anniversary of the Philadelphia office, Philadelphia, 1995. Seated from left: Edward Crawford, David Ford, George Ross, Jim Kautz, Ed Nott. Standing from left: Frank Coulson, Marc Shrier, Jerry O'Grady, Eric Schwartz, Josephine Linden, Arthur Baldadian, Bart Silverman, Eric Dobkin, John McNulty and Mark Keating. (Goldman Sachs Archives, courtesy of Josephine Linden); and Equities New Associates, New York, 1990 (Goldman Sachs Archives, courtesy of Donna Winston).

114 Top row, from left: Equity Trading floor, Tokyo, 1992 (Goldman Sachs Archives); Equity Trading floor, New York, 1987 (Goldman Sachs Archives); and Peter Seccia, Rebecca Shaghalian, Jason Mathews and Tony Pasquariello, Securities Division trading floor, New York, 2010 (Goldman Sachs Archives). Bottom row, from left: Floor of the New York Stock Exchange, 1987 (Maria Bastone / AFP via Getty Images); and Curb Market traders on Wall Street, New York, c. 1925 (Hulton Archive via Getty Images).

115 Top row, from left: Katherine Harig on the floor of the Chicago Mercantile Exchange, Chicago, Illinois, 1983 (Goldman Sachs Archives); Chris Argent and Gary Anderson on the London International Financial Futures and Options Exchange, 1993 (Goldman Sachs Archives); and Trading floor, Plumtree Court, London, 2019 (Goldman Sachs Archives). Bottom row, from left: Trading floor, New York, 2001 (Goldman Sachs Archives); and Tony Confusione, floor broker on the New York Stock Exchange, 1992 (Goldman Sachs Archives).

116 Goldman Sachs' initial public offering on the New York Stock Exchange (Goldman Sachs Archives, courtesy of Marc Bryan-Brown).

117 The Goldman Sachs Group, Inc. commemorative stock certificate (Goldman Sachs Archives). The Goldman Sachs Group, Inc. prospectus (Goldman Sachs Archives).

118 Hank Paulson participating in Community TeamWorks (Goldman Sachs Archives).

119 Hank Paulson and Jim Gorter (Goldman Sachs Archives). Hank Paulson at a Goldman Sachs press briefing (Goldman Sachs Archives).

120 Goldman Sachs' initial public offering roadshow in Hong Kong (Goldman Sachs Archives). London staff awaiting the release of Goldman Sachs' initial public offering (Goldman Sachs Archives).

121 Members of the initial public offering team in the New York office (Goldman Sachs Archives, courtesy of Marc Bryan-Brown). Attendees at the dinner commemorating the 20th anniversary of Goldman Sachs' initial public offering (Goldman Sachs Archives).

123 Cover of 2005 Goldman Sachs Foundation report (Goldman Sachs Archives). 2008 Global Leadership Institute Class (Goldman Sachs Archives). Aston Business School entrepreneurship competition winners (Goldman Sachs Archives).

124 Pine Street logo (Goldman Sachs Archives).

125 Pine Street Partner Orientation (Goldman Sachs Archives). Pine Street Dragon Boat Artwork (Goldman Sachs Archives, courtesy of James Fulton).

126 Corporate advertisements (Goldman Sachs Archives).

127 Corporate advertisements (Goldman Sachs Archives).

128 Clockwise, from top left: Global women partners, New York, January 2019 (Goldman Sachs Archives); Eugene Fife, John Ehara, Geoffrey Boisi and Anthony Moore, 1987 (Goldman Sachs Archives); Hank Paulson, Stephen Friedman, John Whitehead, Robert Rubin, Jon Corzine, Lloyd Blankfein and Robert Kaplan, Retired Partners Dinner, New York, 2014 (Goldman Sachs Archives); John Weinberg, Governor of New York Hugh Carey, and John Whitehead at 85 Broad Street dedication, New York, 1980 (Goldman Sachs Archives); P. Henry James, Robert Rubin and Robert Freeman, New York, 1981 (Goldman Sachs Archives); and Sidney Weinberg and Gus Levy, c. 1960 (Goldman Sachs Archives).

129 Top row, from left: Masa Mochida, Tokyo Equity Trading floor, 1991 (Goldman Sachs Archives); David Solomon, New Analyst Orientation, New York, 2019 (Goldman Sachs Archives); and Ken Brody and Robin Neustein, 1988 (Goldman Sachs Archives). Middle row, from left: Management Committee meeting, New York, 2010 (Goldman Sachs Archives); Jim Crimmins, Tim O'Neill, Glenn Fuhrman and W. Blair Garff, New York, 1992 (Goldman Sachs Archives); and Jon Corzine, Junior Achievement Day, New York, 1998 (Goldman Sachs Archives).

continued on following page

Image Credits

Bottom row, from left: Edith Cooper, Great Place to Work conference, San Diego, California, 2016 (Copyright Kelley L. Cox / Great Place to Work, used with permission); and Richard Gnodde, inaugural townhall at Plumtree Court, London, 2019 (Goldman Sachs Archives).

130 Top row, from left: Gwen Libstag, New York, 1984 (Goldman Sachs Archives); and Goldman Sachs Board of Directors, 2001. Seated from left: Lord Browne of Madingley, John Weinberg and Ruth Simmons. Standing from left: John Bryan, John Thornton, Hank Paulson, John Thain, Robert Hurst and Jim Johnson (Goldman Sachs Archives). Middle row, from left: Keith McDermott, Robert Steel and Terje Johansen, Equity Institutional Sales, London, 1988 (Goldman Sachs Archives); All-China Federation of Industry and Commerce delegation visit, New York, 2005. From left: Tim O'Neill, Kevin Kennedy, John S. Weinberg, Greg Palm, Jon Winkelried and Scott Kapnick (Goldman Sachs Archives, courtesy of Terise Slotkin); and Gus Levy, New York, 1961 (*The New York Times* / Redux). Bottom row, from left: David Viniar speaks at the Goldman Sachs IPO roadshow, 1999 (Goldman Sachs Archives, courtesy of Marc Bryan-Brown); Suzanne Nora Johnson, 1991 (Goldman Sachs Archives); and John Waldron, 2019 (Goldman Sachs Archives, courtesy of Marc Bryan-Brown).

131 Top row, from left: Sidney Weinberg, New York, 1967 (Barton Silverman / *The New York Times* / Redux); Partnership Committee meeting, New York, 2004 (Goldman Sachs Archives); and Philip Culliford, Jim O'Neill, Michael Burton and Isabelle Ealet, 1995 (Goldman Sachs Archives). Middle row, from left: James Flowers, Gary Gensler, Gene Sykes and Andrew Chisholm, 1987 (Goldman Sachs Archives); Nomi Ghez, Perk Thorton, Abby Joseph Cohen and William Kealy, 1992 (Goldman Sachs Archives); and Jon Corzine, Stephen Friedman, Hank Paulson, David Solomon and Lloyd Blankfein, Retired Partners Dinner, New York, 2018 (Goldman Sachs Archives). Bottom row, from left: Adebayo Ogunlesi and Alison Mass, Global Partners Meeting, New York, 2015 (Goldman Sachs Archives); Gordon McMahon (far left) and Kevin Kennedy (third from left) in a meeting, 1985 (Goldman Sachs Archives); and Chris Cole and Dan Jester, 1993 (Goldman Sachs Archives).

132 Goldman Sachs logos (Goldman Sachs Archives).
133 Goldman Sachs logos (Goldman Sachs Archives).
134 *10,000 Women* Graduation, Lagos, Nigeria (Goldman Sachs Archives).
135 Tierra del Fuego, Chile (Goldman Sachs Archives). *10,000 Women* site visit, Hyderabad, India (Goldman Sachs Archives).
136 Kathy Matsui and Hiromi Suzuki (Goldman Sachs Archives).
137 "Women-omics: Buy the Female Economy" cover (Goldman Sachs Archives). "Womenomics 5.0" cover (Goldman Sachs Archives).
138 Signing ceremony to form EADS (Francis Demange via Getty Images).
139 Vodafone acquisition of Mannesmann deal toy (Goldman Sachs Archives, courtesy of Mac Heller). Vodafone logo on the Mannesmann high-rise building (Martin Gerten / picture alliance via Getty Images).
140 "Building Better Global Economic BRICs" research report cover (Goldman Sachs Archives). Jim O'Neill (Dominic Lipinski / PA Images via Getty Images).
141 "BRICs and Beyond" research report cover (Goldman Sachs Archives). Map of BRICs countries in Goldman Sachs 2006 *Annual Report* (Goldman Sachs Archives).
142 Front page of *The New York Times*, September 12, 2001 (From *The New York Times*. © 2001 The New York Times Company. All rights reserved. Used under license.)
143 Page two of *The New York Times*, September 12, 2001 (From *The New York Times*. © 2001 The New York Times Company. All rights reserved. Used under license.).
144 175 Delancey Street ribbon-cutting ceremony (Goldman Sachs Archives, courtesy of Delancey Street Associates). Faubourg Lafitte housing complex, New Orleans (Goldman Sachs Archives).
145 Sumitomo Mitsui Banking Corporation investment deal toy (Goldman Sachs Archives, courtesy of Esta Stecher).
146 Goldman Sachs and Wildlife Conservation Society partnership announcement (Goldman Sachs Archives).
147 Tierra del Fuego, Chile (Goldman Sachs Archives). Guanacos at Karukinka Natural Park, Tierra del Fuego, Chile (Goldman Sachs Archives, photo by Julie Larsen Maher courtesy of Wildlife Conservation Society).
148 Groundbreaking for 200 West Street (Goldman Sachs Archives, courtesy of Terise Slotkin). 200 West Street office building (Goldman Sachs Archives).
149 Goldman Sachs 2007 *Environmental Report* cover (Goldman Sachs Archives).
150 1989 IBD analyst class reunion (Goldman Sachs Archives). 1989 Securities Sales associates class reunion (Courtesy of Rhian-Anwen Hamill).
151 Bengaluru Alumni Networking Event (Goldman Sachs Archives). George Ross and Richard Menschel anniversary dinner (Goldman Sachs Archives, courtesy of Terise Slotkin).
152 Mahzarin Banaji leads "Blindspot: Hidden Biases of Good People" (Goldman Sachs Archives).
153 IFFIm bond featured in Goldman Sachs 2006 *Annual Report* (Goldman Sachs Archives).
154 Lloyd Blankfein and Russell Horwitz leaving the New York Stock Exchange (AP Photo / Mark Lennihan).
155 Lloyd Blankfein (Goldman Sachs Archives). Lloyd Blankfein and Cardinal Timothy Dolan (Goldman Sachs Archives).
156 *10,000 Women* brochure (Goldman Sachs Archives).
157 *10,000 Women* scholars and delegation (Goldman Sachs Archives). *10,000 Women* scholar Su Xiaoyan, China (Goldman Sachs Archives). Panel with *10,000 Women* and *10,000 Small Businesses* scholars (Goldman Sachs Archives).
158 Recruitment advertisements (Goldman Sachs Archives).
159 Recruitment advertisements (Goldman Sachs Archives).
160 Traders on the New York Stock Exchange floor (Spencer Platt via Getty Images).
161 Front page of *Financial Times*, February 9, 2009 (Source: *Financial Times*. Used under license from the *Financial Times*. All Rights Reserved.). Protestors outside the Goldman Sachs Washington, DC office (Bill Clark / Roll Call via Getty Images).
162 Front page of *The Wall Street Journal*, September 22, 2008. (Reprinted with permission of *The Wall Street Journal*, Copyright © 2008 Dow Jones & Company, Inc. All Rights Reserved Worldwide. License number 4666550563958).
163 Warren Buffett addresses the partnership (Goldman Sachs Archives, photo by Walter Smith). Warren Buffett visits a trading floor (Goldman Sachs Archives, photo by Walter Smith).
164 *10,000 Small Businesses* Progress Report cover (Goldman Sachs Archives).
165 *10,000 Small Businesses* LaGuardia College Graduation (Goldman Sachs Archives). *10,000 Small Businesses* scholar (Goldman Sachs Archives).
166 Business Standards Committee report cover (Goldman Sachs Archives).
167 Business Standards Committee meeting (Goldman Sachs Archives). Business Standards Committee co-chairs Mike Evans and Jerry Corrigan (Goldman Sachs Archives).
168 Builders + Innovators signage (Goldman Sachs Archives). David Solomon and Peter Chernin at Builders + Innovators (Goldman Sachs Archives). Builders + Innovators breakout session with entrepreneurs (Goldman Sachs Archives).
169 Signing of Dodd-Frank Act (Brooks Kraft via Getty Images).
170 200 West Street during Hurricane Sandy (Goldman Sachs Archives). Hurricane Sandy Relief and Recovery Community TeamWorks project (Goldman Sachs Archives). Hurricane Sandy Relief and Recovery Community TeamWorks project with Team Rubicon (Goldman Sachs Archives).
171 200 West Street during Hurricane Sandy (Goldman Sachs Archives).
172 Pride flag at 200 West Street, New York (Goldman Sachs Archives).
173 *The Wall Street Journal* article, September 11, 2013 (Reprinted with permission of *The Wall Street Journal*, Copyright © 2013 Dow Jones & Company, Inc. All Rights Reserved Worldwide. License number 4653830872521).
174 Marquee logo (Goldman Sachs Archives). Marquee desktop image (Goldman Sachs Archives).
175 President of Japan Post Holdings (Kiyoshi Ota / Bloomberg via Getty Images). Japan Post Holdings deal toy (Courtesy of Masa Mochida).
176 Analyst Impact Fund winners, 2018 (Goldman Sachs Archives). Analyst Impact Fund finalists, 2016 (Goldman Sachs Archives).
177 Store sign announcing Amazon's acquisition of Whole Foods (Smith Collection / Gado via Getty Images). Amazon acquisition of Whole Foods deal toy (Courtesy of Kim-Thu Posnett).
178 Top row, from left: Allison Nathan, Francesco Garzarelli, Jan Hatzius and Peter Oppenheimer at the EMEA CEO Forum, London, 2017; and Program graduates at the *10,000 Small Businesses* Summit: The Big Power of Small Business, Washington, DC, 2018. Bottom row, from left: Scott Lebovitz, Michael Ronen, managing partner, Softbank Investment Advisers, Julia Steyn, vice president, Urban Mobility and Maven, General Motors, and Brooks Entwistle, chief business officer, Uber International at the Sustainable Finance Innovation Forum, New York, 2018; North American Energy Summit invitation, New York, 2014; and from left, Sarah Friar, Nextdoor CEO, and Anna Skoglund, Disruptive Technology Symposium, London, 2019 (All Goldman Sachs Archives).
179 Clockwise, from top left: China-US CEO Bilateral Investment Dialogue, Beijing, 2014. From left: Evan Feigenbaum, vice chairman, the Paulson Institute; Fenglei Fang, chairman and founder, HOPU Investment Management Company; Lloyd Blankfein; Chen Dongsheng, chairman and CEO, Taikang Life Insurance; and Mark Schwartz; 2015; Gunjan Samtani and Shradha Negi, Women Emerging in Finance event, Bengaluru, 2019; James Paradise, Asia Pacific TechNet Conference, Hong Kong, 2019; GSAM Symposium signage, 2015; HBCU Leadership Summit, New York, 2017. From left, Brian Fortson, Elaine Rene, Amy Watson and Ayanna Clunis; Shared Vision, Global Reach Global Conference, New York, 2004. From left: Esta Stecher, Mike Evans, Michael Sherwood, Robert Kaplan, Sharmin Mossavar-Rahmani, Eric Schwartz and Masa Mochida (Courtesy of Terise Slotkin); Presentation of the Colors, Veterans on Wall Street Conference, New York, 2014; and Joanne Hannaford at the Perspektywy Women in Tech Summit, Warsaw, Poland, 2018 (All Goldman Sachs Archives).
180 Goldman Sachs summer interns, Salt Lake City (Goldman Sachs Archives).
182 *Marcus by Goldman Sachs* logo (Goldman Sachs Archives).
183 Marcus team, London (Goldman Sachs Archives).
184 David Solomon and Lloyd Blankfein (Goldman Sachs Archives). David Solomon and Tyra Banks during *Talks at GS* session at Iowa State Fair (Goldman Sachs Archives).
185 David Solomon at Global Partners Meeting (Goldman Sachs Archives).
186 All photos from the Goldman Sachs Archives.
187 *One Goldman Sachs* schematic (Goldman Sachs Archives).
188 *GS Accelerate* kick-off (Goldman Sachs Archives). *GS Accelerate* entrepreneurs (Goldman Sachs Archives).
189 *Launch With GS* forum (Goldman Sachs Archives). *Launch With GS* visual identity (Goldman Sachs Archives).
190 Daily meeting announcing Apple Card (Goldman Sachs Archives). Apple Card promotional material (Goldman Sachs Archives).
191 Builders + Innovators China sessions (Goldman Sachs Archives).
192 Social impact bond infographic (Goldman Sachs Archives).
193 Goldman Sachs 2018 *Sustainability Report* cover and schematic from report (Goldman Sachs Archives).
194 Firmwide Black Network townhall speakers (Goldman Sachs Archives). Goldman Sachs Global Affinity Networks fair in Bengaluru (Goldman Sachs Archives).
195 All social media posts from Goldman Sachs.
196 150 Outer Ring Road opening ceremony, Bengaluru (Goldman Sachs Archives). 150 Outer Ring Road campus, Bengaluru (Goldman Sachs Archives).
197 Plumtree Court, London (Goldman Sachs Archives). Coffee bar at Plumtree Court, London (Goldman Sachs Archives).
198 eSPORTS digital video, 2018; Stephanie Hui and Lei Zhang, founder and chief executive officer of Hillhouse Capital, *Talks at GS* session at Builders + Innovators, Ningbo, China, 2019; Jake Siewert, Tom Leake and Heather Shemilt, *Exchanges at Goldman Sachs* podcast, New York, 2019; John Waldron with Danielle Weisberg and Carly Zakin, co-founders of The Skimm, *Talks at GS*, New York, 2017; *Music in the Air* infographic, 2016 (All Goldman Sachs Archives).
199 *The Long & Short of It* video series, 2018; Susie Scher and Darren Star, *Talks at GS*, New York, 2018; Jake Siewert and Kathy Matsui, *Exchanges at Goldman Sachs* podcast, New York, 2019; James Esposito and David Beckham, *Talks at GS*, London, 2017; *Blockchain: The New Technology of Trust* infographic, 2017; David Solomon and Harit Talwar, *Catch-Up With David* video series, New York, 2019; Allison Nathan, *Top of Mind* podcast, 2019; and Kathy Elsesser and Emily Weiss, founder and chief executive officer of Glossier, *Talks at GS*, New York, 2019 (All Goldman Sachs Archives).
202 From left: 9 Pine Street, Astor Building, New York (Image courtesy of the Museum of the City of New York); 60 Wall Street, New York (Image courtesy of the New-York Historical Society); 30 Pine Street, New York (Goldman Sachs Archives); and 55 Broad Street, New York (Goldman Sachs Archives).
203 85 Broad Street, New York (Goldman Sachs Archives); 200 West Street, New York (Goldman Sachs Archives); and World Map (Art by Julia Konovaliuk via Getty Images).
216 Goldman Sachs summer interns, London, 2019 (Goldman Sachs Archives).

Acknowledgements

This book was made possible by the dedicated work of many people. Goldman Sachs is deeply grateful to the remarkable team of writers, historians, archivists and design professionals who collaborated with us and contributed to *Goldman, Sachs & Co., Established 1869*. We are proud that many of our own people also devoted significant time to its creation — individuals from all levels of the organization, across businesses and time zones, including retired partners and alumni of the firm. We hope this book is further testament to our commitment to teamwork and excellence, and that both are reflected throughout the rich history we attempted to capture in these pages.

The core team at Goldman Sachs — John F.W. Rogers, Eileen M. Dillon, Aimee Malnati Stromberg, Melanie Edwards and Erik Bringard — expresses their sincere thanks to the following for their roles in the creation of *Goldman, Sachs & Co., Established 1869* and apologize for any inadvertent omissions.

Design: Anne Marie Mascia (A M Mascia Design + Illustration Inc), with montages and infographics produced by David Phan (Sequel Studio).

Archives: Rebecca Altermatt, Alex Johnson and Emilia Mahaffey (all from The History Factory).

Writing Team: Thea Haley (Glen Avenue Communications), Tom White (The White Agency, Inc.) and LaRae Cunningham (Adytum Communications).

Historical Research: Manuel A. Bautista González (The Winthrop Group). The contributions of Andrew Edwards (Oxford University), Richard Salvucci (Trinity University), Peter Thompson (formerly with The History Factory and Goldman Sachs) and Sean Vanatta (Princeton University) are also acknowledged.

Project Advisor: Stephen Chambers (The Winthrop Group).

Printing: Cardinal Graphics NY, Inc.

This book was produced and published by Goldman Sachs & Co. LLC on the occasion of the firm's 150th anniversary in 2019.

POSTSCRIPT

No book of any length could capture all of the individuals who have helped build Goldman Sachs and contributed to the firm's success over the past century and a half, nor could it include every transaction that helped define the firm through its history. The narrative presented here is intended to remind, inspire and capture the spirit of a firm that is ultimately a reflection of, and a tribute to, the efforts of thousands of extraordinarily dedicated people around the world.

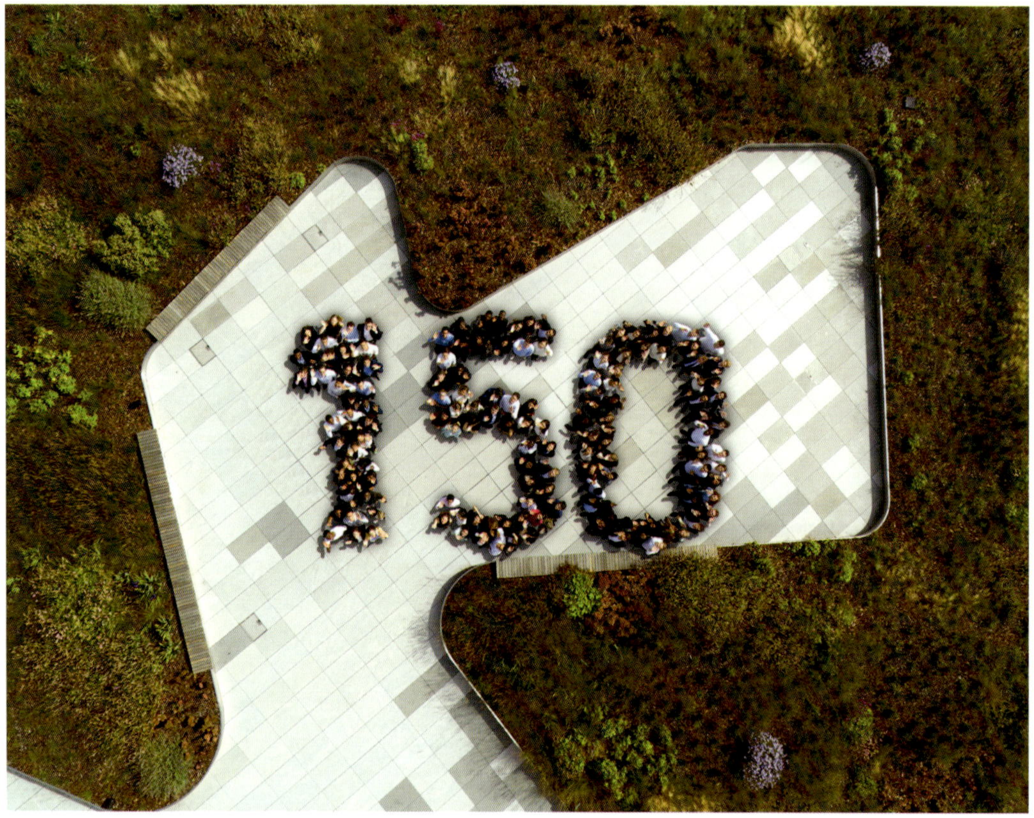
150

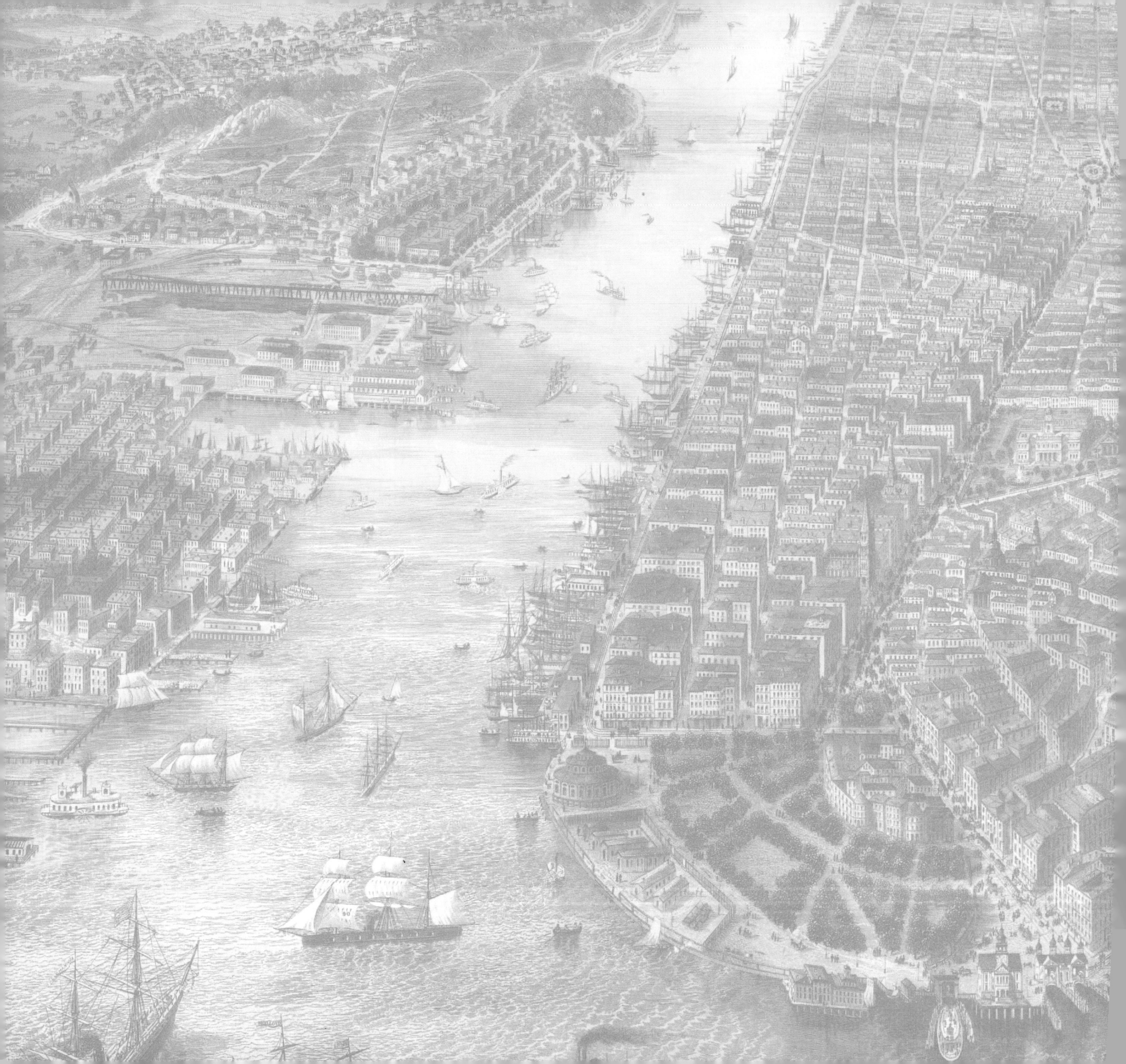